Conducting
a Successful
Capital Campaign

Kent E. Dove

Conducting
a Successful
Capital Campaign

*A Comprehensive
Fundraising Guide
for Nonprofit Organizations*

Jossey-Bass Publishers

San Francisco • Oxford • 1991

CONDUCTING A SUCCESSFUL CAPITAL CAMPAIGN
A Comprehensive Fundraising Guide for Nonprofit Organizations
by Kent E. Dove

Copyright © 1988 by: Jossey-Bass Inc., Publishers
350 Sansome Street
San Francisco, California 94104

&

Jossey-Bass Limited
Headington Hill Hall
Oxford OX3 0BW

Library of Congress Cataloging-in-Publication Data

Dove, Kent E., date.
  Conducting a successful capital campaign.

  Bibliography: p.
  Includes index.
  1. Fund raising—United States.   2. Corporations,
Nonprofit—United States—Finance.   I. Title.
HG177.5.U6D68   1988   658.1'5224   88-42786
ISBN 1-55542-104-0 (alk. paper)

Manufactured in the United States of America

The paper in this book meets the guidelines for
permanence and durability of the Committee on
Production Guidelines for Book Longevity of the
Council on Library Resources.

JACKET DESIGN BY WILLI BAUM

FIRST EDITION
  First printing: November 1988
  Second printing: January 1990
  Third printing: May 1991
Code 8834

A joint publication in
The Jossey-Bass Management Series
and
The Jossey-Bass
Higher Education Series

Contents

Preface   xi

Acknowledgments   xvii

The Author   xxi

1. The Key Components of a Capital Campaign   1

2. Preparing for a Campaign: Three Essential Steps   15

3. Roles of Leaders and Volunteers in the Campaign   29

4. Recruiting, Educating, and Motivating Volunteers   43

5. Building and Stating the Case for the Campaign   56

6. Constructing and Using the Major Gifts Chart   67

7. Establishing the Campaign Structure and Solicitation
   Process   77

8. Identifying, Researching, and Rating Campaign Donors   90

9.   Cultivating and Soliciting Major Gift Prospects   104

10. Managing Campaign Logistics and Day-to-Day
     Operations   122

11. Successful Publications, Promotion, and Public
     Relations   139

12. Concluding the Campaign and Building on the
     Momentum   150

13. Trends Affecting the Future of Capital Campaigns   160

Resources

A.   Communications Materials Checklist   176

B.   Sample Case Statements   178

C.   Sample Program Brochure   209

D.   Sample Question-and-Answer Sheet   231

E.   Sample Campaign Plan of Action/Volunteer Handbook   233

F.   Sample Pledge Forms   270

G.   Sample Newsletters   275

H.   Sample Letterhead and Envelopes   278

     References   281

     Index   285

Preface

Capital campaigns have been part of the development programs of nonprofit organizations for well over half a century. However, the recent proliferation of new nonprofit organizations with emerging development programs, coupled with the increasing ambitiousness of established programs, is changing the face of philanthropy. Increased competition for philanthropic contributions, ever-growing organizational needs, the reduction in or elimination of public grant programs, rising operating costs aggravated by inflation, a more discerning donor public, and other considerations are forcing most nonprofit organizations to rely increasingly on major gift campaigns to meet their objectives. Unfortunately, this is often true whether or not an organization is prepared to undertake the most arduous and important development task—the capital campaign. No longer do good programs automatically receive funding nor old-boy networks guarantee success. In order to succeed, an organization must both prepare properly and perform effectively.

Conducting a Successful Capital Campaign sets forth in systematic fashion the principles that govern all successful campaigns. A small regional historical museum in Virginia conducting a $1 million campaign must take into account the same considerations as a major midwestern state university attempting to raise $50 million. Therefore, rather than concentrate on the differences among capital campaigns (of which there assuredly are many), this book focuses on their similarities (of which there are even more). It attempts to assemble in one publication the primary ideas and techniques central to all modern capital campaigns.

Today educational, arts-related, religious, community, and health care organizations are typically either considering, conducting, or concluding a capital campaign. Yet many nonprofit organizations are inadequately prepared to plan, initiate, or manage such a campaign successfully. This situation is complicated even further by the large number of inexperienced professionals holding demanding, high-level positions within these organizations. The National Society of Fund Raising Executives (NSFRE) indicates that 20 percent of the professionals in fundraising are newcomers to the field. The Council for the Advancement and Support of Education (CASE) estimates that roughly one-third of the professionals with whom it is affiliated have only three years of development experience or less.

Audience

Given these facts, who should read this book? It is written for the executives and staff of a wide range of nonprofit organizations: chief executive officers (CEOs), chief development officers, governing boards, development staff members, key volunteers, and funding agency personnel who desire a fundamental understanding of capital campaigns. This book can be used as a review and guide for the seasoned practitioner; as an introduction to the principles of campaigning for newcomers, volunteers, and professionals without campaign experience; and as a resource for philanthropic agencies in the process of assessing the caliber of programs they are asked to fund. The principles discussed throughout the book are equally relevant to arts-related, religious, educational, community, and health care organizations that are either contemplating or conducting a capital campaign.

It has been a real challenge to present an effective approach to capital campaigns that would prove both universal in its application and valuable in specific situations. Perhaps this is one reason few books on this subject have aimed for such a broad readership. However, judging from my experience as a practitioner, consultant, and lecturer—and from detailed conversations with respected and experienced campaign professionals from all "third-sector" walks of life—I am confident that the principles that govern campaigns are equally applicable to organizations both large and small and to campaigns that are both local and national in scope.

This book takes into account the fact that many organizations that have capital needs and are desirous of launching capital campaigns have very small staffs. One-person offices are common, and sometimes fundraising is only one aspect of a staff member's responsibilities. Many grass-roots organizations have no professional development staff at all. It is possible to conduct a successful campaign under these conditions, but the organization will need to improvise. In many cases, a dedicated volunteer or team of volunteers has conducted a successful campaign in an organization that has no paid development staff. In other instances, a member of the administrative staff has carried out the task. Improvising can and does work when the basic precepts and principles of successful campaigning are followed.

Whenever possible or appropriate, I have provided checklists, formulas, or examples in this book to illustrate fundamental campaign principles. However, two areas—campaign budget and organizational structures—vary too widely from organization to organization or according to circumstances for me to include any precise examples. Therefore, it seemed best to discuss these two issues in somewhat more general terms than the others. Key issues or considerations affecting decisions about budget and structure are in many ways similar, so I have treated them in parallel fashion.

A special effort has been made to use language and examples that are uniformly applicable. The reader will find very few anecdotes or explanations of "how we do it at our shop." Other excellent books, such as Jerold Panas's *Mega Gifts* and James Gregory Lord's *The Raising of Money*, fill this niche in current fundraising literature. Neither is this book designed to be a workbook. The reader will note that forms and charts are kept to a minimum. Both the Third Sector Press and the Public Management Institute publish sample materials that can be adapted to specific organizational situations. *Conducting a Successful Capital*

Campaign establishes the context and rationale behind the use of such materials. The only deviation from this general format is the inclusion in the resources of illustrative materials from four campaigns.

Overview of the Contents

The chapters in this book are organized around the fundamental issues and challenges that must be met if a capital campaign is to achieve success. Chapter One sets forth the global considerations one must take into account when contemplating a campaign. I identify the seven prerequisites for a successful campaign that largely form the basis for the remainder of the book. The chapter also reviews a number of secondary factors that affect the size of the campaign goal and the timing of the campaign.

Thorough precampaign preparation sets the pace for the campaign and ultimately determines its result. An organization must assess its readiness to campaign in the eyes of both its external constituencies and those within the organization. Chapter Two discusses steps an organization should take early in the campaign process.

The human element of campaigns is emphasized throughout this book, particularly in Chapter Three, which looks at the "layman who leads" and the "staff member who serves." The success or failure of most campaigns is ultimately attributed to the effectiveness of the governing board members, the chief executive officer, and the chief development officer. Their respective roles are reviewed here.

In addition to campaign leadership, a dedicated volunteer force is essential to accomplishing the goals of most capital campaigns. Chapter Four establishes the procedures for mobilizing volunteers.

Chapter Five examines the single most definitive document in any campaign—the case statement. This chapter describes the characteristics of the case statement; how it is organized; who should write it; and how to use it in conducting market surveys, enlisting volunteers, and soliciting major gifts.

Chapter Six details one of the most fundamental components of the campaign—the gifts table. It explains the formula for creating a gifts table, and, what is more important, its efficacy in raising donor sights, determining the adequacy of a prospect pool, relating required campaign gift levels to named gift opportunities, and keeping track of campaign progress.

There are likely as many different campaign structures as there are campaigns. Chapter Seven lists seven factors that influence the amount of detail a campaign structure requires. It goes on to describe what special campaign functions need to be implemented by various committees, stressing the particular importance of the major gifts committee.

Before an organization starts campaigning, it should select an appropriate strategy for soliciting gifts. This chapter defines and presents the advantages and disadvantages of various asking strategies. Additionally, the campaign should from the very start establish a criterion for which gifts it will include in the campaign total in the course of the campaign. I include a gift accounting criterion for one campaign as an illustration.

Generally speaking, 90 percent of the campaign funding goal will be realized from fewer than 10 percent of the donors. Obtaining major gifts is critical to campaign success. It is a multistep process that demands a strategy; thorough research; accurate evaluation, careful management, and systematic cultivation of prospects; and skilled soliciting techniques. These steps are described in Chapter Eight and Chapter Nine.

Chapter Ten reviews the many operational aspects of the campaign. Included in this chapter are discussions on the campaign timetable and budget, acknowledging and reporting gifts, donor stewardship, and the selection and use of professional campaign counsel.

In addition to the case statement and program brochure, described in Chapter Five, there are several other pieces of campaign literature that should be developed. These materials and their desired features are described in Chapter Eleven. The discussion in this chapter is supplemented in the resources with some standard sample materials from several successful campaigns.

Achieving financial success on schedule is the ultimate goal of all campaigns. Chapter Twelve discusses how to conclude the campaign successfully, as well as take care of such postcampaign matters as recognizing donors and volunteers, writing final reports, and auditing the productivity of the campaign.

Chapter Thirteen contains a speculative look at emerging campaign trends and at what people conducting campaigns in the 1990s and beyond may experience. The chapter ends with a brief discussion devoted to the pros and cons of capital campaigns and the importance all organizations should place on creating and sustaining a major gifts program in the years to come.

The book concludes with several resource sections containing a sampling of campaign literature taken from four separate campaigns. The resources are included not only to illustrate the outcome of processes described in the text but also to enable the reader to easily develop the support materials needed in any campaign effort. The resource materials include a communications materials checklist, case statements, a program brochure, a question-and-answer sheet, a plan of action/volunteer handbook, pledge cards, newsletters, and stationery and envelopes.

There is a growing body of literature about fundraising, and much of what is being written is extremely well done. I hope others will continue to add to our knowledge about fundraising in general and capital campaigns in particular, and that this book will prove useful to those who do. If after reading this book you feel better acquainted with the principles and practices that guide campaigns, the effort that went into writing it will have been well spent.

Houston, Texas   Kent E. Dove
September 1988

Acknowledgments

In the field of fundraising, new ideas and strategies are often passed freely among professionals with no concept of ownership. For this reason, some of the material in this book represents the thinking of other senior fundraising professionals, shared with me during personal conversations over the years. Some of the material is quoted or condensed from more than 100 outlines and speeches that others have presented at conferences, seminars, and conventions over the last fifteen years. Those who made major contributions to this work in this fashion include: Gene M. Anderson and Addison L. Winship II (gifts range tables); Fran Baxter (prospect management system); John P. Butler III and Joel T. Smith (the future of capital campaigns); Donald A. Campbell, Jr. (defining lead gifts and lead gift donors); Paul B. Chewning (history of fundraising); David R. Dunlop and James C. Kughn, Jr. (working with volunteers); Gary Evans (asking strategies); E. Burr Gibson (the role of professional counsel, and writing the case statement); Martin Grenzebach (market survey, program audit, and postcampaign evaluation); Edward E. Hale and Robert F. Tinker (recruiting and training volunteers, and the role of the governing board, chief executive officer, and chief development officer); Eugene J. Hunckler (gift reporting, and acknowledgment and donor recognition); James Gregory Lord and George Keller (institutional planning); Donald R. Perkins (public relations); Russell R. Picton (effective follow-through); Michael Raddock (selecting campaign counsel); J. David Rose (campaign planning); G. T. (Buck) Smith (planning, cultivating, and soliciting major gifts); Bobbie J. Strand and J. Mark Billian (prospect research); David M. Thompson and Mary Helene Pendel (case statement); and F. Mark Whittaker (prospect research, evaluation, cultivation, and solicitation). I deeply appreciate their contributions.

The resource sections at the end of this volume could not have been compiled without the cooperation and participation of several individuals who deserve special thanks and recognition. R. F. (Dick) Dini, president of R. F. Dini and Associates, introduced me to Bev R. Laws, president of the YMCA of the greater Houston area, who provided the materials from the Second Century Development Fund. Byron K. Welch, president of Welch Associates, introduced me to Nora Starcher, executive director of the Lutheran Hospital (La Crosse, Wisconsin) Foundation, who consented to including the material from the Excellence with Caring Campaign. Marshall Monroe, chair of the board of the National Society of Fund Raising Executives (NSFRE) and director of corporate planning and financial development for the national office of the YMCA, suggested that I contact Richard E. Stoll, vice-president of development at the YMCA of greater St. Louis, and he agreed to share the materials from Making a World of Difference. Martin Grenzebach, president of John Grenzebach and Associates, Inc., who contributed so much to the content of this book, recommended that Darrell D. Wyrick, president and campaign director of the University of Iowa Foundation, and Alan Swanson, vice-president for communications and administration at the foundation, be asked to include materials from Iowa Endowment 2000: A Covenant with Quality.

Sprinkled throughout this book are the teachings and beliefs of J. Jay Gerber. Jay and his associates at Gonser Gerber Tinker Stuhr shared their philosophy of advancement with me years ago. Jay's teachings continue to be the foundation on which my professional beliefs and ideology rest today. Most of the material, however, represents my own thinking on the subject of capital campaigns and how I have seen them evolve during the twenty years I have worked in the profession.

There are three very special people I wish to acknowledge. Curtis R. Simic has been a mentor, confidant, and close friend for more than twenty years. I can think of no one who has done more to guide and to shape me professionally or who has been a better friend. I owe him much. The other two are Richard A. Edwards and Rodney P. Kirsch. Dick has inspired me and challenged me to grow and to mature professionally. He has been a friend, too. This book owes its creation to Rod. He encouraged me to write it, did the research, and spent tireless hours working on the text. He is the most able young fundraising professional I know. I am glad I have had the opportunity to be a professional associate and personal friend of each of these men. I look forward to many more years of close association with all three.

Finally, there are individuals who have helped to shape my life and my thinking in very significant ways, not only about fundraising but also about more important matters. Each deserves mention here, too: William S. Armstrong, Sam Cooper, Philip A. Fox, Paul Fultz, R. N. (Bob) Houser, George Rupp, the late John Stempel, and Herman B Wells.

K. E. D.

This book is dedicated to the memory of my parents;
to my wife, Sandy, my friend and strength;
and to our children, Jason and Kerrye,
the pride and joy of our lives.

The Author

Kent E. Dove is currently vice-president for external affairs at Rice University. He received his B.S. degree in education from Indiana University in 1968, he is a Certified Fund Raising Executive (CFRE) and a member of the board of the National Society of Fund Raising Executives (NSFRE), and he has served three terms on the Council for Advancement and Support of Education's (CASE) Educational Fund Raising Committee. As well, Dove has received CASE's "Apple" award for his efforts in professional education of advancement practitioners. He frequently lectures on a wide range of topics, including capital campaigns, program audits, prospect identification, research and management, managing the development office, the annual fund, and training boards and staff.

Before he accepted his present position at Rice University, Dove served in various educational fundraising management positions at the University of California, Berkeley; Drake University; the University of Alabama; Northwestern University; the University of Tennessee Center for the Health Sciences; West Virginia University; and Indiana University. In addition, he has served as a consultant to numerous third-sector institutions.

Dove's involvement with capital campaigns spans nearly twenty years. As a practitioner, he has participated in the staffing and management of five successful major campaigns and has provided various consulting services to many others. He has been associated with campaigns throughout the United States, and in Canada, as well.

Dove wrote the chapter on capital campaigns in the *Handbook of Institutional Advancement* (edited by A. W. Rowland, 2nd ed., 1986). He is a frequent contributor to various professional publications.

Conducting
a Successful
Capital Campaign

✳ 1 ✳

The Key Components
of a Capital Campaign

A capital campaign is an organized, intensive fundraising effort on the part of the third-sector institution or organization to secure extraordinary gifts and pledges for a specific purpose or purposes (such as building construction, renovation, equipment acquisition, or endowment funds) during a specified period of time. The nature of campaigns, like the nature of society itself, is in continuous transition. New campaign models are emerging, and campaign goals are beginning to include operating as well as endowment components. In the period since World War II, it has become clear that one of the most permanent features of our environment is change. And it appears that change will move at an even faster pace in the future than it has in the past. John Milton (1660) said it best: "the ship of the Commonwealth is always under sail."

While we will certainly do things differently in the future from the way we have done them in the past, it is equally certain that the significant essential features that characterize capital campaigns will endure. This book is about the abiding principles that define and provide the context for a successful capital campaign or ongoing major gifts program, not the exceptions to the rules, of which there assuredly are many. Certainly, few principles in campaigning are immutable. The nature of a campaign is as complex and challenging as human nature itself, because each campaign essentially and fundamentally deals with people, their motivations, needs, desires, aspirations, and hopes, even more than it deals with formulas, organizational charts, and timetables. But a check of the record over time and through all types of philanthropic and charitable organizations shows beyond any doubt that those that abide by these principles win more often, win more convincingly, and win not only the day but also the future more of the time.

Those who occasionally win by other methods almost always are lucky, and some would rather be lucky than good. For goodness' sake, take and enjoy all the luck available; everyone does. There is nothing wrong with being lucky. Successful campaigns organized and managed "by the rules" generally enjoy their fair share of luck, too. But it is better to be good than to be lucky. Those who are good, those who operate their campaigns within a prescribed structure, will make their own luck as they go along—opportunities will be met by preparation. The others will have to wait for luck to come along, but that may not happen at strategic times during the course of their campaign, or it may not happen often enough to win the campaign victory. And winning is important; often, especially when the case is truly compelling, it is essential.

This book is about the means used to reach an end. Do not be misled, however. The ultimate objective is not simply to raise money. And the means is never people just "giving away" financial resources. Successful campaigns seek and secure investments in a better society, a higher quality of life, an enriched culture, and they showcase humankind at its best, expressing love and hope and caring for others with greater needs. There is clearly an evangelical aspect to fundraising that motivates most professionals and volunteers. Never lose sight of that. If it is lost, society will lose a central thread that holds together the fabric of philanthropy and charity as they are known today, as they ought to be known. Such a loss would be incalculable.

Philanthropy and charity are as old as humankind itself. However, fundraising as practiced in the 1980s, particularly the capital campaign, is a twentieth-century phenomenon. In tracing the roots of giving in the American society and the development of the fundraising function, we find several benchmark periods. In 1641, Harvard College sponsored the first systematic effort to raise funds for higher education when it sent a trio of preachers to

England on a begging mission to raise funds (Chewning, 1984, p. 16). Once in England, these fund raisers found they needed a fundraising brochure and relayed the need back to Harvard. In response to this request came *New England's First Fruits,* largely written in Massachusetts but printed in London in 1643. It was the first of countless public relations pamphlets and brochures.

The first attempt to stage a community chest fund drive was undertaken in Philadelphia in 1829 by Matthew Carey. A total of 137 subscribers giving a total of $276.50 was the net result of America's first federated fundraising effort. In this effort are found, in embryo, the elements of modern fundraising: the paid solicitor, the advance promotion, the classified prospect list, and the federated drive.

During the late nineteenth and early twentieth centuries, capitalists such as Andrew Carnegie and John Rockefeller began underwriting libraries, museums, research projects, and even entire universities. As a result of both the rise of industrialization and the new willingness of major donors to give to third-sector institutions, major gift fundraising became an established practice. Fundraising and public relations firms, such as the John Price Jones Corporation, were established to assist nonprofit organizations that did not have the staff or expertise to conduct these efforts on their own.

One of the first successful major campaigns was directed early in this century by Charles Sumner Ward and his colleague Lyman L. Pierce, campaign directors for the YMCA. Over the course of three decades, Ward's fundraising techniques raised more than half a billion dollars for this organization. Because of his efforts, Ward became known as the master campaigner, and his strategies were copied by many other successful fund raisers. They became the foundation on which today's capital campaigns are still built.

The importance of a capital campaign to any institution at critical moments in its history cannot be understated. Throughout this century, it has been the one public undertaking that exposes the hopes and aspirations of an institution to critical market segments who ultimately are asked to invest the time, energy, and financial support crucial to its quality and, at times, its survival. The role of campaigns and their impact on the future of institutions are becoming ever more important. There are several factors principally responsible for this. Institutional budgets are tightening and becoming more strained; the size of enrollments/patient loads/ service markets is leveling off or declining (the decreases in hospital patient care loads and average days per stay are most noteworthy); and competition for contributions is increasing. There are more recognized charities in North America today than ever before; Alan Arlett, president of the Canadian Centre for Philanthropy, reported that in 1986 new charities were being registered at a record rate across Canada (personal communication). Sixty more people per month are joining the National Society of Fund Raising Executives (NSFRE) than were two years ago; membership is at an all-time high. At the same time, public grant programs are being reduced or eliminated as a part of the current federal administration's strategy (according to Gabor, 1987, federal cutbacks have created the greatest need in years for philanthropies); the donor public is becoming both more pressed and more discriminating as resources are becoming more scarce; and fixed operating costs are escalating more rapidly than the rate of inflation. Given these factors, capital campaigns are becoming a standard feature of virtually every size and type of third-sector institution.

Modern capital campaigns can be grouped in three categories according to the size of their fundraising goals: less than $25 million, $25 million to $100 million, or more than $100 million. By far the largest number of campaigns have goals of less than $25 million. Campaigns in the $100,000 to $1 million range, if they are true capital campaigns, will be less numerous in the future than they have been in the past. Why? Simply because few true "capital" needs can be met by campaigns with goals in this range. Even modest construction projects these days often require more than $1 million. The number of campaigns in the $25 million to $100 million range is significant and growing. In virtually every major population center in North America there is at least one campaign with a goal in this range under way today, and the list of colleges and universities with announced campaign goals in this range is too long to enumerate. What is even more surprising is the number of announced campaigns with goals of $100 million or more—forty-three in higher education alone in the summer of 1987 according to a telephone survey conducted by the Chronicle of Higher Education ("Fact-File . . . ," Sept. 2, 1987, p. A76). And the next size barrier has already been broken with the announcement in February 1987 of Stanford University's current campaign, with a goal of more than $1 billion. (New York University has also announced a $1 billion goal, but its campaign is divided into three phases, and the third phase is not scheduled for completion until the year 2000.) It must be remembered, however, that the basic ground rules for success are the same for every campaign, whether the goal is $100,000 or $100 million. History is convincingly clear on this. It is these basic ground rules that must be the focus of everyone who plans and implements a campaign.

Seven Prerequisites to Success

Before a campaign is formally undertaken and publicly announced, precampaign work, sometimes even pre-precampaign work, is necessary. First and foremost in any capital campaign effort is the need for commitment on the part of the governing board, administration, and volunteer leadership. A decision must be made that the effort will be one of teamwork. A campaign cannot be successfully undertaken by staff alone or by outside professionals alone. Any successful campaign must have:

- Support and time commitments from all key groups—the governing board, the chief executive officer, prospective major donors and key volunteer leaders, the professional fundraising staff, and the institutional family
- An organization with a clear image of itself and a strategic plan for its growth and improvement
- Objectives based on important and legitimate institutional plans, goals, budgets, and needs
- A compelling case for support, always presented in a written document and, in larger, more complex campaigns, in additional support materials
- A market survey addressing internal and external preparedness
- Leadership enlisted and educated

• Major donors ready and able to give substantial lead gifts before
any public announcement of the campaign

The presence or absence of these fundamental factors
determines an institution's ability to campaign successfully. Discussions about them are interwoven throughout this book. They are its
substance, because they are essential and critical to success. A lack
of any single factor can cause the campaign to be delayed or even
cancelled.

Other Significant Variables

Several other elements that may affect the success of a
campaign should also be taken into consideration. These secondary
factors tend to determine the size of the goal and the timing (both
length and starting date) of the campaign rather than whether the
campaign should be undertaken. These significant variables are:

Age of the Organization. Older organizations tend to be
better established than others. They have longer track records of
service and past success; they often have better defined, older
constituencies; and their support bases are often more developed. As
a university president once asked, "Do you remember the last time
a college 100 years old or older was closed?"

Caliber of the Constituency. Research on patterns of charitable giving by Americans suggests that, on the whole, heads of
households contribute more than others. The amount of contributions is generally correlated with level of income, occupation of
wage earner, employment status, level of education, and age (The
Gallup Organization, 1982, p. 3). Another important piece of
research, *The Charitable Behavior of Americans* (White, 1986),
recently commissioned by the Rockefeller Brothers Fund and
conducted by Yankelovich, Skelley and White, Inc., confirms many
of these conclusions. According to this survey, major influences on
giving include income level, life expectancy, age, religious involvement, and marital status. Older, more prosperous individuals,
especially the religious, give proportionately more. Organizations
with constituencies that are older, wealthier, better educated, and

more skilled do better. The evidence is all around. Look at the examples in any community.

Range of the Institution's Giving Program. The most productive fundraising programs characteristically include four key functional elements: an annual giving program, a planned giving program, a major gifts program, and a prospect research program. Organizations that lack any of these programs or have failed to fully develop them tend to be less well prepared for the campaign activity than those that have them already operating effectively; consequently, they may have to accept lower campaign goals. Pickett (1984) demonstrated this point convincingly in his sampling of institutions of higher education.

Size of Constituency and Geographical Spread. The individual demographic factors mentioned earlier are certainly the most important determinants of the ability of a constituency to support a capital campaign. However, it is also generally true that organizations with larger constituencies tend to have a better base from which to work. (This will not always be the case, of course. An organization that provides services for indigent or low-income groups may well have a very large client list but few major gift prospects within this constituency who are able and willing to give at the levels required to support a capital campaign effort.) The geographical distribution of the constituency is another factor to be considered in determining the preparedness for a campaign and the size of goal that is realistic. Less time, money, and staff are needed to organize and manage a campaign in a small geographical area, such as a city or a section of a city, than to conduct one over a wider area, which presents more complex organizational problems. The national campaigns, especially those being conducted by large educational institutions such as Stanford University, demonstrate this.

Previous Fundraising Success. Realism is necessary in determining capital campaign goals or, indeed, whether an institution is even ready to enter into a capital campaign. How long ago was the last one conducted? For how much? Was it successful? Past performance as well as current trends in giving must be analyzed. An institution annually raising $500,000 is not likely to be prepared to mount a successful campaign for $30 million. While there is no ironclad prescription for using recent and current giving totals to project capital campaign goals, a random review of several successful recent campaigns suggests that organizations normally set goals that range from four to six times their current total annual development income. A major consulting firm suggests that the cumulative total of gifts for the past five years represents a good starting target when determining a campaign goal. An organization that has raised $20 million in that time will probably end up with a "new money" campaign goal of $15 million to $25 million. One must be especially careful in using such rules of thumb to determine a goal if the comprehensive campaign model described later in this chapter is used. It must always be remembered that part of the comprehensive goal is ongoing annual support, and the amount of this support should not be included in the capital component of the total goal. Caveat: The use of mathematical assumptions alone to make projections is overly simplistic.

Quality of Program and Impact of Services. Institutions that provide higher-quality programs and a broader range of services tend to have greater access to a wider segment of the philanthropic market. Quality of services and the impact these services have on the constituency being served are extremely important variables to be considered in determining campaign preparedness and goals. High-quality organizations such as the Mayo Clinic, Boys Town, the Girl Scouts of America, better YMCA/YWCAs around the country, and the "best" churches and synagogues in a community are more competitive in the most competitive environments—known philanthropists, foundations, and corporations. These funding sources must always choose among numerous organizations requesting donations and most often select those that demonstrate the highest qualifications.

Location of the Organization. Organizations located in urban areas tend to have a better climate in which to seek significant contributions than those located in rural areas. Residents of larger cities and geographical areas in which individual wealth and corporate headquarters are concentrated tend to be more experienced and sophisticated with regard to campaigns and more generous in their support of them. Communities with United Way campaigns also tend to be more receptive to and supportive of capital campaigns. There are regional differences as well, in both the United States and Canada. Organized fundraising by nonprofit organizations is generally more mature and sophisticated and involves more realistic expectations on the East Coast than in the Midwest and on the West Coast in the United States, and in eastern Canada than in western Canada, although there are specific exceptions to this in both countries. There are other factors to be considered, too. In the United States, there is a noteworthy concentration of foundation wealth on the island of Manhattan, and a significant portion of the support provided by these foundations tends to go to East Coast institutions. The state of Texas has a number of large foundations, many of which restrict their giving to organizations within the state. On the other hand, in states such as North Dakota, South Dakota, and Alabama, with fewer large foundations and corporate headquarters, there is much less charitable giving. The concentration of population and/or wealth and institutional proximity to it are often important variables. However, every community has a power structure, and any organization that is planning a campaign can maximize its potential by effectively involving these key community leaders.

The Human Factors. Human emotion and motivation are factors that should never be underestimated. There are three factors that transcend all others in motivating people to give—urgency, importance, and relevance. An earthquake hits Central America and destroys a hospital; a tornado rips through the Midwest and flattens a church. There is an urgent need, and people respond to it immediately. Never mind that the organization affected may not have an organized fundraising operation or the essential elements of capital fundraising, donors will react to an urgent situation. The decision to give is often spontaneous (Panas, 1984, p. 176).

Importance is the second strong motivator. If something is important enough to people, they will see that it gets done. If a community decides that a YMCA/YWCA building is important to it or that a program to shelter and feed the homeless and hungry should be at the top of its agenda, this importance alone can transcend other factors in getting the job done. Again, never mind that the organization falls short in critical ways. Even if the prospective donor does not feel the urgency of the situation or deem it relevant personally, if it is perceived as being important—particularly if it is perceived as being important to peers and colleagues whose esteem the prospective donor values—support can be and will be generated. The third factor is relevance. People respond to things that are personally relevant, often on a totally emotional basis. Individuals give emotionally, not cerebrally (Panas, 1984, p. 172).

Other Factors. Other factors that affect a capital campaign may be local or temporary in nature, and it may be impossible to predict their occurrence or impact. An example of this is the economy. When the last recession hit the automobile industry a few years ago, it became more difficult to mount a campaign in the state of Michigan. The economic condition in Oregon in recent years dampened enthusiasm for campaigns there, even when all the other essential elements were present and the need pressing and urgent. The psychological effect of the energy crisis that hit Texas in 1985 makes it difficult today to contemplate mounting major campaign efforts, although there already are promising signs of an economic recovery. In October 1987, "Black Monday" hit America's stock market, sending reverberations around the world. Its impact on campaigns is now rippling across North America. The timing of other campaigns and fundraising drives is another consideration. In the face of competing and conflicting capital fundraising efforts, an institution may decide to alter its own time frame or to proceed more cautiously because the leadership it desires to attract is already committed to other efforts or other efforts have already overextended its constituency's ability to give.

Factors such as these will undoubtedly need to be considered from time to time as an organization plans its campaign. An institution that finds itself less than well prepared to meet such contingencies need not abandon its plans to campaign. However, it may have to slow its pace or postpone its efforts for a time until it has acquired the necessary strength or the situation has altered so as to allow the campaign process to proceed. Failure to do this will place the campaign at risk and possibly predestine its failure.

Forms of Capital Campaigns

While the general principles of capital campaigns tend to be universally applicable to any type of organization, there are different campaign models. Four rather distinctive forms are found today: the historical capital campaign, the comprehensive campaign, the single-purpose campaign, and the continuing major gifts program.

Historical Capital Campaign. The historical capital campaign is a fundraising effort designed to secure gifts of capital assets to meet capital needs of an organization, to build buildings, and, in some instances, to build the endowment. It is characterized by a highly motivated volunteer group working in a tightly organized and managed manner to meet a specific overall capital goal with one or more objectives during a specific time period, usually three years or less. The volunteers make every reasonable effort to see all constituents and special friends face to face, because the campaign is viewed as a "once-in-a-lifetime" program: historical capital campaigns typically are spaced many years, even decades, apart, and they usually occur only once during the donor population's giving life. They are often superimposed on the ongoing development effort. In some instances, other fundraising efforts, especially annual campaigns, are suspended or downplayed during historical capital campaigns. It is common to create a separate campaign office, budget, and staff for the sole purpose of supporting the effort.

The historical capital campaign is still used in a variety of situations—a church that is building an addition, a YMCA/YWCA constructing a swimming facility, and a Scout organization creating a summer camp are a few examples. However, at least four important changes in campaigning have made the historical model less fashionable today and have led to the increasing use of two other models, the comprehensive campaign and the single-purpose campaign. First, historical capital campaigns seek gifts of capital assets to meet capital needs of the institution. Today's capital campaigns are often designed to meet other needs, and more and more today the gifts are being made in all forms, including capital. Second, the historical capital campaign typically is an infrequent, atypical, all-out effort by an institution and is marketed in this way to the prospects, and this type of campaign is no longer as common as it once was. Many institutions today hardly complete one campaign before announcing the next one. The third factor is sheer economics—the cost of fundraising. The historical capital cam-

paign attempts to reach all constituents and friends of the institution on a one-to-one, face-to-face basis. The number of constituents,
the geographical distribution of the constituents of organizations
serving wide areas, and the frequency of campaign efforts today
simply preclude—financially, not to mention logistically—this
kind of activity for many of America's third-sector institutions.
Finally, an institution conducting a historical capital campaign
runs the risk of restricting or damaging other established, ongoing
giving programs, a risk fewer and fewer institutions are willing or
able to take.

Comprehensive Campaign. The comprehensive campaign is
a major comprehensive development program with specific goals
and timetables. It almost always includes under one umbrella
current operations, one-time goals, and endowment objectives. It
generally lasts for three to five years, although some campaigns are
longer, and some are conducted in phases. Gifts and pledges of all
kinds, including annual as well as planned and deferred gifts, are
often sought and counted in the campaign dollar total. In many
instances, there is less dependence on volunteers and increasing
involvement of administrators and staff, not only as cultivators but
also as solicitors, who concentrate on maximizing the gifts of major
donor prospects through intense personal solicitation, often
soliciting both special and general prospects by telephone or direct
mail. This type of campaign is related to the total development
program, often encompassing other ongoing giving programs. The
comprehensive campaign model is especially attractive to larger,
more complex organizations that want to keep the total fundraising
effort under one umbrella or to create a more substantial total goal
than the "new money" goal might otherwise be.

Single-Purpose Campaign. Also currently popular is the
single-purpose campaign—a campaign to raise money for a single
building, for an endowment fund, or for any other single objective.
It is often targeted at one particular special-interest constituency
group, and it generally is not undertaken as a part of the entire
development effort, although it is related to it. This form of
campaign activity is leading many institutions to employ a full-
time professional fund raiser, sometimes with a staff, whose
responsibility is major and special gifts and who carries a corre-

sponding title. Many institutions today are continually into and out of single-purpose campaigns and, occasionally, into two or three or more at the same time. This particular campaign model is used almost exclusively by larger, administratively more complex institutions. It is generally best to conduct a single, unified campaign regardless of the size or complexity of any institution; but that is not always possible, and sometimes is not even desirable, in complex organizations.

Continuing Major Gifts Program. The fourth campaign model is the continuing major gifts program as an integrated part of a planned, ongoing development program. Realizing that there is a limit to the number of times extraordinary fundraising efforts can produce quick and effective solutions to today's problems, institutional leaders are accepting two premises: (1) that strategic organizational planning will become an accepted, even required practice in all nonprofit organizations and (2) that this type of planning will eventually lead to better management practices and better managers for the institutions using it and for their development programs.

Where a strategic planning approach is used, development programs become multiyear, planned efforts designed in supportive concert with institutional strategies. This results in perpetual campaigning to satisfy capital as well as other needs through a coordinated, ongoing fundraising effort with major "campaigns" harmoniously integrated into the ongoing program, thus making the "campaigns" far less obvious as extraordinary fundraising efforts than with the other models. A major gifts program is designed to be more proactive in gaining financial support for a planned future. It is administered by a professional staff.

This should not suggest that institutions utilizing the strategic planning method will not from time to time continue to engage in intensive, time-specific "capital campaigns" with defined goals. They will. Besides the sheer volume of dollars that can be raised when a heightened sense of urgency and importance is created, and the psychological and motivational strategies that can maximize giving in a campaign's excitement, institutions will occasionally simply want to bring to themselves the special attention that a campaign provides. What is different in the planned environment that is future oriented is that those who campaign will do so because they choose to and not because they have no other plausible alternative. Therefore, announced capital campaigns, as they historically have been known, will probably become less frequent. But when undertaken, they will, curiously, have many of the traditional characteristics of the campaigns that Ward organized seventy years ago.

The selection of a campaign model to be used in a particular situation will be influenced by a number of factors, including the commitment to and quality of strategic institutional planning, the current level of maturity and sophistication of the development program, the development staff's experience and ability, the availability of campaign leadership, the impressiveness of the case, the potential of the major donor prospects, and the range and scope of the anticipated campaign effort. There is no one correct model for all institutions or all situations. In fact, there may be opportunities to incorporate features of more than one of the models to best serve a particular situation.

✳ 2 ✳

Preparing for a Campaign: Three Essential Steps

This chapter discusses three essential aspects of the early stages of campaign planning—strategic institutional planning and its impact on the campaign, the purpose and organization of the market survey, and the use of an internal audit to determine institutional preparedness.

Strategic Planning

The first requirement for any capital campaign is a clear image of the institution and a plan for growth and improvement in order that it may better fulfill its purpose—a strategic plan. It is an approach that asks most institutions to be more intentional, more organized, and more strategic than they have been in the past. Any development program presupposes that the institution knows what it is going to develop. No amount of public relations can serve as a substitute for an institution's having a reason for being.

Everywhere today, board members and local leaders are asking questions about the future of their third-sector institutions. They want to know their aims and goals. They are interested in an institutional audit of the organizations that they are asked to support. But many institutions have neglected—or avoided—the self-analysis and planning that would define aims and set goals. An institution without a strategic plan is at the mercy of pressure groups. It is in danger of being manipulated by an influential individual's whim, a board member's pet project, or uninformed community opinion.

15

It is the business of all nonprofit institutions to do strategic planning. Without a strategy based on a knowledge of the philanthropic marketplace, they will have only random ideas without a guiding purpose. James Gregory Lord says it thus:

> As the Roman philosopher Seneca said, "When a man does not know what harbor he is making for, no wind is the right one." Or, as Yogi Berra put it more recently, "You've got to be very careful if you don't know where you are going, because you might not get there." Many forces outside individual institutions are trying to legislate how they ought to be doing their jobs. So an institution has to have a plan for its future particularly when it is preparing to embark on a fundraising campaign, if for no other reason, because people deserve to know how the institution intends to use the money—and what kind of benefits are expected. What makes planning even more valuable is the opportunity it presents for involvement. If an institution's leaders are on the ball they will use the planning process to get people involved in mapping an organization's future—especially those people who have the power to bring about that future. Authentic involvement in a planning process promotes a sense of ownership among prospective donors and volunteers. People are simply motivated to work for and invest in the realization of plans they themselves have helped to develop.
>
> The act of planning also focuses and clarifies thinking. This is another way in which the process itself is more important than the resulting document. Furthermore, with regard to fundraising, planning makes an institution look good. Most donors don't want to know all the details—but they do want to be assured that an organization knows its future and sees a path for getting there. They want to know that not-for-profit organizations are using the skills of the business world, and that they are treating the eleemos-

ynary enterprise in an intentional, organized, and strategic manner. Any institution will make an excellent impression if it can tell those it is trying to attract, either as volunteers or as potential donors, that it has conducted surveys among the people it serves, designed a strategic plan, and produced a financial plan for the next three to five years or more.

This kind of planning is exactly what one philanthropist wanted when he asked a hospital trustee: "What's your mission? And I don't mean that formal stuff, either. What are you doing? What does your five year plan look like? What services are you going to add? To abandon?" More and more prospects are asking these tough questions. Too many organizations still have no answers, or only the vaguest ones. The sharp organizations, those that are attracting big money, are ready with their plans. Corporations, foundations, and wealthy individuals, after all, are only asking that not-for-profits follow the same discipline that they—the prospects—have been practicing for years. Let's be clear, what's being talked about isn't the kind of "long-range planning" many organizations already do, but real strategic planning. The difference is important [Lord, 1985, pp. 32–35].

Traditional long-range planning is an administrative tool. Predictions are made on the basis of past performance, current resources, and demographic trends. Strategic planning, the kind George Keller (1983) describes in *Academic Strategy*, is an entrepreneurial process whereby an organization attempts to design its own future on the basis of the external environment, its opportunities, and its constraints. Strategic planning looks at forces outside the institution's control, forces such as rising expectations for certain kinds of training or services or a declining service population. Through this kind of planning, any organization can examine its options, decide what its future direction should be, and develop an action plan, a budget, and a timetable for meeting its objectives.

Conducting a Market Survey

In order for an institution's board to establish monetary and programmatic goals for its capital campaign, the organization needs to conduct both internal and external evaluations of its programs. To determine goals for a successful capital campaign, an inventory of needs and a determination of priorities are imperative. There is a great deal of difference between an institutional wants list and a needs list. It is absolutely essential that the wants list be carefully pared to a substantiated and documented needs list. The needs list is initially generated in house. It evolves from the planning process to determine all important needs that might be met with private funding. Then the needs must be ranked in priority order. Institutional planners should always be cognizant of the importance of identifying goals that appeal to the constituency. Legitimate institutional needs should not be dramatically altered or abandoned because of lack of constituency appeal, although they may necessitate special "educational" programs for the constituency before a campaign can move forward, but items of little or no interest to the constituency generally should not appear as major components of a campaign goal. When it is possible, goals should be brought under one umbrella to make the campaign a unified one. This makes sense in terms of both organizing the fundraising volunteers and ensuring institutional cohesion. How much constituency appeal a particular campaign component has can best be determined by a selective surveying (market survey) of key constituents. A market survey is a test of an institution's philanthropic potential.

Before undertaking a market survey, the institution must have an institutional plan anticipating funding needs, a financial plan for approved projects and programs, advocacy and gift support from board members, a sales and production staff, a comprehensive financial development program, prospects capable of providing the support expected, and a case for substantial support. These essentials of fundraising are the constant threads that run through the fabric of all capital campaigns.

The major purpose of the market survey is to provide an accurate assessment of the factors that might affect the campaign and to investigate and evaluate the external opportunity for an institution to mount and successfully accomplish a large-scale major gifts campaign. An essential objective is to determine, on the basis of reactions to the case statement, attitudes toward the institutional priorities and the campaign goal and, if warranted, to suggest changes in either or both. Other objectives are to educate potential major donors and campaign leadership, to identify and evaluate those best suited to give leadership to workers and/or major donors to the campaign, and to provide the institution with an analysis of all information gathered.

According to Martin Grenzebach (1986a, p. 1), there are certain prerequisites for any fundraising campaign to achieve success.

> The institution must enjoy a *positive image* within its constituency and within the business, financial, and industrial communities; there must be a clearly *perceived need,* well defined in the minds of those who know the institution best and which can be made to inspire a sense of commitment in the thinking of those who are asked for financial support; there must be a *presence of available funds* ample enough in depth and breadth that, when properly motivated, those who hold the key to these resources will release enough of them to the institution in such measure as to meet its goal; there must be *capable leadership,* holding the complete respect of the community and willing to give the necessary time and talent to the institution and its causes; and there must be a generally *favorable economic climate* within the constituency and/or the community, such as is occasioned by a sound economic outlook and the reasonable absence of conflicting campaigns and competing enterprises.

Grenzebach (1986b) also describes the process of conducting a market survey. One to five days of consultation are required to develop the design of the study, assemble and evaluate the list of prospects to be interviewed, draft and review the interview contact letter and needs statement, develop interview strategies, draft the interview questionnaire, and assemble and mail any ancillary marketing materials that may be required. Most consultants assume the following responsibilities:

- Preparation of an explanatory letter to be sent to those who will be interviewed.
- Assistance in preparation of a realistic needs list and brief case statement relating to the needs.
- Development of the questions to be employed in the interview process and possible alternative questions for select interviews.
- Assistance in establishing the interview schedule and executing that schedule.
- Correlation and analysis of the information obtained and provision of recommendations based on the findings.
- Preparation and presentation of both a written and an oral survey report to the board of the institution [Grenzebach, 1986b, pp. 3–4].

Market surveys are conducted through personal interviews with a carefully selected cross section of board members, community leaders, service users, alumni, friends, and other key constituents. The interview population is selected on the basis of close relationship to the institution, familiarity with people and situations pertinent to fundraising, potential as donors, and ability to influence others to work and give. Under ordinary circumstances, an interview sample of fifty to seventy properly selected respondents will provide the information that is needed for an institution to determine the feasibility of a capital campaign. However, many organizations often interview and survey larger numbers of respondents to inform them about the campaign and begin their involvement. The size of the sample is determined by the size and complexity of the institution's constituency and the campaign's design and goal.

For a sample of fifty to seventy people, the interview portion of the study generally requires three to five weeks. The initial list of major constituents should be supplemented by basic profile information on each interview candidate. In order to accomplish the appropriate number of interviews, the list of names should be about twice as large as the sample needed. Every prospective interviewee receives an initial contact letter and brief case statement describing the funding needs of the organization. These letters are followed up by telephone calls to each individual to schedule the survey interviews. Confidential interviews are conducted by professional counsel or by institutional staff under the direction of counsel. A significant but smaller number of the interviews are conducted with selected administration and staff.

Every effort must be made to conduct the interviews objectively. It is important that each person interviewed be assured that the conversation will be held in strict confidence. The privileged information thus obtained becomes invaluable in the process of evaluating the potential for a successful capital campaign. Generally, the value of face-to-face interviews does not rest solely with the apparent facts obtained. It must be remembered that in some instances what appear to be facts are merely subjective observations. However, as the interview process continues, those conducting the interviews are in a unique position to check and cross-check the reliability of various opinions and to assess the perceptiveness of each person interviewed. It usually becomes clear which responses should be given greater weight, and those are emphasized in the market survey report. Normally, each face-to-face interview takes from thirty minutes to an hour to complete. In addition to the traditional face-to-face interview, focus groups, telephone interviews, and direct-mail questionnaires are increasingly being used to supplement and further validate these surveys, although these methods have limitations and should not supplant the face-to-face interview as the principal technique. It is extremely important that the organization understand that a market survey used to determine the feasibility of a campaign should not deal at length with the presentation of a campaign plan or timetable. These items should be covered in detail after the market survey has been accepted formally by the organization's board.

After the interviews have been conducted, an additional six to ten days are usually required for evaluation and analysis and the preparation of a final report. If the organization is not conducting an internal program audit and is not using ongoing consultation, the modern survey will check the following internal systems: individual, foundation, and corporate records; quality and range of information maintained; ongoing efforts to expand and update prospect files and other donor records; the gift processing system and financial record-keeping procedures; and other data-processing support services, such as daily and monthly tracking of prospects, donors, and corporate and foundation proposals. In addition, attention must be paid to quarterly and annual gift progress and management reporting; the word-processing support services for the development program, including correspondence, proposal preparation, and other text and manuscript services; and the basic techniques of donor research and internal staff prospect rating. One to two days should be reserved for presentation of the survey to the administration and the board.

The market survey report typically includes the following:

- Suggested goal for the campaign, if such a campaign is feasible.
- The anticipated strengths and weaknesses of the campaign identified by the survey.
- A recommended strategic plan for the campaign.
- The potential leadership available as compared to the leadership required to make the campaign successful.
- A list of major donor prospects.
- A recommendation on services needed to establish and carry forward the campaign and a proposed campaign structure.
- If it is not feasible to conduct a campaign, recommendations for upgrading the institution's development performance and circumstances so that it will become feasible.
- A draft letter expressing appreciation to those who have been interviewed.
- Significant development information obtained through the survey interviews but not necessarily

pertinent to the campaign's feasibility [Grenze-
bach, 1986b, pp. 4–5].

The market survey should provide an accurate and perceptive
assessment of the constituents' views of the institution, their
awareness of and support for the needs being advanced by the
institution, information regarding the correct timing of a capital
campaign and whether the right leadership is available, and,
undoubtedly most important from a financial standpoint, whether
sufficient money can be raised to undertake the program.

Beyond this, there are other significant benefits that a market
survey provides, including a significant public relations value; an
opportunity for constituency leaders to review the institution;
valuable development information that is gleaned from the
interviews; an opportunity to have a positive impact on business
and civic leaders by including them in the survey sample; and
information from the interviews that is helpful not only with regard
to formulating the campaign plan but also for institutional
comprehensive planning. Properly done, it can minimize the cost
and maximize the success of the campaign, and it is very often the
first public step taken in cultivating key support for the campaign,
especially with those close to but not directly included in the
immediate family of the institution.

Increasingly today, institutions are deciding in advance that
they will campaign and then using the market survey to inform
potential volunteer leaders and major donors that a campaign is
being planned as well as to gain the benefit of outside expertise in
establishing a strategic game plan for the fundraising effort. In
these instances, the purpose of the market survey is different, and
its presentation accordingly has a different focus. The organization
must understand whether it seeks a true feasibility study or is
already committed to a campaign (unless counsel can dissuade it on
the basis of the findings of the survey) and is using the market
survey fundamentally as an educational technique to advance its
efforts. It must communicate its situation to counsel before the
market survey is undertaken so that counsel can appropriately
structure its efforts and reports to the organization.

An organizational feature that is emerging today is the

creation of a market survey committee. The purpose of such a committee is to provide a way to develop a sense of direct involvement and active leadership of its members during the early, key planning stages of the campaign, in addition to providing knowledge and background about significant campaign issues. Members of the committee typically are asked to (1) review a draft list of those to be interviewed and make recommendations; (2) when necessary, facilitate access for the consultant to those who are being interviewed; (3) meet with the consultant to review and comment on the detailed design of the survey instrument; and (4) review and comment on both the draft and final versions of the market survey report. Membership includes a chair, possibly the individual who will be asked to serve as general chair of the campaign, and high-level representatives from the major constituency groups the campaign will target as well as from the board. The committee functions best when there are no more than ten members, with five to seven being optimum in most cases. Because dedicated volunteer leadership is essential to a campaign's success and because involvement eventually leads to investment of time, energy, and resources, a few wise institutions today are involving key prospects at this very early stage. Many more will adopt this approach as it becomes more widely known.

Conducting an Internal Program Audit

For a capital campaign to be successful, it must be well organized and well managed both internally and externally. Too often, institutions devote most of their time and attention to external preparedness while doing little or nothing to address the internal conditions, both within the institution as a whole and within the development office itself, that can enhance or handicap a campaign. In such situations, it is unfortunate that so much is done to raise significant sums of money by institutions not internally prepared to handle the effort, thereby forfeiting many of its lasting benefits. One of the first requirements for internal preparedness is that all internal constituencies of the organization be made aware of the campaign and made to feel they have an active part to play in it. Key administrators should be consulted or informed about all proposals on fundraising activities that relate to their specific areas. At the same time, key institutional personnel should be actively involved with providing the kind of information that will lead to the eliciting of large campaign gifts. Even before the capital campaign is undertaken, it is advisable to conduct an internal program audit.

What exactly is an institutional development audit? It is a formal, comprehensive evaluation of an institution's development program and its relationship to the people in the institutional areas that it touches. It is conducted by an auditor (an experienced, qualified fundraising professional) or an auditing team that gathers both objective and subjective data by observing and interviewing as well as reviewing institutional literature and written reports. This information is then analyzed to assess an institution's fundraising program.

What will an audit do in advance of a capital campaign? It will establish the facts about an institution's program, as opposed to feelings or perceptions about it; suggest new and better ways of doing things at this critical point at the beginning of the campaign; justify the role of the development program and its budget, both to the institutional leaders and to the development staff; and involve management and volunteer leaders in the program and encourage their help and support.

In addition, an audit conducted immediately before the capital campaign can help those at the top of the institution—senior management and board members—to better understand what the development officers and program do, how it is done, why it is done, and what results can be expected. By providing a comprehensive overview, the audit can establish a firmer understanding of the development operation. This can encourage the kind of synergy between top management, key volunteers, and development professionals that is essential to making the capital campaign a success.

In order to develop a comprehensive overview, Grenzebach (1986c) recommends that the audit include an evaluation of the following areas:

- The articulation of the case for support.
- Fundraising progress over the last five years.

- A review of current operating goals and priorities for development, including current and past years' activities, current staffing structures and personnel, and the breadth of institutional resources.
- An examination of the annual giving participation level in terms of both percentage and overall dollars.
- A review of the current relationship within the organizational structure between other components of the advancement effort, if any, and the development program.
- A review of the depth and breadth of local, community, and state corporate and foundation support, solicitation progress in those areas, and the utilization of board relationships and volunteer-based activities with these corporations and foundations.
- An examination of the specific corporate and foundation relations programs—identification, analysis, research, cultivation, and solicitation of gift prospects; management and tracking mechanisms employed with these programs.
- Identification of the strengths and weaknesses of board members and other top leadership.
- An examination of the institutional support groups, if any—the strength of various fundraising boards, the quality of the program(s), their relationship(s) to the institution.
- A review of the current level of involvement on the part of the chief executive officer, the board, and other high-level institutional officers in advancement activities—in particular, their current level and expertise in solicitation activities.
- A review of the involvement and understanding of institutional administrators with regard to the development program and public relations, the needs determination process, and a designation of special gift opportunities and major gifts–targeted solicitation.

- An examination of the formal relationship and level of cooperation of the development program with other components of the institution.
- A review of research, records, and system support functions.
- A review of the quality of proposal preparation and internal proposal review.
- A review of the planned giving program and how it is incorporated into the development program— number of mailings, request procedures, record keeping, planned gift proposals presented to gift prospects.
- An examination of the donor relations program— acknowledgment strategies, cultivation events, gift clubs, and donor recognition activities.
- A review and/or structuring of a detailed annual operating plan for development, which specifies monthly, quarterly, and annual goals together with reporting mechanisms and review methods.
- Any other special aspects of the institution that require review or examination [Grenzebach, 1986c, pp. 1-4].

Many people representing the institution's various constituencies should be involved in providing the answers to the questions posed. The auditor should interview board members, the chief executive officer, senior managers, the chief development officer, the professional development staff, representatives of the secretarial/clerical staff, other key individuals within the institution, important volunteers and lay leaders, and, possibly, influential and affluent community members. The auditor should make every effort to conduct the interviews objectively and should assure each person interviewed that the conversation will be confidential. The interview process should go until the auditor is certain that enough information is available to provide a complete report to the institution. Finally, the auditor should supplement these interviews with personal observations on such factors as space allocation, visual impact of publications, and so on. The audit report should be presented in writing. It will often be supplemented by an oral report to the board and chief executive officer.

For the purposes of preparing for a capital campaign, it is best that the audit be conducted by external evaluators. It may be done by an individual, a team of individuals, or a professional consultant with expertise in this area. Advantages of using independent auditors are that they can bring expertise and experience to the task that generally are not found among institutional personnel and that they are free from the biases that often are found in organizations. It is important to use an external auditor to conduct an audit of the program right before the capital campaign. The stakes are so high that the institution cannot run the risk of having the job done any less professionally, less objectively, or less well than it can be.

✳ 3 ✳

Roles of Leaders
and Volunteers
in the Campaign

"A good fundraising program has two kinds of leadership—the layman who leads and the staff member who manages and serves. The better each is and the better they work together, the better the results will be. Leadership in itself, let it never be forgotten, is always the key factor in successful fundraising, whatever the cause, whatever the goal, and whatever the scope of the campaign" (Seymour, 1966, p. 179).

The chair of the governing board, the general chair of the campaign, and the chief executive officer of the institution have the principal roles in a capital campaign—especially in the early phases. They are responsible for setting the pace and establishing the right mood for the campaign. They also have to be confident that the planning stage is completed correctly and precisely and that all the tools necessary for a successful campaign are present, especially a market survey, a case statement, and a comprehensive campaign plan. The success or failure of most campaigns is ultimately attributable to them.

Dramatically increased fundraising competition in recent years has had a significant impact on top volunteer enlistment. Today there are more large, important campaigns and relatively fewer qualified, interested individuals to fill key leadership roles. Experienced volunteers now ask tough questions before they commit themselves to a project. The responsibility for enlisting and

29

motivating these top volunteers falls to the chief executive officer, professional staff, and key members of the board. It is they who must be prepared to convincingly win the commitment of top volunteer leaders.

Campaign Leadership

The selection of leadership is of the utmost importance in a campaign. Top leadership should be excited and exciting. It should come primarily from within. Any institution should be able to find within its board, service user groups, advisory groups, and other "family" types of constituencies the bulk of the leadership it will need during a campaign. The power structure of a community may also provide supplemental leadership. Community leadership falls into four main groups: (1) those who have inherited both wealth and its tradition of public service; (2) the newly rich and newly powerful, Horatio Algers of the modern world; (3) the top professional managers of key corporations; and (4) the respected and admired men and women in the community. An absence of leadership at this level is an early warning sign that the institution is not yet adequately prepared to undertake a campaign.

Top leadership should consist of respected individuals who have an immediate name recognition with the institution's publics; who are strongly identified with the institution and have a history of association and active involvement with it; who have established a substantial record of major gift support to the institution; and who will be forceful, dynamic leaders with colleagues and friends who are also leaders representing the institution's various constituencies. For a campaign to be successful, it is necessary for top leadership to make a commitment of time, effort, and giving.

An organizational chart and job description should be prepared for the leadership that clearly describe specific responsibilities and the amount of time that will be required, including the number of meetings necessary to complete the task. Recruitment should begin at the top and work down so volunteers recruit the people who work for them.

The Role of the Campaign Chair

The duties of a campaign chair generally include (1) serving as the campaign's chief executive officer; (2) enlisting chairpersons for the principal functioning units of the campaign organization; (3) cultivating and solicitating a limited number of appropriate prospects; (4) assuming specific responsibility for the personal and/or corporate commitments from members of the campaign steering committee and all the principal operating chairs; (5) serving as chair of the campaign steering committee and presiding over its meetings; (6) making day-to-day decisions regarding the problems of the campaign, in consultation with the chief executive officer and chief development officer and others at the institution when important considerations arise; and (7) acting as spokesperson for the campaign in all news stories, campaign publications, special events, and other functions.

As the general campaign chair is the chief operating officer of the capital campaign, the best that an organization has to offer is barely good enough. The person who accepts this position is the key to the campaign and, more often than not, the measure of its success. No one is too big or too important for this leadership post. The person chosen must be a person of proven capabilities who has influence and affluence and is willing to use them on behalf of the institution; one who is dedicated to seeing that the job is done on schedule; one who commands respect without demanding it; one to whom others will readily respond, because people give to and work for people, not causes; and one who has intimate knowledge of the institution and the full scope of its program. Additionally, the job requires one who has persistence that compels others to follow suit; is easily accessible; is willing to follow the campaign plan and procedures and accept direction; is willing to devote sufficient time to leadership, aware that early phases of planning and recruiting may require a considerable amount of the chair's time; has the determination to overcome obstacles and invalid excuses; and is willing and prepared at the start of the campaign to make a personal pledge that is generous, thoughtful, and proportionate. (In the event that the chair represents a corporation, a significant commitment from the company should demonstrate leadership for other business and industry prospects.)

The Role of the Governing Board

Members of governing boards have four main functions: (1) to define the concept of the institution, to set institutional goals, and to approve plans for reaching the goals; (2) to approve the top administrative officers and to motivate them, not just rubber-stamp administrative recommendations, to give affirmative support to administrators, and to lend board leadership to administrative leadership; (3) to audit and assess the performance of the institution in all of its parts and the work of the top executives in the pursuit of established goals; and (4) to take appropriate action on the board's assessments of what must be done to reach institutional goals and build a more effective institution (Stuhr, 1977, p. 46).

In order to effectively carry out these four functions, boards are often asked to make decisions that lead their institutions into capital campaigns and then to act effectively within the campaign structure. In a capital campaign, the individual board member's help is needed in setting the goals, encouraging the staff, formulating plans, identifying, cultivating, and soliciting major gift prospects, readily accepting major posts in the campaign (the community expects the institution's lay leaders to accept the key jobs), and taking on sufficient dollar goals for themselves to launch the campaign.

Leadership from the governing board, says Thomas E. Broce (1979), is the single most critical factor affecting the success of a campaign and even in determining whether an institution should conduct a capital program. Without the board's visible and unanimous commitment, it will be difficult if not impossible to motivate others to participate. And it is the governing board members, independent of others, who must eventually commit themselves to seeing that a stated goal is reached because they themselves are unanimously determined that it will be.

Gerber (in Stuhr, 1977) reinforces Stuhr's points, stating that leadership from the top in recruiting workers, cultivating, soliciting, and giving is absolutely critical to a successful capital campaign. While additional people are needed as volunteer leaders, workers, and givers, the added emphasis that the board leadership gives cannot be matched by any other group. More than anything else, the role of board members is to establish a policy framework within which the institution operates and to set an example for others. With regard to the capital campaign, board members set an example for others by taking a place in the volunteer organization and becoming workers, by making gifts that are generous and appropriate to each member's means early in the campaign schedule, by being informed and enthusiastic about the campaign and the institution, by working to bring other volunteers into the program, and by communicating to others in the constituency about the institution and the campaign.

The board as a whole must be involved in a significant way from the start, says Homer J. Livingston, Jr. (1984) speaking to a development workshop. The executive, finance, and development committees are board committees that must be informed about and supportive of the project. Much of the money to be raised will come through the efforts of board members. It is mandatory to get their approval to raise money for the project, and it is imperative that they be sold not only on the project but also on the institution. The more enthusiastic they are about the institution's leadership and the institution itself, the better job they will do in raising money.

As a part of its overall responsibility, the board should review the timing of the campaign. How does it relate to prior drives? What have similar institutions recently done, begun doing, or announced? Has anything recently happened to affect the institution that makes this a particularly propitious or unpropitious time? Another area of board responsibility, not generally considered a part of the campaign but nevertheless very significant, is the investment of the funds as they are received. The investment committee of the board should determine in advance the amount of funds expected to be received and formulate an investment plan. If the funds will be needed relatively soon, some kind of short-term investment is probably called for, whereas if the funds are earmarked for endowment, longer-term debt or equity may be considered. The most important thing to do is to get the donations working.

The plan for a major campaign is ordinarily developed by

the administration of an institution. Administrators are involved daily and are probably more aware of needs than outside board members. This is not to say there will not be occasions when the board will suggest a campaign. But the initial step will usually be the chief executive officer of the institution discussing a need with the board chair. This will likely be followed by discussion with the executive committee of the board. Given preliminary approval, the staff generally will be asked to prepare a detailed report of the specific needs and the costs and benefits involved for formal submission to the executive committee of the board. Following review and approval of need, with possible input from the finance and development committees, the concept is submitted to the full board for approval. If the board approves, a capital campaign then is usually referred to the board's development committee for planning and overall supervision of its implementation.

The development committee and the development staff are the likely organizers of any capital campaign. The board's role in this area is first of all to ensure that the campaign is properly planned. It should look at the organization and structure, people involved, individuals, corporations, and foundations being solicited, how they will be solicited, how much they will be asked for, timing of efforts, and marketing aids being used.

Having approved the concept and the plan, board members should be asked to give. But they should first be thoroughly cultivated and involved through the process described in Chapter Four. Involvement in planning, both institutional and campaign, is extremely important, because involvement begets investment. The institution should evaluate both the potential and probable giving ability of each board member and ask key board members to help rate fellow members as well. As a part of the involvement and cultivation process, expose board members to the first draft of the case statement and seek their active reaction and involvement in the formulation of the final draft. It is important that the institution not take board members for granted and that they be cultivated at the highest level.

Before soliciting board members, consider the possibility of a formula for board member giving—a certain percentage of net worth or of annual income, for example. Also formulate a policy for counting deferred and planned gifts from board members and others. This method may help board members to enhance their participation in the campaign. Also consider the degree to which a board member's giving might be a leverage factor in setting the total goal: "If the board gives $1 million, we would have a chance of raising $4 to $5 million." Most importantly, involve a key group of the board in answering these questions and establishing the board goal. Once this goal has been established and the board has been fully involved and properly cultivated, it is time to solicit the board.

Remember, *the single greatest mistake made in fundraising in general and in capital campaigns specifically is not asking for the gift.* The institution must ask its board to give early in the campaign to serve as an example for others—the local community, other potential major donors, service users, and friends. But once board members are ready to be solicited, plan each solicitation carefully. No board member should ever give before being asked to do so. When board gifts, as well as other gifts, are offered in advance, they are generally much smaller than if they had been properly solicited. Choose solicitors carefully, and make sure each solicitor has made a personal commitment first. Members of the board should be solicited by the chief executive officer and/or other members of the board. Team solicitation, preferably with two callers on the prospect, is the most successful method. In making a solicitation, it is important to know the board member's areas of interest and relate them to the campaign. The biggest gifts will be generated when board members are asked to provide support in an area of personal interest. It is also extremely important to note that capital gifts are not to be made in place of annual gifts. Carefully consider the best asking method—the separate ask, double ask, or triple ask described in Chapter Seven—before approaching board members and others.

In successful campaigns, the contributors from board members and the foundations and firms they control can range from 20 percent to more than 50 percent of the total goal of the campaign. There are, of course, some exceptions to this. But there must always be a core or nucleus group ready to provide this kind of financial leadership, and it most often includes strong board participation. One hundred percent participation from the board in a capital campaign program is a powerful signal to other donors that the institution has vitality and vigor and the confidence and enthusiasm of its governing board, who, above all, should know the institution best.

Once they have given, the role of board members becomes that of solicitors. All board members should be responsible for some part of the campaign. It is not necessary that the campaign chair be a board member, but, ideally, every member of the board should be in a leadership position, with a group of nonboard solicitors working for and with them. This makes the board's involvement better known and demonstrates the board's backing of the program, and it gives the solicitors someone knowledgeable about the institution to answer their questions and to go with them on calls. Board members should be used to identify potential solicitors, such as people with a past, present, or future involvement with the institution. Board members presumably have useful contacts in the community and should use them in bringing in as solicitors people who could be significant givers. They should ensure that enough people are involved to get the job done in an organized manner and that they are the proper people, that they have sufficient contacts to be useful solicitors or can be significant contributors themselves.

Every community has leaders whose very involvement in a campaign gives it credibility. Board members should encourage these kinds of people to participate. As well, several of these people should be numbered among an institution's board. Board members should be asked to make important fundraising calls; their participation will add to the significance of the call. However, they need not be involved with all the calls. Being a board member is a part-time responsibility, and most board members probably have another, full-time position. They cannot afford to spend a great deal of time making calls, so board member calls should be carefully selected. Board members are most helpful in calling on people they know or on people of similar standing in the community or corporate world. If an institution has a CEO of a significant corporation on its board, it should use that person to make calls on other CEOs.

In summary, here are the responsibilities of the board in a campaign:

- Reviewing the need for the campaign
- Helping to structure the organization and the timing of the campaign
- Suggesting people as solicitors and potential donors
- Setting levels for prospects
- Ensuring proper research on prospects
- Reviewing all printed material to be used in presentations
- Making an early lead gift commensurate with individual ability
- Being a volunteer solicitor in the campaign
- Doing follow-up and cultivating other major donor prospects, as appropriate
- Ensuring that proper investment is planned for the funds

The Role of the Chief Executive Officer

The CEO and senior management determine the personality of an institution. They give it life and vitality. It is increasingly clear that the CEO is central to the success of today's capital campaigns. Wallace B. Graves (quoted in Stuhr, 1977) says that the CEO's role in the capital campaign can be described by four functions.

The chief executive officer must personify the character and the goals of the institution being led. Every constituency of the institution expects this of the chief executive officer. Successful results from development efforts depend on the chief executive officer's ability to exemplify the character and life-style, the hopes and aspirations of all those who comprise the institution at any given moment. Bene-factors are becoming more discriminating in their selection of institutions to support. They want to know what the institution is trying to accomplish and how it expects to achieve its objectives. Therefore, any institution needs an easily recognizable image, one [that] is unusually appealing. It is the chief executive officer who must know the institution thoroughly.

Second, the chief executive officer must com-municate these goals to the institution's constituent body. The chief executive officer must understand how the institution's constituents perceive its character and goals and must provide them with the synthesis, a structure within which [the volunteers and the CEO can] carry out their representations. People respond most generously to institutions whose representatives exude clarity, solidarity, and confidence respecting their missions and the means for their pursuit.

Third, a chief executive officer must create a strong development staff. Chief executive officers need to find chief development officers with whom they can share their public relations and fundraising programs in an environment of complete confidence. These two should complement each other in administrative skills and working styles. Together, the chief executive officer and chief development officer must build and keep a strong staff, people who are creative in the production of institutional publications and . . . sensitive and talented in public relations activities, people who can find those who can be interested in supporting the institution and who can help the chief executive officer and their chief development officer cultivate this interest and consummate gifts.

Finally, the chief executive officer must be primarily responsible for fundraising. How the chief executive officer accomplishes this mission depends greatly upon individual personality and style of operation. No matter what other valuable contributions a chief executive officer makes to the quality of the individual institution being served, this person will have failed if the institution's financial needs are not provided for. This does not mean the chief executive officer cannot get a lot of help from others. In fact, the job cannot be done without it. If a chief executive officer has a good development staff, keeps the board informed and properly involved, . . . has the cooperation of key staff members and just a little bit of luck, success in the everlasting quest for funds will be possible. But it falls to the chief executive officer to have money on the mind most of the time, not as an obsession, but in service of the institution's mission [Stuhr, 1977, p. 72].

With the help of the board, the CEO must see that the organization has plans sufficiently specific to identify its needs. The plans must be institutionwide. The CEO should participate in the planning process but not make the plans. The plans should include items that the development staff can clearly articulate and passionately believe in. These become the basis for any capital campaign. If the institution is worth supporting, the plans will have something exciting to sell.

Speaking to a development workshop in 1976, Lewis Nobles, president of Mississippi College, said:

There is no way that a chief executive officer of any organization can sidestep leadership in fundraising. In the areas of making solicitation calls, cultivating major gift prospects, and contacting foundations and corporations, the leadership of the chief executive officer is particularly important. But, this individual's time must be conserved and well spent and specific involvement tailored to play to personal strengths.

The chief executive officer must be prepared to manage the function as well as to lead it. This may well mean delegating responsibility and authority as well as exercising [them]. It is vital in the stimulation of volunteers to assist with these endeavors, but not necessary to directly become personally involved with everyone and every step of the process. The relationship of the chief executive officer to donors, but especially to major donors, should be personal and individual to the extent it can be. The chief executive officer is called on to represent the total institution to the best of [his or her] ability. A managed program involving strategic contact with, and continued interest in, those persons and organizations who are best able to support an institution is the major basis for any large gift and represents the mode of operation for the chief executive officer not only during the capital campaign but also over a longer period of time. The staff and volunteers should assist the chief executive officer in this process, and the chief executive officer must not only let them assist but also delegate appropriate responsibility and authority to enable them to assist effectively.

The chief executive officer's enthusiasm, knowledge of [the institution's] direction, sensitivity to the climate of the institution and to the donor's particular interest in it, and strong articulation of [and belief in its mission] will provide the subject matter for any number of presentations during the campaign. Patience and perseverance in building through innumerable small steps builds the interest of someone only peripherally interested in the institution [and] an alertness to every opportunity to speak for the institution—these are the characteristics that must be consciously built into the job of the chief executive officer during the campaign.

Indeed, the essential role of the chief executive officer in the development of private support is to be the energizing, vitalizing central force that will provide an institution with an enduring future. In this entire area of leadership, however, it cannot be forgotten that financial resources never take the place of ideas, convictions, and diligence in the making of a great institution [Stuhr, 1977, pp. 73-74].

The Role of the Chief Development Officer

In any capital campaign, the institution's chief development officer will be the catalytic force—an educator, manager, researcher, communicator, facilitator, leader, guide, and stimulator. This professional should hold a rank equal to that of other administrative cabinet officers and report directly to the chief executive officer. The principal purpose of the chief development officer in a capital campaign is to obtain understanding and support for the total program. This individual must be an effective manager of staff, provide support for the chief executive officer, governing board, and key volunteers, and see that calls are made on prospects, not just planned and talked about. The role of the development staff is often in the background. More than anything else, the role of the chief development officer is to give structure and direction to any capital campaign effort.

How is this done? While every manager is different, and each one has an individual style—and no single management style is always best in all situations—it nevertheless can be said that the following characteristics are usually attributed to successful campaign managers. Most members of the modern professional development staff and today's volunteers believe the campaign director should be less authority oriented and more a provider of work conditions, a helper in problem solving and goal accomplishment. Most importantly, the campaign director should keep out of the way and permit people to manage their own work to the degree possible. The manager's role is to provide a climate in which staff members can gain confidence in each other, in which goals are felt to be understandable and meaningful, and in which all people can participate successfully.

The management function is important to the overall production of the entire staff and all volunteers. The campaign director should have two primary goals: to be a contributor through actual involvement in the professional activity and to provide leadership and guidance for both the staff and the volunteers. Actually, the leadership function today is considered to be more coordination of effort than actual fundraising. The two roles are interdependent. Because most staff members and volunteers will agree that the campaign manager leads through demonstration, this individual should possess considerable knowledge of the profession, better than average skills, and an ability to employ successful techniques in making a contribution to the campaign.

Since the campaign director works in a group environment where all functions are so interdependent and related, that individual must take advantage of the diverse talents of the group members, both staff and volunteers. Rather than working through others in a traditional sense of assigning tasks to subordinates, the director should have the ability to work with peers, associates, and even superiors to get the job done. This, of course, places a premium on good and flexible personal qualities. The campaign director should build an overall approach on the best practices of traditional management, augmented by new approaches, directions, techniques, and attitudes.

The campaign director's role should be built on a recognition that a great deal of the organization's planning, organizing, directing, and controlling can and will be accomplished by others, each of whom is a manager, if only of his or her own time and effort. In other words, the campaign director should provide the necessary climate to facilitate the best work of all subordinates, both staff and volunteers. A successful campaign director generally (1) recognizes the needs of staff and volunteers; (2) delegates authority and/or responsibility; (3) solicits and cultivates donor prospects; (4) involves staff and volunteers appropriately in every level of decision making; (5) provides meaningful support, direction, and leadership; (6) recognizes the challenge of changing times and human motivations; and (7) provides adequate feedback and recognition of achievement.

Chapter Ten explains in detail the specific duties and responsibilities of the chief development officer, the campaign director, and the development staff in any capital campaign.

✳ 4 ✳

Recruiting, Educating,
and Motivating Volunteers

Leadership selection is perhaps the most critical of all decisions to be made. All volunteers are not equal! Some are of the utmost importance to the success of a campaign; others have lesser capabilities.

Volunteers are people who offer themselves to perform a service of their own free will. There is no substitute for the influence a volunteer can have on certain prospective donors. In many cases, the staff's influence is negligible compared to that of the right volunteer. But always remember that while all volunteers can do something, only a few can do a lot. And since the success of any capital campaign is usually dependent on what a handful of donors do, it becomes critically important to the success of the campaign that the right volunteers be enlisted, *right* meaning that they have the ability to influence the people who will make or break the success of the undertaking.

Every volunteer will do something within reason to help the institution. However, volunteers usually do nothing to help unless asked to do something specific. It is not the number of meetings attended that determines the volunteer's power. Some volunteers are of critical importance because of the one principal contact they can make with the top-flight prospect. It is the responsibility of staff to be certain that those with proven performance records or with the best credentials receive the best assignments and that the other volunteers are brought along through training to a higher level of performance. Always make assignments on a peer-to-peer (for

43

example, CEO to CEO) or peer-down basis (for example, CEO to vice-president), and always be certain that the top potential donors are assigned to the top volunteers.

Almost every institution has access to top leadership, although some do not believe this to be true. (If an institution truly does not have such access, it probably cannot mount a successful campaign.) Successful volunteers have certain recognizable traits, among them that they are respected in the community, visible, able to influence others, success oriented, involved in causes outside their work, able to attract other top leadership, comfortable in most settings, and self-assured.

In looking for volunteers who are willing to work for the institution, first look to the organization's own family of constituents. If it is a college or university, then its alumni, parents, and friends constitute the closest family members. For many community service organizations, those closest would include the individuals who utilize the services of the organization and their families. Other places to find volunteers include the corporate community, the church constituency, if the organization is church related, and other volunteer organizations and local citizens.

Recruiting Volunteers

Any organization wants the most capable, the most visible, and the most committed people out front. The people who fill such roles usually are found among the prominent members of its constituency or community. They are recognizable immediately not only for what they do for a particular institution but also for what they do professionally, civically, or politically. Ask busy people to do the job. The secret in utilizing the time of busy people is to have them do what is critical to the project and no more. The next level volunteer can do what is next critically important.

Recruitment of volunteers is a shared responsibility and is usually done most successfully from the top down. The campaign chair should be recruited by the top people in an organization. Before recruiting the chair for a capital campaign, the institution should have searched for the right person, figured out what it wants from that person, and prepared the institution's case statement as an enlistment aid. Having done all these things, the institution should not send in a low-level manager to ask for the commitment. Send top guns—the chief executive officer and the board chair.

In recruiting the next level—cochairs and the campaign cabinet—the campaign chair reviews the pool of potential draftees with the staff and then participates in the recruitment visits. The campaign chair should do the actual asking but should be accompanied by the chief executive officer and the board chair. Though some feel that the CEO and board chair need not be involved, that would be a mistake. The last thing an organization wants to do is convey to its newly committed campaign chair that he or she must do the job all alone. The organization must convey the sense of a well-built, well-staffed rolling bandwagon. The development staff can assist the division chairs who make up a cabinet in the recruiting that they do. This process continues all the way down through the organization until, ultimately, volunteers recruit volunteers, without staff present.

The recruitment process is a key part of the training and motivational process as well. No clear-thinking volunteer will accept a responsible assignment without asking a lot of pertinent questions. An organization must anticipate such questions and organize accordingly. Inform, but do not propagandize. Explain problems. The objective is to fully inform volunteers about the project and the campaign objectives and to give them confidence that they can do the assigned task successfully and will enjoy the experience. Enjoyment of the task is one of the greatest motivators, and it is the staff's responsibility to make it a satisfying experience. Choosing the right people for the right tasks, thereby ensuring success, is the best way to do this, says James C. Kughn, Jr. (1982).

Because the kind of people sought for top jobs are known in the community, it is not too difficult to learn a great deal about them. It behooves an organization to learn as much as it can about them. The more an institution knows about the community's top leaders, the better prepared it will be when the time comes to ask them for their help in achieving its goals. Edward E. Hale (1980)

provides a partial checklist for ensuring a successful first encounter
in the recruitment of a key leader:

- Relying on the case statement, point out in some
  detail the importance of the campaign to the
  institution in general, those who will benefit from
  the services of the organization, and those who
  will come later. Stress the philosophical side of the
  case. People respond to ideas first, mechanics
  second.
- Meet personally with the prospective volunteer
  leader at a place and time most conducive to an
  unhurried discussion.
- Make it clear what the job is that is being offered.
- Assure the prospective volunteer that the institution will provide all the backup needed to conduct
  a successful campaign.
- Assure the prospective volunteer that the top
  leadership of the institution on the board and
  among the institution's friends will be willing to
  help.
- Clarify the amount of time needed to do the job.
- Describe the goals and how they were set. Let
  the prospective volunteer see that they are obtain-
  able.
- Answer all questions fully.
- [After providing the] institutional [background,
  describe aspects] of the program that the institution thinks will be most meaningful to the candidate.
- Decide before the meeting who among those
  calling on the person will actually ask the person
  to take a volunteer assignment in the campaign.
  Try to work out ahead of time how the prospective
  volunteer will be approached.

Working with Volunteers

The staff serves behind the scenes in a supporting relationship to top volunteer leadership. In working with volunteers, the staff function should be carried out with a "passion for anonymity." Staff should coordinate and stimulate. They should furnish technical know-how, supply mechanical and clerical support, furnish resource information, and keep records. Finally, staff help to motivate and energize the volunteers. But at the center of the activity—in the spotlight—are the volunteers themselves.

At a CASE conference held at Dartmouth College, David R. Dunlop (1981) recommended the following principles to guide staff.

Before the first meeting with a volunteer, it is well for the staff to find out certain things about the volunteer: birthdate and place; religious affiliation; business background; family status; homes; directorships; political affiliations; and clubs, honors, and awards. Some might question the value of taking the time for such details. But while some of the benefits are obscure, attention to these details is worthwhile if only to avoid embarrassment.

At the initial meeting with the volunteer leader, first impressions are important. The staff member should try to appear presentable, considerate, reliable, well organized, and knowledgeable. To be presentable, avoid appearing too different. People feel more comfortable around people who seem similar to themselves. Individual manner, speech, and dress will affect how volunteers feel about staff.

To show consideration, begin the first meeting with the volunteer by asking how much time the individual has to spend. Of course, respect the time limit the volunteer suggests. Use a watch, if necessary. Doing so shows the person that the staff recognizes the demands on the volunteer's time and values the time given. To appear well organized, use an agenda openly. Give the volunteer the original and work from a copy. Let the volunteer see items checked off as they are covered. Doing this reinforces a sense of accomplishment and refocuses attention on the agenda items still to be discussed. To build confidence in staff reliability, take notes openly.

Doing so stresses the significance attached to the thoughts and ideas being discussed.

To show that the staff is well organized and plans ahead, consult volunteers about stationery to be used in their work for the institution. While some volunteers may permit the use of their own business stationery, others will not. Some volunteers have several other pieces of stationery from which to choose. Staff should understand the criteria for the use of each. Also ask whether the volunteer's secretary could provide samples of the volunteer's writing style as a guide for drafting letters and other material. If staff will be preparing printed materials to go out over the volunteer's signature, ask for three or four sample signatures in black ink. And, of course, have a pen with black ink and paper ready for the volunteer when this favor is asked. Ask whether staff may consult the volunteer's secretary for the salutation to be used in writing the key people with whom the volunteer will be dealing on behalf of the campaign. By giving attention to these details, staff members demonstrate to the volunteer the forethought they have given to the volunteer's work altogether.

An additional show of consideration comes in asking the volunteers the best time for staff to call them and when they would like to avoid being interrupted. To give a sense of urgency to the work the staff plans to do together with the volunteer, set the time and place of the next meeting. Doing this suggests timing for the accomplishment of tasks even if specific deadlines have not been set.

In routine contact with volunteers, be prompt. The emphasis on promptness should go beyond being on time for appointments. It is a matter of faithfully delivering whatever has been promised, when it is promised, be that a report, a draft of a letter, an opinion, or a staff member for a meeting. Courtesy requires that staff members not keep volunteers waiting on the phone. If a secretary places calls for staff members, never keep a volunteer waiting for the staff member to come on the line. Think of how discourteous it appears when a call interrupts a volunteer's work and then keeps him or her waiting.

Document the work accomplished at each meeting with volunteers. Put in writing each key decision, strategy, or plan and then invite the volunteer to make additions or corrections to the record. This practice not only makes sure there is understanding of the decisions but also provides a timely reminder and reference for the work being done. A volunteer's suggestion should never be rejected at the time it is offered, no matter how unworthy it may seem. If the staff does not see merit in a volunteer's idea, simply say that it is something the staff would like to consider further or that the idea is new and there is a need to consult others about it. Then hope when reporting back to the volunteer at least some worthwhile element can be found in the idea. This delayed response not only allows the volunteer to save face but also gives everyone more time to consider the suggestion.

Never delegate proofreading of material that will bear a volunteer's signature. The responsibility is the staff member's to make sure the copy is perfect. When it is perfect, submit it to the volunteer "for your consideration or approval," not "for your signature." No matter how many drafts have been gone through, always extend to the volunteer the opportunity to make additional changes gracefully. Remember that when volunteers are asked to sign something, it is then their work, and they have the final say in its preparation.

Be candid with volunteer leaders. Sometimes staff members are tempted to offer optimistic encouragement rather than candor. It may be okay to do this in publicly announcing or discussing campaign progress but not with the campaign leaders. Staff behavior shows an attitude. Keep it on the professional side. The objective of staff relationships with volunteers is not to become bosom buddies. Harold J. Seymour used to say, "A party may be a party to a layman, but remember a party is a business meeting to you." Do not be an expert. A know-it-all attitude defeats the very relationship the staff is trying to build with the campaign volunteers. No one likes the person who is right all the time.

Educating Volunteers

The adage "easier said than done" certainly applies to educating volunteers. Orientation is necessary, and so are meetings.

The campaign needs the power and stimulus that result when people come together to consider and attack a problem. But in order to have a successful training session or meeting, the staff needs to provide plenty of advance notice to the volunteers; a well-planned agenda—have a copy for everyone, and mail it in advance; a purpose and a result—decisions made, action taken; minutes to summarize what is to be done as a result of the meeting; and someone in charge who will start on time, keep the meeting on track, and stop on time.

Volunteers expect professionalism from staff. The staff must provide good training and the tools to complete the campaign successfully. As professionals, they must do their work in a businesslike manner and in a businesslike atmosphere with well-prepared materials and a comprehensive training program. It is the ultimate objective of the institution to have the volunteers catch fire with enthusiasm. A carefully planned volunteer training session can help do this, and carefully planned meetings can keep fanning the flame. Among the points to be covered at any orientation session are the following:

- A clear explanation of each person's role in the campaign—a chart will help to show this
- The points in the case statement that have caused the campaign to take on philosophical meaning
- Information and effective tools for each person to complete the assignment
- Questions fully answered
- Instructions for the volunteers—what they are to do, with whom, when, where, and why
- Careful selection, rating, and assignment of prospects
- Guidelines on preparing for a successful call
- Clear instructions on what to do and what not to do on a call
- Instructions on what to do after a call
- Where to call if there is a problem
- How to handle objections
- The importance of large gifts

Other elements that may be included as appropriate are:

- A tour of the institution's facilities
- Presentation of architectural designs and floor plans if a renovated or a new building is a goal of the campaign
- Role playing of a major donor solicitation call
- Presentation of any audiovisual aids that have been prepared to make the case or assist volunteers
- A time line to make solicitations
- Appropriate remarks from the board chair, chief executive officer, and campaign chair
- Introduction of the staff members and the assignment each will have during the campaign

The quality of the orientation session depends on the person in charge, those in attendance, the expectations before the meeting, the planning that went into the meeting, where it is held, how the room is arranged, the program, and the enthusiasm of the leaders.

During the volunteer training session, the explanation of the campaign plan, the campaign timetable, and the campaign objectives should be the shared responsibility of the institution's chief executive officer, the top campaign leadership (usually the campaign chair), and the chief development officer. If the chief development officer is also serving as campaign director, it is especially important that the volunteers recognize this fact so they will know this person as their contact within the organization. The campaign director should be the one to explain the mechanics of the campaign and the materials in the worker's kit during the training session. This is important not only because the professional knows the materials best but also because it demonstrates the competence of the director and builds confidence that the program is well conceived and carefully planned.

There are many kinds of volunteer training sessions, including workshops. Bringing campaign leadership to the institution or to a resort area for a one- or two-day workshop requires a tremendous investment. For nationwide campaigns, the institution needs to recruit campaign leadership far in advance, usually six to ten months before the campaign begins, so it can be certain to get the workshop included in the busy schedules of its key volunteers. Once at the workshop, they will have full opportunity to meet key institutional personnel and, ideally, some of the beneficiaries of the institution's services to hear firsthand about the institution and its objectives. For those coming long distances, it may be their first time back in many years. It can be inspirational and should help prepare them further for their leadership work. They also see who else is involved, and this alone can be rewarding. Of course, a limited-area campaign also should bring the leadership on site, but the logistics are not as difficult. A meeting at a resort area, or any off-site location, means that there can be no distractions by phone calls or other intrusions.

The volunteers' worker's kit is a staff responsibility. The staff must prepare all the explanatory materials that will enable each volunteer to be a complete advocate of the program. Volunteers should feel equipped to answer the major questions that will be asked by the prospective donors. Included in the worker's kit should be the case statement for the institution, a description of the campaign objectives, the campaign plan, information about how to give noncash gifts, pledge cards, rating cards, range of gifts needed, report forms and envelopes, plus supporting materials. Chief among the supporting materials is a volunteer's guide. While this type of guide is prepared in many different forms and formats, it should always stress the following points to each volunteer:

- Know the case. Be able to present it concisely and with enthusiasm.
- Make your own gift. It gives you a psychological boost and helps you ask others.
- Be positive; never be apologetic. Assume that the prospect is going to give. Remember, you are asking not for yourself but for an institution worthy of support.
- Make personal calls only. See prospects face to face; do not use

telephone calls or letters, except to arrange or confirm meetings. (If volunteers will not do this for the organization, it is better off without their services.)

- Keep sights high and emphasize that this is a capital campaign. Ask the donor to consider the amount suggested on the rating card.
- Go back if necessary. It is best not to leave the pledge card to be returned later. If the prospective donor wants to consider making a gift, tell him or her that you will get back at a specified time. Decisions for major gifts take time, so be prepared to make a number of visits if necessary.
- Obtain multiple-year (usually three- to five-year) pledges. Most donors can give more if they can spread payments over a period of years. However, some donors will not pledge for more than a year but will make a gift. If so, ask whether the institution can seek a renewal of the gift each year of the campaign period. Many are receptive to this approach.
- Get the job finished—do not procrastinate. Take the best prospects first. Success will build confidence. Report gifts promptly so that others will see your success and the institution will be able to announce progress toward the campaign goals.

At this point, it is almost necessary to discuss what can be done about hesitant or reluctant solicitors and what the staff member can do to help. First, recommend that the volunteers make their own gifts first. It is a fact that the volunteer's commitment is a source of psychological strength when asking another to make a commitment. Second, suggest that the volunteers team up to make calls on their prospects so that each can bolster the other. The team approach should be used for most major prospects, so suggest this approach to unsure or reluctant volunteers. Third, for some volunteers, asking for the gift is the most difficult part of the personal visit. Give them phrasing that helps take the sting out of the request. For example, if the volunteer asks the donor, "Would you consider giving (the rating amount) over the next three years to help (name of organization) reach the goal?" the prospective donor cannot be offended. The solicitor is asking for consideration of a request, not telling the donor what to do. It makes the appeal, but not in a hard-sell, aggressive way.

Servicing Volunteers

Servicing volunteers is vital, says Kughn (1982). Volunteers do not often provide their own steam, try to solve the problems that crop up, or motivate themselves. Volunteers should have assignments consistent with both their interests and abilities. Before giving a volunteer an assignment, ask, "Is success possible for this volunteer?" The key to effectiveness is assigning volunteers tasks they can and want to do in the campaign. The tasks must be important.

The organization has the right to expect certain things from volunteers. In addition to taking a specific assignment, they should be expected to inform the staff if something should occur that affects their ability or willingness to do the job; promptly report all progress concerning their prospects; never overstep or exceed their assignments without first clearing the changes with the staff; let the staff know if conflicting interests should arise that might place the institution at a disadvantage; and check with the staff before departing from the agreed-on plan.

The staff must always remember that most volunteers agree to serve on a board or committee in the hope that they can be of constructive help. Typically, volunteers look to the institution and ask it to show them how they can best serve. They assume the institution will be wise enough to give them a task that is within their experience and capabilities and that is important to the institution's goal. They expect to be used wisely and successfully.

It is an axiom of any capital campaign that no institution can hire enough fund raisers to do the job alone. Volunteers are invaluable in the basic element of all fundraising, research, as well as being absolutely indispensable in cultivating prospects and in selling the program. It has been repeated over and over again that an institution receives important sums by having important people ask important prospects for support of important projects. Give volunteers the time, attention, and service they require and deserve. It will pay great dividends.

✳ 5 ✳

Building and Stating
the Case for the Campaign

Campaigns are built on the institution's case statement. This chapter defines what a case statement is, how it is organized, how it is used, and how it is presented to an institution's constituencies.

Seymour writes of the case statement, "This is the one definitive piece of the whole campaign. It tells all that needs to be told, answers all the important questions, reviews the arguments for support, explains the proposed plan for raising the money and shows how gifts may be made, and who the people are who vouch for the project, and who will give it leadership and direction" (Seymour, 1966, pp. 42-43).

The guidebook for the NSFRE's survey course for its certification examination defines it thus: "The case statement is a centralization or documentation of all information describing the organization: needs, goals, objectives, strategies and tasks, staff, facilities, budget, institutional plans, financial history, personnel, staff competence to serve the mission, or the cause that the organization represents. It is a 'data base'" (National Society of Fund Raising Executives, 1985).

The absence of an effective case or someone capable of formulating it properly can mean that its preparation will consume precious time when it is at a premium at the beginning of a campaign effort. Seasoned campaign directors know that case statement preparation is often the first, and can be the most formidable, challenge in any campaign effort. The case statement is one of the initial key management requirements for successful institutional development of a campaign.

Experience has shown that a sophisticated and carefully developed case and the active involvement of key governing board members, other top volunteer leadership, and major potential donors are the most critical elements affecting an institution's ability to receive financial support. They represent a basic step, along with institutional planning, documented research and evaluation of the constituency, leadership enlistment, volunteer organization, qualified staff, and adequate budget, toward winning greater philanthropic support.

Mary Helene Pendel (1981) believes that the case statement must be a motivational document—that is, it must be persuasive, not merely an essay of either glorification or need for survival. The case statement must:

- Serve to justify and explain the institution, its program and needs, so as to lead to advocacy and actual support.
- Attempt to win the reader with the nature of the vision [that] characterizes the leadership of the institution and to reassure the reader of the wisdom and responsible nature of its management.
- Characterize the organization so that it is distinctive in the eyes of the reader (this does not necessarily mean unique).
- Be positive, forward looking, and confident, with all the facts and projections reasonable, clear, vital, and accurate.
- Carefully set forth the fundraising plans in terms of policy, priority, and enduring benefits. (The following questions must be anticipated from the reader: Why this institution? Why now? Why me? How?) The case must be clear and concise, even though it may, in fact, be lengthy.
- Be a substantial plan for the future, not a burden-

some revisiting of the past, no matter how honored or glorious. . . . In a real sense, it is a pro-
spectus. It invites investment.

A case is a reasoned argument for an organization to receive
the support it can demonstrate it needs to continue to live and
flourish as an essential community resource. Only after the
institution has isolated, defined, and researched its target market
(donor market, service market, client base) is it ready to develop its
case. The institution's case, then, poses the institution's mission,
goals, plans, and programs in terms of the role these play or can
play in the life of the larger society. The "case" must be the
institution. It aims, above all, to be persuasive, to motivate the
reader to respond.

The case statement should contain a view of the organization
and a brief history. The document is not a fully developed essay on
the philosophy of the organization but a statement about the
perspective it takes on the issues being addressed by the immediate
campaign. It is almost never typeset. Its appearance is most effective
when it has the format of a looseleaf binder of typewritten,
photocopied pages—obviously a draft document meant to be
reviewed and revised, a working document that is kept on a word
processor and is updated periodically to remain immediately
relevant. Distribution should be limited to board members and
others who are interested enough in the organization to take the
time to read it and who have the interest and ability to act upon its
recommendations and requests. Where good planning is being
done, the case statement and the institution's planning document
are companion pieces.

Organization of the Case Statement

The organization of case statements takes many forms, and
there seems to be no one formula for success. However, there are
certain essential elements that are included in every good case
statement. It describes the organization's mission in terms of human
and social issues that are of central concern to the organization. It

states the organization's objectives in specific, quantifiable terms. It describes a set of tasks or strategies for reaching the objectives within a given period of time. It reports on the facilities, staff designations, and budget required to carry out the tasks, including control procedures for continuing evaluation. It identifies those who will benefit from the services offered by the organization. It puts forth the reasons why anyone should make a contribution to support the organization and thus the cause that it is serving. Finally, it stresses the strengths of the organization. Avoid the trap of publicizing weaknesses or needs. Emphasize the positive; sell strengths, successes, and opportunities. Demonstrate the potential of the institution. Show how it can become even better and, therefore, more valuable if supported.

In addition to these essential elements, the case should include information relative to the service areas or the environment in which the organization functions. It should provide an analysis of the service area and examine the significant changes happening in the market or service area and anticipated impact of these changes on the organization, such as a comparison of endowments with those of other universities or of patient/physician load per square foot of facility with that at comparable care facilities. It should provide demographic and psychographic data as well as socioeconomic indices. It should include the institution's plans (immediate, short-range, and long-range) and describe its future capabilities. It should list current and anticipated long-range needs, as well as annual, special, capital, and endowment requirements, all drawn from the institutional plan. A good case statement also includes a listing of personnel in the organization, including curriculum vitae of key staff and governing board members; an analysis of recent gift history; the financial history of the organization, including recent financial statements and audits; and a general history of the organization.

Good case statements, to be complete, include messages of endorsement and commitment from top leadership, a detailed plan for using the resources sought and the compelling rationale for providing them, a budget detailing the gift opportunities, and a listing of those who will lead the campaign as well as those who have management responsibility for the institution.

Outline of a Case Statement

In collecting, organizing, and presenting the written case, the printed document that is shared publicly, it is best to have an experienced professional do the writing and to use highly qualified designers and printers. If such people are not immediately available, they should be sought out. There are professional firms that specialized in preparing case statements, as well as highly talented individuals who work independently.

Preparation of the case provides an important opportunity for involving institutional insiders, prospective volunteer leaders and major donors, and the organization's power structure; in fact, the case cannot be properly developed without the benefit of their insights and perspectives. Research in the institutional files, personal interviews to gather pertinent data, and keen observation are all tools of the case statement writer.

David M. Thompson and other members of his firm Frantzreb, Prey, Ferner, and Thompson drafted the following typical outline of a case statement for working purposes. The institutional staff can use this as a checklist to pull together material pertinent to the case.

Preface or Summary (This section should express the essence of the case in one or two pages and state overall goals to be achieved.)

I.   *Institutional Mission*
   A.   Role in society
   B.   Philosophy of purpose
   C.   Mission, goals, and program
   D.   Salient factors in its history—heritage and distinctions that have endured
   E.   Factors that appeal to
      1.   Service users (a collective term used to describe those who receive services/benefits from a third-sector organization including students, patients, members, clients, recipients, etc.) and their families
      2.   Institutional family

3. Governing board members and volunteers
4. Friends and community
5. Past donors
6. Potential leadership and financial resources

II. *Record of Accomplishment*
   A. Service growth—regular and special programs
   B. Service users—meeting their needs
   C. Institutional family
      1. Nature and quality
      2. Role in teaching, research, policy, preservation, collection, services
   D. Service users/constituents
      1. Further education/services
      2. Careers/speciality goals
      3. Civic leadership
   E. Community service
   F. Improvements in environment and physical facilities
   G. Financial growth
      1. Annual operations
      2. Capital—current and endowment
      3. Methods used to finance accomplishments
   H. Philanthropic support—distinctive gifts and bequests
   I. Where the institution stands today

III. *Directions for the Future*
   A. Distinctions that must continue to endure
   B. New directions
   C. Objectives, curriculum, programs, services
   D. Service users
      1. Number to be served
      2. Nature of constituency
      3. Qualifications

E. Institutional and administrative projected
    requirements
F. Governance projected requirements
G. Financial policies
    1. For tuition, fees, charges
    2. For investment management
    3. For business management
    4. For private gifts and grants
    5. For public support
H. Physical facilities
    1. Campus/environment
    2. Buildings
    3. Equipment

IV. *Urgent and Continuing Development Objectives*
A. Priorities and costs
    1. Endowment for
        a. Service users
        b. Professional staff/faculty, physicians, curators
        c. Library/equipment restoration
        d. Laboratories/service units
        e. Operation of buildings
        f. Facility maintenance
    2. New buildings
    3. Redevelopment of present facilities
    4. Property acquisition
    5. Debt reduction
B. Master plan

V. *Plan of Action to Accomplish Future Objectives*
A. Goals
B. Programs
    1. Support current operations
    2. Support capital expansion
    3. Support special programs or projects
    4. Role of estate planning
C. Organization
D. Timing

  E. Resources
   1. Constituent sources
   2. Range of gifts needed—gift table
   3. Opportunities for memorials and tributes
   4. Methods of giving, including planned gifts and deferred giving
 VI. *The Institution's Sponsorship*
  A. Membership of the governing board
  B. Membership of the development groups
  C. Church/government [sponsorship]
   [Thompson and others, 1978]

Uses of the Case Statement

Pendel (1981) identifies six ways in which the case statement is most profitably used. First, it is used by the institutional family as an internal document to resolve, sharpen, and focus planning and policies into a written statement that interprets the institution to others. Second, an abbreviated form of the statement should be used in testing the market (market survey). Third, the statement serves to rally present leadership around the policy, planning, and sales story. It is the expression of the institutional policy and plans agreed upon by the governing board and aggressively promoted by the development program and other volunteer groups. Fourth, the statement serves as a vital tool in campaigning for leadership. It is easier to enlist new governing board members and top volunteers when there is a statement that argues the case for stability and security as well as for leadership and gift support. In addition, communicating the case will enhance effectively the ability to recruit quality staff and administrators. Fifth, the statement serves as a supporting tool in the solicitation of large annual, capital, and special gifts through tailored appeals to selected prospects with considerable gift potential. Sixth, it serves as a basic reference guide for proposed publications and communications of various kinds to be distributed to the institution's various constituencies.

A thorough, honest case statement will transform apathy for an institution into a sense of a cause that moves people into action.

When done properly, the case statement can challenge the entire institution toward greater service and enthusiastic support.

Presenting the Case Statement

While the traditional case statement is sufficient for most campaigns—a building drive to provide a shelter for the homeless or a neonatal care unit for a hospital, for example—many modern campaigns, especially for complex and large institutions, present the case through multiple publications. A series of documents can be more understandable, attractive, and effective in educating and persuading than a single piece. While there is no standard way of dividing the case into components, it is not unusual, particularly for public institutions such as tax-assisted colleges and universities, for it to be presented in the following segments:

- A "historical piece" indicating a long-established tradition of private support for the public good, if the institution has such a tradition of philanthropy. If it does not, a more general argument based on a solid rationale can still be made and is often required to persuade certain potential leaders and givers.
- A financial case delineating the economic benefits derived by the community from the institution, highlighting the role of private support in the budget and encouraging the investment of private dollars in the campaign.
- The traditional program brochure, which makes the arguments for the immediate campaign.
- A companion piece outlining gift opportunities and ways of giving.

In complex organizations such as large universities, museums, medical centers, and hospitals, it is not unusual to find several separate objectives within the overall campaign goal. In such situations, separate case statements are often prepared to support each of the major campaign objectives, and individual pieces may also be prepared for each unit of the organization that has a major objective within the overall campaign goal.

The Case-Stating Process

The case-stating process, says Curtis R. Simic (personal communication, 1985), is "the process of making 'insiders' out of 'outsiders.'" While the case statement will continue to be the centerpiece of the presentation of capital campaigns, in future campaigns, particularly larger, more complex campaigns and campaigns where specific issues demand extraordinary attention, it will be only one part of the overall case-stating process. As Simic argues in support of this larger process, acceptance of a campaign by both volunteers and prospective donors often requires frequent and repeated reinforcement. Therefore, the case-stating process usually involves a series of presentations, oral, written, and audiovisual, to introduce the campaign to all of the organization's constituencies.

Those asked to provide leadership—both as workers and as givers—must be fully informed about the campaign and its objectives. In addition, these vitally important constituents must also accept the premise of the campaign, understand its logic and its persuasion, and be moved to act in its behalf. This most often requires a series of events, often repetitious, rather than a single presentation to any one group of key constituents. A single presentation will not teach everyone all they need to know, let alone permit these key individuals to ask all the questions they need to ask to be knowledgeable, fully satisfy themselves about the urgency, importance, and relevance of the campaign, and invest themselves fully in its behalf.

Individuals with the strongest ties or involvement are at the center of an institution's orbit. They are the most likely to read and to react to the case statement. Prospects more distant from the center represent diminishing interest. The program brochure and the question-and-answer pamphlet are often more appropriate publications to be used with these prospects. In addition to the case statement, then, the institution should also prepare a program brochure. Many institutions consider this a case statement. Unfortunately, it is not; rather, it is often a shortcut that has been taken because the institution has neither the will nor the ability to prepare a proper case document. Even with a well-stated case, a program brochure is a necessity. But it cannot and does not replace the case statement.

The principal differences between a case statement and a program brochure are length of the document, quality of printing and use of typographical features, and scope of distribution. The brochure should be attractive but not too elaborate or overwhelmingly expensive. This type of document is often best hand delivered. When mailed, it should be accompanied by a personal note. The format should be flexible, particularly in a comprehensive campaign encompassing several objectives.

A second companion piece is a pamphlet, usually of four or six panels, consisting of questions and answers that focus directly and concisely on the major objectives and issues of the campaign. This piece is designed for those who currently are not close to the organization or the campaign and who will not give attention, at least initially, to lengthy, detailed arguments for support. It is designed to be carried easily by a volunteer or a prospect and to be read in two minutes or less. It can either be mailed or presented in person. It is designed for very wide distribution.

✳ 6 ✳

Constructing and Using
the Major Gifts Chart

A standards-of-giving chart, or gifts table, is the concrete mathematical demonstration of the essential importance of major gifts to a successful capital campaign and is important to both volunteers and donors. It can and should serve several functions throughout the course of the capital campaign. It indicates the number and size of various gifts that will be needed if the institution is to reach its goal successfully. It also serves as a reality test, especially with the board and major donors from whom leadership gifts are expected. It is a vital part of the market survey used to determine the feasibility of the projected goal. Once a gifts table is firmly established, it defines the goals that must be met in order for the campaign to succeed and, hopefully, raises the sights of prospective donors. It also establishes specific guidelines for volunteers to use in terms of the gift solicitation patterns. The gifts table is also an essential management tool; it provides the purest and truest indicator of progress to date in any given campaign. Finally, it is a valuable evaluation tool after the campaign.

Constructing a Gifts Table

Certain mathematical assumptions are followed in arranging a gifts table. The 80/20 rule says that 80 percent of the money will come from 20 percent of the donors. This is a common rule of thumb, although in very recent years, many campaigns have seen 90 percent of the money come from 10 percent of the donors, and in at least one case 99 percent of the money came from 1 percent of the donors. In his book on fundraising principles, Seymour (1966, p. 32) stated the rule of thirds. Succinctly put, it says that the top ten gifts in any campaign will represent 33 percent of the goal; the next hundred will represent another third of the goal; and all the rest of the gifts will represent the final third of the campaign goal. When plotted on the gifts table, all these equations generally work out mathematically to about the same kind of representation, except, of course, when 99 percent of the dollars come from 1 percent of the donors (a rare situation, although it may become more common in future years). Tables 1 through 5 present typical gift tables for a $2 million campaign, a $4 million campaign, a $6 million campaign, a $25 million campaign, and a $60 million campaign, respectively.

A traditional gifts table is constructed as follows: The lead major gift, the single largest gift needed, is calculated to be 10 percent of the campaign goal: in a $1 million campaign, the lead major gift needed to predict success is $100,000. Then, each successively smaller gift is half the amount of the previous one, and the number of donors needed is doubled, as illustrated in Table 6. Of course, this simplistic approach does not always produce an appropriate gifts chart. One reason for this is that in the majority of campaigns, those with goals of less than $10 million, there is a clear trend toward fewer and fewer major gifts accounting for more and more of the total goal. Reports from recent campaigns suggest that at times as few as four to six gifts, and often no more than ten to fifteen gifts, account for 50 to 70 percent of the total goal in successful campaigns in this goal range. Gifts tables are now being designed to reflect this (see Tables 1, 2, and 3). The trend is evident in larger campaigns, too. Table 8 shows 35 percent of the goal in a $51 million campaign provided by just twelve gifts; Table 9 shows 48 percent of a $25 million goal coming from only eleven gifts. In very large campaigns, those with goals of more than $100 million, the projected amount of the lead major gift is sometimes set at less than 10 percent of the total goal. When this is done, the percentage of the overall goal expected to be met by major gifts is not reduced; rather, the portion of the goal expected to be received through other

Table 1. Standards of Giving Necessary for Success
in a $2 Million Campaign.

	Gift Range	Number of Gifts	Total
Major gifts	$400,000	1	$ 400,000
	250,000	1	250,000
	150,000	1	150,000
	100,000	2	200,000
	50,000	2	100,000
Special gifts	25,000	10	250,000
	10,000	15	150,000
	5,000	25	125,000
General gifts	less than 5,000	all others	375,000
			$2,000,000

Table 2. Standards of Giving Necessary for Success
in a $4 Million Campaign.

	Gift Range	Number of Gifts	Total
Major gifts	$500,000	1	$ 500,000
	300,000	1	300,000
	200,000	2	400,000
	150,000	3	500,000
	100,000	5	500,000
Special gifts	50,000	10	600,000
	25,000	14	400,000
	10,000	25	375,000
General gifts	less than 10,000	all others	425,000
			$4,000,000

major gifts is increased to compensate for the smaller lead major gift that is expected.

A standards-of-giving table is a sobering thing, and rightly so. It says, in effect, that without gifts of the order indicated, the entire effort has little if any chance for success. In the mood of urgency created by this awareness, campaign leaders are better prepared to offer specific suggestions to prospective donors, and volunteers are better able to base each approach on the specific standards of giving needed to ensure the campaign's success. Goal

Table 3. Standards of Giving Necessary for Success
in a $6 Million Campaign.

	Gift Range	Number of Gifts	Total
Major gifts	$750,000	1	$ 750,000
	500,000	1	500,000
	300,000	3	850,000
	200,000	4	800,000
	150,000	4	700,000
	100,000	6	600,000
Special gifts	50,000	10	600,000
	25,000	14	400,000
	10,000	25	375,000
General gifts	less than 10,000	all others	425,000
			$6,000,000

Table 4. Standards of Giving Necessary for Success
in a $25 Million Campaign.

	Gift Range	Number of Gifts	Total
Major gifts	$2,500,000	1	$ 2,500,000
	1,000,000	4	4,000,000
	500,000	4	2,000,000
	250,000	6	1,500,000
	150,000	10	1,500,000
	100,000	23	2,300,000
Special gifts	50,000	42	2,100,000
	25,000	54	1,350,000
General gifts	10,000	135	1,350,000
	less than 5,000	all others	2,100,000
			$25,000,000

setting and gifts tables inevitably are interrelated, says Addison L. Winship II, certainly to the extent that one of the important ingredients in setting a campaign goal has to be a realistic assessment of what the big gift potential is (Addison L. Winship II, personal communication, March 25, 1986).

The mathematical development of the gifts table should take into account known information about major gift possibilities. For instance, if a campaign goal of $25 million is contemplated, and it

**Table 5. Standards of Giving Necessary for Success
in a $60 Million Campaign.**

	Gift Range	Number of Gifts	Total
Major gifts	$6,000,000	1	$ 6,000,000
	5,000,000	1	5,000,000
	2,500,000	3	7,500,000
	1,000,000	6	6,000,000
	750,000	8	6,000,000
	500,000	10	5,000,000
	250,000	12	3,000,000
	100,000	20	2,000,000
Special gifts	50,000	50	2,500,000
	25,000	100	2,500,000
General gifts	less than 25,000	all others	14,500,000
			$60,000,000

**Table 6. Illustration of Mathematically Developed Traditional
Gifts Table—$1 Million Goal.**

	Gift Range	Number of Gifts	Number of Prospects Needed	Total
Major gifts	$100,000	1	4	$ 100,000
	50,000	2	8	100,000
	25,000	4	16	100,000
Special gifts	12,500	8	24	100,000
	6,250	16	48	100,000
	3,125	32	96	100,000
	1,560	64	128	80,000
General gifts	less than 1,500	many		320,000
				$1,000,000

is felt that one gift of $10 million is a virtual certainty, a gifts table should be established with a gift of $10 million as a part of it, even if its circulation is limited until the gift is actually received. This is outside the guidelines of the mathematical principles or other standard assumptions that normally guide the construction of such a table, but it is reasonable under this circumstance and demonstrates good logic and common sense if it is properly used as a sight-raising technique or as an assurance technique for that one potential donor who might make a magnificent ultimate gift. However, be certain of that gift before circulating the table publicly, because if the gift fails to materialize, such a skewed gifts table obviously will create a problem for the campaign from the beginning.

Known gift needs should also be taken into account. In a recent campaign, the institution included in its goal forty endowments to partially fund professorial positions. The gifts table (Table 7) was designed with this knowledge and reflected the need.

If a $10 million building has three floors and each can be named for a $2.5 million gift, have three $2.5 million giving opportunities available. If there is a need for fifteen endowed scholarships at $100,000 per scholarship, show at least fifteen $100,000 gift opportunities. It is a sign of poor planning, and a source of possible embarrassment, to have a list of named and memorial gift opportunities that is not in concert with the gifts table.

The Gifts Table as an Essential Management Tool

The gifts table is used during the market survey to indicate to those being interviewed the size and number of gifts that will be needed to ensure the success of the campaign at the dollar level being tested. One of the most vital pieces of information any market

Table 7. Gifts Needed to Raise $270 Million.

Gift Amount	Number of Gifts Needed	Total
$20,000,000	2	$ 40,000,000
15,000,000	2	30,000,000
10,000,000	3	30,000,000
5,000,000	6	30,000,000
2,500,000	10	25,000,000
1,000,000	20	20,000,000
750,000	30	22,500,000
500,000	**40**	**20,000,000**
250,000	75	18,750,000
100,000	100	10,000,000
less than 100,000	many	23,750,000
		$270,000,000

survey provides is an assessment by the respondents of the feasibility of the tested goal in relationship to the gifts table. Used as a part of the market survey, the gifts table is one of the strongest indicators as to whether a goal has been set appropriately, too high, or too low. As a result of the market survey, the goal often must be decreased and the gifts table for the campaign itself correspondingly adjusted.

Once the gifts table has been determined, it is important for the institution to do solid prospecting. It is a generally accepted rule of thumb that an institution must have at least four legitimate gift prospects for each major gift required (see Table 6). As the institution moves down the gifts table, fewer prospects are required for each gift—three prospects for each special gift and two for each general gift. This is because a prospect in the upper gift ranges who does not give a gift as large as anticipated may give a smaller gift, thereby contributing to the goal of a lower category on the gifts chart even before that phase of the campaign is undertaken.

Once the campaign commences, the gifts table is an essential management tool. It is not uncommon to hear a campaign director report, "We have 80 percent of the goal in hand and ten months to go in the campaign." On the surface, this may appear to be a favorable report. However, if the lead major gift, the top gift on the chart, has yet to be received and there is little or no probability that it will be received, the report is far less encouraging than it might be if in fact all the gifts at the top end of the range had been secured. Both volunteers and staff should use the gifts table as a "score card" during the campaign.

Table 8 illustrates how a gifts table can be used to indicate the number of gifts required in a range and those received to date. It is a far more accurate indicator of progress in a campaign than any other representation. The actual campaign from which this example is taken exceeded its goal of $51 million by nearly $4 million, and 86 percent of the total funds were received from fewer than 3 percent of the donors. As the table indicates, the amount of gifts received in all the top major gifts ranges exceeded the requirements that were projected at the beginning of the campaign. This gifts chart reveals a trend now obvious in many capital campaigns, that the rule of thirds is being supplanted by a greater proportion of funds received through major gifts at the top end of

74   Conducting a Successful Capital Campaign

Table 8. Major Gifts Chart of a Campaign with a Goal of $51 Million.

Gift Range	Number of Gifts Required	Number of Gifts Received	Amount Required	Amount Received	Percentage of Goal
$1,000,000	10	12	$14,000,000	$19,200,000	35
500,000	12	14	7,000,000	9,000,000	16
100,000	80	82	10,500,000	15,100,000	28
50,000	75	64	5,000,000	4,100,000	7
			$36,500,000	$47,400,000	86

the range in successful campaigns. In addition to the campaign illustrated in Table 8, at least two other very recent indicators support this theory. While supervising a campaign at Dartmouth College, Winship surveyed six other large university campaigns with goals of more than $100 million (Addison L. Winship II, personal communication, March 25, 1986). The review of the gifts table strongly suggested that a successful campaign should be expected to raise between 45 and 50 percent of its goal in gifts of $1 million or more. His evaluation of these campaigns showed that 74 percent of the total gifts to these six campaigns were in amounts of $100,000 or more.

Anderson (1986) reported the same findings from a survey of campaigns with goals ranging from $300,000 to $300 million. In the campaigns he surveyed, consistently 75 percent of the campaign goal was received in gifts of $10,000 or more. He also reported that the overall mean value of the top ten gifts in these campaigns came to around 45 percent of the campaign total. This pattern was fairly consistent for all campaigns covered in this analysis. The Winship survey of larger campaigns showed only a slightly different pattern. The trend in all campaigns is clear and consistent.

Can a campaign succeed without receiving the lead major gift established on the gifts table? Yes, it can. Table 9 provides an example of an actual campaign that succeeded without receiving its projected lead major gift. But a campaign probably cannot succeed without the total of major gifts received equaling or exceeding the percentage of the total goal expected from the major gifts category.

Table 9. A Campaign That Succeeded Without Its Lead Major Gift.

	Gift Range	Donors Needed	Donors Committed	Total Gifts Requested	Total Gifts Received
or gifts	$2,500,000	1	0	$ 2,500,000	$ 0
	1,000,000	4	7	4,000,000	9,536.107.51
	500,000	4	4	2,000,000	2,500,000.00
	250,000	6	6	1,500,000	1,513,000.00
	150,000	10	10	1,500,000	1,934,520.10
:ial gifts	100,000	23	12	2,300,000	1,319,890.00
	50,000	42	15	2,100,000	897,783.80
	25,000	54	35	1,350,000	1,031,990.37
	10,000	135	58	1,350,000	709,192.52
		279	147	$18,600,000	$19,442,484.30

Tables 8 and 9 show the results of two actual campaigns that more than met their major gift goals. With success at the major gifts level, even if the lead major gift is not received, a campaign can succeed; without success at this level, a campaign is almost certainly doomed to failure.

An Unworkable Gifts Chart

One of the most common fallacies regarding gift ranges and distribution patterns is the notion that a campaign can succeed if everyone in the constituency gives the same amount. For the purpose of illustration, this theory suggests that a campaign with a prospect universe of 1,000 can achieve a $1 million goal by having each prospect give $1,000. It never works. Why? This type of approach is not fair or equitable to donors. Wealth is not distributed democratically in this society. If everyone is asked to make a gift that is "generous within their own means," each donor will not be expected to give the same amount; much will be expected of a few, and many more will be expected to do as much as they can. Not only will everyone not give the same amount to any given campaign, many will choose to give nothing at all. In addition, this approach limits the amount asked from those who could give more, and seldom do donors give more than they are asked to give.

The Gifts Table as an Evaluation Tool

The gifts table can be a valuable evaluation tool after the campaign is completed. Table 9, from a recent campaign, illustrates the trend toward a growing emphasis on major gifts and a weakening of support in the traditional special gifts range. The same trend is in evidence in the campaign depicted in Table 8. This phenomenon is being reported by other campaign directors across the country. This may be occurring because the middle class has less disposable discretionary income available today. Indeed, some research suggests that the middle class is shrinking and that, while some in this group are moving up the economic ladder, more are falling back down it (Rose, 1986). A recent study done by the Gallup Organization for the AAFRC Trust for Philanthropy (1987) compares individual giving in 1985 and 1986. It shows that 42 percent gave more in 1986 than in 1985; that 57 percent of those giving more said their reason for giving more was that they had more to give; and 28 percent of those giving less cited as a reason that they had less to give. Taken collectively, all of this information suggests that major gifts at the top end of the gifts chart will be more and more important to the success of any campaign. This argues strongly for a concentration of effort at this level and suggests that institutions interested in entering into a campaign must have prospects able and willing to give at the major gifts level if the institution is to have any real hope of success, whether the campaign goal is $250,000 or $20 million.

✴ 7 ✴

Establishing
the Campaign Structure
and Solicitation Process

The responsibility of professionally staffing a campaign falls primarily to the chief development officer, the campaign director, and the development staff. The chief development officer should bear the primary responsibility for preparing a comprehensive campaign plan, organizational chart, and campaign schedule before the campaign is launched. These should include a leadership recruitment system and schedule and a public information plan and schedule covering media, printed materials, typescript materials, and audiovisual materials. The development staff should see that provisions are made for production of a prospect list as well as an evaluation system for all campaign prospects; this system should include evaluation committees for larger gift prospects and formulas for giving for smaller gift prospects. There must also be a campaign budget and expense control system, a system for recruiting volunteer workers, informational meetings for those recruited, and training workshops for volunteers and leaders.

It is important that the development staff establish a progress reporting and control system for prospects. This should include a prospect pledge card assignment system, a worker assignment system, a report meeting schedule, progress report mailings, a worker activity system, and a prospect reassignment system with a pledge card redistribution system. A gift tabulation system and a campaign audit system should be well thought out and planned for in advance, including the section listing posting, master listing posting, and auditing of all cash and pledges. Additionally, steps should be set forth to address organization, volunteer recruitment and training, the public kickoff, subsequent report meetings, and follow-up and clean-up necessary to the success of area campaigns. There should also be a gift acknowledgment system, a collection system, and a final follow-up system.

Not only is it important for the campaign director to work effectively with the volunteer organization and the top levels of institutional administration, but this officer must also make sure that the entire institutional community is aware of the campaign and feels that it has an active part to play. Key administrators should be consulted or informed on all proposals and fundraising activities that relate to their specific areas. At the same time, key institutional personnel should be actively involved in the cultivation and solicitation process.

Campaign Organization

An organization chart for a typical capital campaign will generally resemble that shown in Figure 1. Organization charts can and do take many forms. However, every campaign organizational pattern should minimally incorporate the structural features shown there. This is the basic pattern from which other, more complex patterns are developed.

The exact structure of any campaign organization will be determined by (1) the campaign methodology chosen, (2) the type of "ask" methodology chosen, (3) the extent to which the organization intends to "rifle shot" its campaign versus a "shotgun" approach, the latter requiring a more extensive volunteer structure, (4) the size and diversity of the institutional constituency, (5) whether the campaign is a community campaign or wide-area campaign, (6) the extent to which the campaign will rely on volunteers to do solicitation, and (7) the mix of face-to-face, telephone, and direct-mail solicitation that will be incorporated into the campaign structure.

A chair and members for each committee should be enlisted according to the following pattern. The chair of the board and the

Figure 1. Capital Campaign Organization Chart.

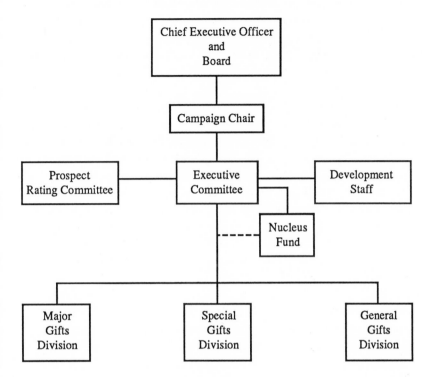

chief executive officer should enlist the general campaign chair in a personal visit. The general campaign chair, the chair of the board, and the chief executive officer, working as a team or, as applicable, in pairs, should enlist members of the campaign executive committee. Again, these visits should be made in person. The enlistment should be as official and dignified as possible. Each volunteer should be given a job description with definite assignments and specific results expected within a definite time period. Professionals find that sharing the results of the market survey and/or a preliminary version of the case statement is often very helpful in selling top prospective leaders on the campaign. This makes them feel that they are in on the ground floor, which they are.

Volunteer enlistment is a top-down process. Once the board

chair and the chief executive officer have enlisted the campaign chair, and the three of them have enlisted the key campaign leadership, each member of the volunteer structure in turn should be expected and required to enlist the individuals who will work with them throughout the campaign. In all cases, even at the special and general gifts level, it is best for leadership to be enlisted through a personal visit.

The success of any campaign depends on an overall volunteer organization designed to facilitate rather than restrict effective prospect solicitation. Organizational concepts must be realistic and practical. Overorganization can be cumbersome and stifling. The best organizational structure permits efficient flow of communication and easy performance of functions by everyone involved. The size of a volunteer organization is dictated by the scope of the campaign, the size of the constituency, and geographical requirements. The effective rule of thumb regarding volunteer solicitors and prospects is one prospect per volunteer at the major gift level; two to three prospects per volunteer at the special gift level; and five prospects per volunteer at the general gift level. Often, the pattern followed is three to five major gift prospects per volunteer, four to seven special gifts prospects per volunteer, and, occasionally, ten or more prospects per volunteer for general gifts solicitation. This is less effective, but it is reality for many organizations.

Committee Responsibilities

Any campaign structure requires a number of committees, or at least one committee functioning in a number of ways. A typical campaign includes a policy committee, an executive committee, and committees on prospect evaluation, major gifts, special gifts, general gifts, and public relations (the role of the public relations committee is discussed in Chapter Eleven). Depending on the campaign model and structure chosen, there also may be a need for an institutional family campaign committee, community campaign committee, corporate campaign committee, and foundation campaign committee.

The development committee of the board generally functions as the policy committee. It determines the general policies of the program and sets the goals. It approves the organizational pattern, staffing and budget requirements, and proposed timetable. It also sets guidelines under which memorial gifts or named gift opportunities may be established and determines guidelines for gift acknowledgment and donor recognition. The top development officer staffs this committee. Its recommendations are presented for approval to the governing board.

The executive committee provides general direction and active management of the program. It coordinates activities of volunteers and sets the operating schedule. The executive committee generally includes the chairs of the several campaign operating committees, advisory groups, and top administrators. The chief executive of the institution and the chair of the board should be ex officio members. This committee, too, is served administratively by the top development officer. This committee normally reports to the chief development officer and/or the chief executive officer.

The prospect evaluation committee should be active early in the program, measuring both interest and financial capability. It evaluates what the prospects can give (not what they will give) in terms of both effort and contributions. Confidentiality and anonymity are absolutely essential to this committee. The research staff of the development office is assigned to this committee.

The major gifts committee has a critical task of evaluating, cultivating, and soliciting the institution's most important prospects. Because 90 percent or more of the campaign goal will probably come from 10 percent of the donors or fewer, it is important that the most affluent and influential group possible be enlisted to serve on this committee. The members of this committee must be the best volunteers who can call on the best prospects at the appropriate time to secure maximum investments. Often, committee members are assigned only one or two prospects to work with at a time. This group constitutes one of the most important task forces in the campaign organization. It is the responsibility of this team, under the direction of its chair, to persuade its members to take appropriate assignments and to keep them in steady and productive pursuit of their prospects. Because this committee is so important, the selection of its chair should be carefully considered. Generally, the chair should be a resident of the community in which the campaign is taking a place or, in the case of a wide-area campaign, able to commute readily to the organization's location, capable of making a major gift, active in the business or social community, and someone with considerable influence who is not afraid to ask for major gifts.

In brief, the tasks of the major gifts chair are (1) to put together a strong committee willing to seek gifts in the major gifts range; (2) to work closely with the campaign chair in all matters affecting the committee's responsibility; (3) to make a personal gift that is generous within his or her own means; (4) to ask for certain major gifts personally; (5) to hold regular meetings of the committee in which its members can screen and rate new prospects, take additional assignments, and report on progress; (6) to follow up periodically with members of the committee and make regular, timely reports to the committee on the progress of the campaign; (7) to see that members of the committee are fully informed about the campaign and that each member has made a personal commitment in accordance with his or her ability; and (8) to work with the other committee chairs to identify and develop other individual leadership gifts throughout the campaign structure.

The special gifts committee deals with substantial gifts just below the major gifts level. The duties of committee members are similar to those of members of the major gifts committee. The ratio of one worker to two to four prospects is commonly used. Liaison may be provided by development staff other than the top development officer.

General gifts solicitation is generally the cleanup phase and in most modern campaigns is targeted to the general constituency of the institution. Personal solicitation is encouraged, but telephone solicitation and direct-mail solicitation are often used. For personal solicitation, one worker to five prospects is the generally accepted ratio. Telephone solicitation, second in effectiveness to direct-mail solicitation, is growing increasingly more popular; mail techniques are the least effective of the three. Some campaigns have recently reported success with combination phone and mail programs.

The Solicitation Process

As has been repeatedly demonstrated through many years of fundraising experience, personal solicitation is both the most economical and the most effective form of campaign solicitation. Telephone solicitation is an extension of the personal visit but usually is not nearly as effective. Phone-mail solicitation, which should be used for prospects the institution cannot reach personally, is an increasingly effective method, although some believe that overuse is already causing it to lose some of its effectiveness. The principal purpose of a broad mail campaign is to elicit new interest and to cultivate those who may give more later. If mail must be used for individual solicitation, pave the way by telephone where feasible.

But how, exactly, does an institution go about structuring its gift solicitation and determining the scope of solicitation for its particular campaign? Gary A. Evans (1978) outlines three distinct approaches to asking for gifts to be considered.

Separate Ask. With the separate ask, donors are solicited at two separate times, once for an extended commitment to a capital gift and once each year for annual giving. The advantages of this type of ask are that (1) two separate solicitations clarify the difference between capital giving and annual giving; (2) it may make worker training easier, since those who volunteer for capital funds solicitation need only inform the donor that the capital fund is distinct from annual giving and that donors will be asked at a different time to consider annual support; and (3) a special solicitation for annual giving may give it more emphasis, since it will not appear subordinate to the capital campaign. A separate ask also presents problems: (1) donors may resent the second request coming only a few months after they have made a major commitment to a capital campaign; (2) more volunteers may be required if the annual fund solicitation is to involve more than direct mail; and (3) if solicitations come at separate times, some donors may merely shift their annual fund giving to the capital campaign and later decline to support the annual fund, thus not having increased their total contribution. Although the separate ask can be used with any of the four types of campaigns described in Chapter One, it is not particularly well suited for the comprehensive campaign, because the institution choosing the comprehensive model has done so to create harmony and unity within its total program, and this approach creates division.

Double Ask. Among institutions that have a continuing

program and reasonably satisfying experience in annual campaigns, the double ask—soliciting the donor for both the capital gift and the annual gift at the same time—is becoming an increasingly popular method for coordinating annual and capital campaigns. People who are not ready for solicitation for capital gifts continue to be solicited for annual gifts, those who are ready are asked for both. The advantages of the double ask are that (1) assuming that capital funds are solicited personally (and they must be with major donors), this system automatically provides for face-to-face solicitation for the annual gift as well; (2) this system provides an efficient use of volunteers, since the volunteer for capital solicitation will handle annual giving at the same time; (3) it reduces the "harassment" of the donor by providing for a single approach during the year; and (4) it keeps alive the concept of annual giving while also bringing attention to the capital campaign. However, the double ask also presents some problems. Donors may not appreciate the distinction between the types of gifts and simply say, "Look, I'll make a gift to the institution; you divide it up as you want." It may also make worker training more difficult—the more forms of solicitation a worker must present, the greater the potential for confusion.

There are two forms the double ask may take. The first is the multiple-year-capital/one-year-annual. Here the donor is asked to make a pledge to the capital campaign to be paid over a period of years and at the same time asked to make a contribution to the current annual fund, with a reminder that another solicitation for annual giving will occur each year as the capital pledge is being paid. The second is the multiple-year-capital/multiple-year-annual. With this form, the donor is asked to make a pledge to contribute over the next three to five years, allocating a portion to capital and a portion to annual giving. The disadvantage of this approach is that it limits the possibilities of presenting the case to the donor annually if the donor has made a commitment to both capital and annual funds.

Triple Ask. With the triple ask, not only are the capital and annual gifts solicited at the same time, but a planned gift commitment is also sought. The advantages and disadvantages of the triple ask are similar to those of the double ask. This is a very sophisticated form of ask, requiring an extremely well planned approach by the staff and volunteers and a donor prospect who is extremely knowledgeable. It is to be used selectively and sparingly—only where the situation warrants it.

Scope of Solicitation

Having considered the ways in which the annual fund and capital campaign can be combined, Evans (1978) suggests that an organization must consider the scope of each solicitation. That is, will the organization solicit everybody for everything, or will it limit solicitation of certain prospects to capital gifts and solicit others for annual gifts only? Once an organization has decided to continue annual giving in some form while conducting a capital campaign, which is increasingly the case, the traditional practice has been to solicit all constituents for both gifts. The advantages are obvious: everyone is given the full opportunity to participate in the several elements of the total development program, and by going to the entire constituency with the capital funds campaign, an organization might have the opportunity to discover a few major donors not previously known to it. There are also problems with this approach: maximum solicitation of constituents requires maximum commitment of staff and volunteers (as noted in Chapter One, it may be impossible for an institution with limited numbers of staff and able volunteers to approach its entire constituency), and soliciting everyone for everything is expensive; indeed, it may not be cost-effective.

Each time a solicitation moves to a larger and larger number of prospects, the sights of donors drop. When ten donors give a total of $10 million, the level at which people are contributing is perfectly clear. When 5,000 givers contribute $500,000, the level of giving is equally clear, but less impressive, and the sights of major donors may be reduced. When it is known that everyone will be asked to provide the capital funds required, the burden is lifted from the handful with potential for major support, and they may wait for the masses to provide the funds needed.

A new concept is now emerging in capital fund solicitation: solicit for capital gifts only those with capital potential; ask all others for annual giving. To do this, an organization must identify the people capable of making significant multiple-year capital gifts and solicit them for that purpose. All other constituents will be solicited only for annual giving, since the organization has made the judgment that they do not have capital potential. The advantages of this type of approach are twofold. First, it allows the organization to focus staff time and its best volunteers on the top major prospects. Once an organization moves a campaign to larger and larger numbers, it dilutes staff time and volunteer attention. By focusing only on major donors for major gifts, the organization can more effectively use the "rifle shot approach." Second, this approach makes the annual fund an integral part of the overall objectives. It requires a total development goal that includes annual giving, thus permitting annual fund donors to feel that they are part of the program.

There are four problems with this type of approach. First, the major donors may resent the fact that only a small number are being asked for capital gifts. Second, the masses may feel they have no role in "laying the bricks" if their gifts go only for current operations. (It is possible to overcome this by emphasizing the total development program, especially if the relative merits of sustaining the ongoing program while the capital drive is in progress are highlighted.) Third, if only selected capital prospects will be approached for capital giving, the organization must continue a never-ending search for new major donors. This will require a strong annual giving program as a means for identifying capital donors. Fourth, unless the masses clearly understand their vital importance in meeting the overall objectives, they may develop the habit of letting the big donor do it all. The large number of annual giving donors should not come to believe that an institution is dependent on only a handful of people.

Having decided whether to drop the annual fund or integrate it into the effort, whether to exercise the separate ask, double ask, or triple ask, and whether to solicit select constituents for capital gifts or everyone for every purpose, it is important next to coordinate this package with the planned or deferred giving program. Again, options are open to the institution. The first is to exclude planned giving. This means that an organization would exclude from its campaign goal any charitable life income trusts, annuities, or promised bequests unless the donor died and the money came to the institution during the course of the campaign. A second option is to count everything—even the promise of a bequest from a four-year-old. A balance somewhere in between is suggested.

In planning for a major development program, it is reasonable to include in the goal an expectation for income trusts, annuities, and other irrevocable commitments. This allows the institution to talk to potential donors about irrevocable gifts with retained life interest. Donors may be more apt to make a decision if they know that establishing a life income trust will make them participants in the campaign. Many institutions include in their campaign results the face value of all life income gifts at the time they are made, with no subsequent changes in fundraising reports when the donor dies and the trust is paid to the institution. Other institutions prefer to include only the actuarial value of the gift, making annual adjustments.

Bequests are a bit more difficult. Certainly it is not wise (and perhaps not even honest) to include in an institution's campaign results the potential bequest from a very young person. On the other hand, it may be unwise to exclude completely the promise of a bequest from a donor who is advanced in years and willing to add a codicil to the will for a major gift in order to have the satisfaction of participating in the total development program.

Institutions should think about what is both fair and a good incentive for fundraising and then set up clear guidelines in advance. An institution may decide to include all estate notes from people over sixty-five years of age and all promises of bequests from those seventy and older, for example. In any event, the institution should make its decision before it sets its goal. It certainly would be unwise if a goal reflected only direct needs for cash required in the near future and then the institution counted toward that goal all promises of bequests, some of which may not materialize for many years. It is extremely important to exercise good judgment in a campaign where bricks and mortar are a major issue. It is imperative not only that an institution receive the commitments to build the structure under consideration but also that a cash flow be established to pay for construction and reduce debt in a timely and equitable fashion. The use of planned gifts to meet construction payments schedules is a highly risky business.

A final consideration is not only what to count but also, especially in the case of noncash gifts, how to value gifts for accounting and recording purposes. Within the educational sector, the guidelines of the Council for Advancement and Support of Education (CASE) and the National Association of College and University Business Officers (NACUBO) are becoming an accepted, standardized approach to resolving this issue. These guidelines can be obtained from CASE, 11 Dupont Circle, Suite 400, Washington, D.C. 20036. Any organization can look to these guidelines as a model approach, realizing that different circumstances may suggest the need to modify these standards to make them applicable and useful.

With these observations and caveats in mind, an institution might consider the following guidelines from an actual campaign as a basis for consideration and discussion. Under these guidelines, the institution will count toward the total campaign goal all of the following:

- All outright gifts made between the determined starting date and the conclusion of the campaign
- All pledges that are (1) initiated between the determined starting date and the conclusion of the campaign and (2) documented in writing by the donors
- All distributions from estates or trusts received during the campaign period (unless previously counted as a bequest or other planned gift to the campaign or otherwise already counted by the institution)
- The value of future bequests, if unconditional and supported by a copy of the will, codicil, or testamentary trust
- The full fair market value of planned gifts in which the institution or its foundation has a remainder interest held irrevocably by the institution, its foundation, or another trustee
- The present value of the income interest of charitable lead trusts held by the institution, its foundation, or another trustee
- The cash surrender value of life insurance policies and similar

instruments when all of the incidents of ownership have been given to the institution or its foundation

- All private gifts and grants for newly established purposes
- Government grants awarded in support of stated campaign goals and objectives

It is important to establish such guidelines at the beginning of the campaign, when they can be considered and decided in a calm, rational way, without the influence of the pressures often present when an institution is midstream in a campaign and pressing to achieve success.

✳ 8 ✳

Identifying, Researching, and Rating Campaign Donors

As a general rule, more than 90 percent of any campaign goal will be realized from fewer than 10 percent of the donors. There is no way to overemphasize the importance of major gifts to the success of a capital campaign. In order to obtain major gifts, an organization must involve itself in the major donor cultivation process. These gifts do not just happen—someone makes them happen as a result of a well-thought-out plan. This chapter discusses the steps involved in successfully generating major gifts.

Defining Major Gifts

What exactly is a major gift? In campaigns with goals ranging from $5 million to $50 million, a major gift is generally defined as any gift of $100,000 or more, a special gift as any gift of $10,000 to $99,999.99, and a general gift as any gift of less than $10,000. In campaigns with goals of more than $50 million or less than $5 million, the definitions may be different. A lead gift is a gift that serves to establish a trend for giving by others believed to be capable of making gifts at the same level. It is possible to secure lead gifts in the major, special, and general divisions of the gifts table. A nucleus gift is a gift received at the earliest stages of the campaign, usually a major and/or lead gift and most often given by an institutional "insider," a board member or previous major donor. Nucleus gifts collectively provide a nucleus fund to create a giving momentum to launch the campaign.

Characteristics of Major Gift Donors

Major gift donors have strong values and deep beliefs, says
Donald A. Campbell, Jr. (1985). They believe in people and have
great respect for knowledge. They often desire to provide opportunities they did not themselves have, to help the less fortunate, to
improve the quality of life, to solve problems in society, and to
preserve and perpetuate values of humankind, especially those that
they hold dearest. Major gift donors usually are quite religious,
have a deep belief in the free enterprise system, and are generally
conservative. They already know someone in or something about
the institution they will be asked to support. Someone has already
made an impression on them. They have come to believe in
someone, or something, the institution represents—the chief
executive officer, a member of the board, a volunteer, or a professional staff member, or some part of what an institution stands for.
They have values that are comparable with the institution's and are
probably regular donors to the institution or to one that is similar.

They view giving as an investment, and through their
investments they desire to solve a problem or issue, seek ways to
express themselves (self-actualization), and expect to see and
understand the "return on the investment." They will not seek but
will accept (in fact, expect) recognition. They may want to honor
or memorialize someone else rather than themselves, although
many will in fact honor themselves. They have the resources to
make a major gift. In some instances, these resources may not be
liquid at the moment. Their spouses and families are usually
involved in the gift decision. Major donors tend to stay with
programs and activities that have been of interest to them over a
long period of time. Those who will give major gifts to an
institution in the future generally have given to it in the past.

Identifying Prospects

A prospect is any individual, foundation, corporation, or
organization that has the potential and is likely to give. In cases
where potential exists but probability does not, it is mandatory for
the institution to move these prospects through what G. T. Smith

describes as the cultivation cycle (G. T. Smith, conversation with the author). The cultivation of potentially large donors is a systematic and continuing effort to develop a power structure, either actual or potential, for an institution. It involves five steps: identification, information, interest, involvement, and investment.

In nearly every instance, the final four steps constitute a continuing cycle of learning additional information about potential donors, heightening their interest through the dissemination of information, both through personal contact and mailings, encouraging a meaningful involvement such as volunteer service or active participation, and ultimately receiving significant financial investment. Involvement is the highest level of cultivation in that it requires that the prospect be brought into active contact with the organization through service on a committee, as a member of the board, or in some other, equally important way.

Effective Research

Prospect research is a process whereby the staff evaluates the organization's constituency to identify individuals, foundations, and corporations capable of making a substantial commitment to the capital campaign so that effective solicitation strategies can be designed. The objectives of research are (1) to identify people and their relationships with other people; (2) to determine interests in, associations with, and gifts to the institution; (3) to discover ownership, control, influence, and wealth of people, corporations, and foundations; and (4) to reduce great quantities of information to readable, understandable, concise reports pertinent to the current campaign.

To do this, the professional staff must correlate, control, and interpret data to (1) develop a strategy for action; (2) determine assignment of the prospect to the appropriate projects; (3) identify the prospect with the right groups; (4) assign the prospect cultivation to the right people; and (5) establish a time schedule for implementation of the cultivation and solicitation program.

The best prospects for major gifts to any organization are those who are committed to it and have already given. Many will have already accepted positions of leadership within the organization. Prospect research involves both basic and sophisticated processes. F. Mark Whittaker (1983) outlines the basic information that must be gathered:

- name, nickname
- address(es)
- telephone number(s)
- business title, address, and phone number
- marital status
- the names, number, and ages of children
- date and place of birth
- education (secondary and higher/academic area)
- spouse's name
- spouse's education and business
- family connections to the organization
- family connections to other organizations
- job history
- honors and achievements
- clubs and organizations
- political affiliation
- religious affiliation
- personal interests
- estimated net worth
- net salary
- stock holdings
- directorships
- family foundations
- favorite charities
- gift record
- names of secretaries
- attorney
- banker
- close friends

It is also important to keep a record of contacts, including:

- last visit to the organization
- date, place, and purpose of last contact

- results
- next steps
- staff assignment
- volunteer assignment

Among the sources of this information are institutional records, including those kept in the development office, the chief executive officer's office, and the alumni/public relations office, as well as institutional publications and the institutional staff. Other especially good sources of information are board members, service users, and friends who can provide information from personal knowledge. Printed and published materials that are excellent sources of information include local, regional, and national newspapers, *Who's Who in America* (and its separate editions on women, government, finance, industry, the East, the West, the South, and business), magazines such as *Forbes, Fortune, Business Week,* and others, clipping services, proxy statements, *Standard & Poor's, Dun and Bradstreet, Moody's, Taft Corporate Directory,* state directories of corporations and executives, chambers of commerce, corporate annual reports, foundation annual reports, foundation directories, foundation grants indexes, *Taft Information System and Monitor,* state foundation directories, the *Chronicle of Higher Education, Philanthropic Digest,* and *Foundation Directory.*

Once research is completed, the development staff should review the information to determine whether all the needed information is there, and whether the prospect belongs in the prospect pool. Prospects who do not belong should be deleted from the list early on in the review process and their names given to the annual giving staff. The next step is an "in-house" financial rating of the prospects. The rating includes prospects' *potential* to give (what they would give if the institution were their number-one philanthropic cause and they wanted to make the biggest gift of their lives) and a *probable* gift size (a gift they could pledge over the next eighteen months, without much solicitation, that would be payable over the next three to five years). For an individual, figure the potential gift as 3–5 percent of the person's total assets outside of personal real estate and life insurance. To determine the probable gift, look at the prospect's giving history (including the largest previous gift), other obligations, financial health, type of investments, rate of return, family obligations (parents, children), attitude toward giving, the strength of ties to the institution, and "conspicuous consumption"—the visible signs of wealth, private schools, estates, vacation homes, and so forth.

For corporations and foundations, look at their obligations to other nonprofit organizations. Add 20 percent to the prospect's largest gift or multiply its last annual giving commitment by 10. That is the probable gift. In determining how much to ask for, think of the organization as representing sources of other income as well (family, foundations, corporations). Combine the "give" and the "get." Corporations may have five or six channels of potential funding: corporation contributions, corporation foundations, matching gifts programs, research and development, marketing, advertising, and the discretionary budget of the executive office.

Once the potential and probable gift sizes have been determined, it is time to evolve a strategy. Look at the nature of the prospect's asset base. Is it liquid? In stock? Define how the institution wants the prospect to give. Are there tax considerations? What are the prospect's possible interests at the institution? How do those interests tie into its priorities? Who is the best person to make the first contact, and who is the best to make the solicitation? Determine the next move: whether to get more information, visit the prospect, invite the prospect to attend some function, and so on.

Corporate Research. J. Mark Billian (1985) says research on corporate prospects needs to address three vital questions: How financially healthy is the business? What are its current products and interests? Does it have any existing relationship with the institution that wants to approach it? The following basic information should be gathered on each corporate prospect (Billian, 1985):

- full name and correct address
- corporate assets
- type of business
- list of corporate officers and directors
- if there is a corporate foundation, a list of its officers

- sales volume
- previous giving record
- decision-making process
- gifts to other institutions (more difficult to determine if there is no corporate foundation)
- connections with the institution—if it is an educational institution, a list of alumni employed by the corporation; if it is a hospital, a list of patients it employs; and so forth
- history of institutional dealings with the corporation
- local subsidiaries and officers
- corporate gift committee—names, connections, and kindred interests

Corporate financial analyses are available through printed sources such as *The Million Dollar Directory, Standard & Poor's,* and the Moody series of industrial manuals. In addition, a number of data bases are available on line, in particular PTS PROMPT and F&S, available from Predicast, Inc., through Dialogue. Publicly held companies must also file annual 10K reports. These are not only excellent resources but also available free for the asking. Finally, Dun & Bradstreet business profiles provide in-depth research on thousands of companies, both public and private.

From the viewpoint of corporate and foundation relations, it is equally important to learn something about company products, research and development, and future marketing plans. An annual report can supply some of this information. Other sources might include the institution's office of sponsored research, if it has one, which may be aware of research and development interests within the corporation. Philanthropic publications such as *Taft Corporate Giving Watch* and *Philanthropic Digest* list corporate contributions, which can be reviewed for trends in grants for research and development. In addition, several data bases list awards of government contracts. Finally, newspapers and journals can provide a glimpse of the future. Articles in magazines such as *Fortune* and *Forbes* may provide a vision of the direction in which the corporate prospect is moving. Local newspapers are an equally valuable resource.

Working with the appropriate in-house staff, the institution needs to expand on the basic questions about relationships with corporate prospects. For an educational institution, for instance, how many alumni are employed by the corporation? Do any members of the institution's staff serve on the corporate advisory boards or science advisory panels? Does the corporation rely on the institution in any way for services? What about funding history— has funding come from the corporation or from the corporate foundation? Enlightened corporate self-interest is based on these relationships, so it is important to understand these components when planning a campaign approach. Except for a few national corporations and corporate foundations, and the local corporate community, this category of prospects has become more specialized in recent years. Most do not give outside of areas where they have plants, programs, or people. Very often "quid pro quo" consider-ations, stockholder concerns, for example, determine the grant policy of national corporations.

Corporations tend to support campaigns in areas where they have plant operations and, particularly, headquarters operations. Corporations will also support campaigns if they have subsidiaries in the service area of the institution. Besides major corporations, other sources for support of a campaign include local independent businesses, vendors, and businesses that are owned by or that employ people who are affiliated with the institution, whatever their geographical location. In dealing with any prospects, but especially corporation and foundation prospects, a campaign should never extend its boundaries beyond the circle represented by its volunteer leadership. This is a cardinal rule that is often not followed in campaigns.

Foundation Research. J. Mark Billian (1985) says that foundations are the easiest of the three types of prospects to research in that they usually have specific funding interests that are known that can easily be determined by potential applicants. These in-terests are usually dictated for the most part by policy and history of grants. The information sought about foundations is basically the same type of information sought about corporations. This information includes:

- the full, correct name of the foundation
- precise street address and phone number

- the officers or directors of the foundation and their professional connections
- brief historical sketch—when founded, by whom, and for what purposes
- current assets
- amount of recent grants—by year and by individual recipient
- decision-making process
- pattern of giving—to what kinds of institutions and for what programs, with specific examples
- the institution's best "contact"—the person to visit or send a proposal to
- connections with the institution
- history of the institution's contacts with the foundation
- recent IRS 990 form with income and grants made
- guidelines and areas of interest published by foundation
- most recent annual report [Billian, 1985]

Again, there are several excellent printed and computerized sources for this information. Once of the most widely used comprehensive references is a source book, *Profiles*, published by the Foundation Center; another is the *Taft Foundation Reporter*. These profiles detail financial assets, interests and giving focus, grants to other institutions, and proposal submission requirements. One of the most valuable components of these references is the index by giving interests. A quick review of this information will tell an institution in almost every case whether a foundation is actually a prospect for its campaign. Should an institution be seeking a source for funding of a publication in the health sciences, for example, this index can point out foundations that have stated their interest in funding this particular area. The result is, of course, that chances are great for finding a donor who will be interested in considering the institution's proposal.

The best foundation prospects for a campaign are those geographically nearby. The likelihood of investment is much greater when the foundation is located in the institution's local area, state, or region. A foundation is also more likely to support a campaign if it shares similar philosophies with the institution. It is important to match interests between the organization and the foundation. If there are individuals associated with the foundation, especially on the board, who are directly or indirectly affiliated with the institution, the chances that it will receive favorable consideration are enhanced. Any review of foundations requires a systematic study of all sources to locate those foundations that might have matching interests.

Remember to talk to members of the institutional board and others close to the institution to see whether they can help to establish links with the foundation. It is extremely important in a capital campaign that the effort to secure gifts from foundations be focused on those foundations that are most likely to support the institution. In many instances, the great majority of foundations will not be interested in a particular program. Again, it makes no sense to pursue nonprospects.

Rating Prospects

Once effective research has been done and prospects identified, the next step is to evaluate prospects. Prospect rating is often done by staff, but it also must be done by volunteers in order to validate the staff effort. The purpose of external prospect rating is to accurately determine an individual's *ability* to give. The evaluator should not be concerned with what the individual *might* give—or even whether he or she *will* give. Further research subsequent to the evaluation and future cultivation and solicitation activities will address these questions. During the rating done by volunteers, the sole criterion should be what a donor can do given personal circumstances. The staff member should not participate in the evaluation other than to explain the purpose of the session, to keep the session moving, and to clarify and answer questions as to form and procedure. There are four rating session techniques commonly used.

With the *group discussion* procedure, evaluators engage in a roundtable discussion until they agree on a rating. A group leader should conduct the session. A professional staff member should be present to record the observations made but should make no comment to the evaluators that could influence a rating. This is the best method of evaluation, but its success depends on the group leader's ability to initiate discussion and the group's willingness to participate openly and forthrightly, as well as the evaluators' informed ability to make the ratings.

With the *group/individual ratings*, each member of the group is given a rating book and works individually, without discussion, to rate the prospects and offer appropriate written comments. The professional staff member collects the evaluations at the end of the session and tabulates the information after the meeting. The major disadvantage here is a lack of exchange of ideas or information within the group. The advantage is that the confidentiality of this method may lead the evaluator to provide a higher evaluation and more pointed and useful comments. The success of such sessions will often depend on getting someone who is well known and well connected to serve as host or hostess.

With the *individual/one-on-one* procedure, the professional staff member meets individually with the volunteer evaluator and verbally goes through the prospect list, recording pertinent comments on the evaluation form. The advantage of this process is that the evaluator can feel a complete assurance of confidentiality. No one else will hear the comments or know the evaluator's personal feelings about the prospect. The disadvantage is that the validity of the evaluation is limited to the extent of the evaluator's knowledge. There are no second and third opinions. And the evaluator may not know a number of the prospects well enough to rate them, thus necessitating additional rating sessions with other evaluators.

With the *individual/solitary* procedure, evaluators are given a list of prospects and rating instructions and left on their own. The evaluation book is either picked up or mailed back by a mutually agreed upon date. This procedure should be used only in special circumstances. Its advantage is that it gives the evaluator time to reflect and to substantially consider the rating and comments. When properly done, it generally leads to a very thoughtful, thorough evaluation. Its disadvantage is that often an individual will put off doing the evaluation, thereby frustrating the process.

No matter which technique for evaluation is used, the

evaluation should be done by knowledgeable individuals. Second-hand and hearsay information is of little or no value. Speculation is just that. Bankers, lawyers, investment counselors, insurance executives, the socially prominent, and those actively involved in organized philanthropy in communities with organized efforts make the best evaluators. Evaluation of individual prospects should continue until an adequate data base is established. Many institutions acquire at least three evaluations, preferably all within a fairly narrow range (say, $10,000, $15,000, and $12,000), before assuming that the evaluation of a particular prospect has been validated.

Estimating an Individual's Giving Potential. When considering giving potential, any information known to the evaluator about an individual's financial circumstances should be part of an evaluation. Factors to be considered when assessing the giving potential include accumulated or inherited wealth, stocks and bonds, real and personal property, full or part ownership in business enterprises, access to family or other corporations, foundations or trusts, and annual income level.

There are no absolute rules to suggest how much an individual might be capable of giving to philanthropy on the basis of accumulated assets and income. However, a useful framework for making decisions is shown in Table 10. These guidelines are suggestions and should be used only as a starting point to help focus institutional thinking about an individual's potential to make charitable gifts. Remember, the institution is rating potential, not inclination to give. Measurements of inclination to give tend to be less precise and more subjective. Factors to be considered include level of interest, number of years of giving to the organization, involvement with the organization, and cumulative previous giving.

The goal of these kinds of evaluation sessions is twofold: (1) to uncover fresh information about important prospects (first priority) and about all other prospects (second priority) and (2) to promote the cultivation and involvement of the volunteers who participate in the process. Other benefits may accrue, too; this is often a valuable staff training tool, it is a way of identifying suitable solicitors, it can raise the sights of volunteers who eventually will

Table 10. Income Asset Gift Rating Formula.

Income Level	Assets Accumulated	Suggested Gift Potential (to be given in cash over five years or through a planned gift vehicle)	Rating
more than $500,000	more than $10,000,000	$500,000 or more	500K or higher
$100,000–$500,000	$1,000,000 to $10,000,000	$250,000 to $500,000	250K
less than $100,000	$1,000,000 to $10,000,000	$100,000 to $250,000	100K
$100,000 to $250,000	less than $1,000,000	$50,000 to $100,000	50K
$50,000 to $100,000	$500,000 to $1,000,000	$10,000 to $50,000	10K

become donors, and it is an opportunity to educate the participants about the campaign.

Keeping the Evaluation Session Manageable. It is extremely important to keep the evaluation session manageable from the standpoint of the volunteer. Too many names to evaluate at a single sitting can be counterproductive. No evaluation session should be scheduled to last more than one and a half hours. How many names can be rated in ninety minutes? It depends on the rating method being used, the level of prospect being evaluated, and the ability of the evaluator. Some evaluators working alone can rate as many as 500 prospects in a session; a group discussion session may cover only 100 to 150 prospects. If evaluators are asked to rate too many prospects or the session is too long, the level of concentration will drop off toward the end of the session. Therefore, it is generally recommended that all lists be kept as short as possible.

✳ 9 ✳

Cultivating and Soliciting
Major Gift Prospects

Once prospects have been identified, researched, and evaluated, the organization must begin to cultivate them. Cultivation is a continuous process. It often takes several steps, and anywhere from six months to six years, to obtain a major gift. On average, campaign directors indicate that it now takes eighteen to twenty-four months to successfully cultivate and negotiate major gifts.

Major Donor Solicitation Guidance System

Bringing in major gifts is a matter of hard work, imagination, and good taste. Certainly, major gifts occasionally come from an unexpected source, but usually many cultivation contacts by staff and/or volunteers are necessary to bring prospects to the point of making major gifts. Thus, the pursuit of the extraordinary gift should be a well-planned, properly funded, adequately staffed part of any campaign effort. Prospect management is a systematic approach to identifying and tracking major gift prospects. Whether using large and complex data bases, straightforward word processing, or a manual system, prospect management systems rely on, and at the same time encourage, careful planning and follow-through. By recording vital information on major gift candidates and donors, an institution may know at any given time who its best prospects are and where it stands in relation to them.

According to Fran Baxter (1987), director of the prospect management system at the University of California, Berkeley, the concept of prospect management is a relatively recent trend in development, made possible by the widespread use of computers in fundraising. Data-processing technology, which has revolutionized gift processing, acknowledgment, and record keeping, will play an increasingly important role in shaping development activities on the front end—long before solicitation occurs.

Prospect management enables an institution to focus attention on the individuals and organizations that hold the most promise for major gifts. These top-tier prospects are generally a small percentage of an institution's master file, but they account for the greatest proportion of gifts. Whether the threshold for a major gift at an institution is $500 or $50,000, the prospects with the potential to give that or a greater amount are candidates for prospect management.

All institutions with sound fundraising programs—no matter what their level of automation—practice some sort of prospect management with their major contributors and prospects. However, computer applications in prospect management allow an institution to record and track a greater level of detail on major prospects than is possible in any manual system, and they are safer than relying on the information that staff and volunteers carry around in their heads.

A well-designed and -maintained prospect management system can improve major gift fundraising and help an organization to measure the effectiveness of its development program. It can provide detail on a single prospect, select all prospects with a common trait, or give an overall view of a campaign's progress. The objectives of most tracking systems are to manage effectively cultivation and solicitation processes that are highly individualized; to identify and quantify measures of progress in the cultivation and solicitation process; to maintain momentum over long periods of time; to provide information that will educate, motivate, and reward volunteers and staff involved in the major gifts effort; to focus attention on top prospects; to facilitate regular reporting to volunteers and staff; and to develop a written history of prospect cultivation that will provide an institutional memory of communications with major supporters.

There are a number of tracking systems available today, ranging from manual to those using word processing or spreadsheets through very sophisticated systems using state-of-the-art computer hardware and software. The criteria for selecting a tracking system include: size of major prospect pool, size of development staff, complexity of fundraising program, existing computer capability, and budget. Systems developed for prospect management need not be complex, but they should accommodate all of the data needed for identifying, assigning, and tracking major prospects.

When planning for a prospect management system, an institution should consider its information needs, the size of its file, and its equipment. If the equipment is already in place in the office—both computer (hardware) and programs (software)—this may have an effect on the data and number of records that can be tracked. Ideally, the first two considerations—needs and size—should determine the kind of equipment selected. A number of systems are on the market that have been developed expressly for prospect management. If one of these meets an institution's specifications for data, file size, and system cost, it will save developing a system from scratch.

It may also be possible to use an existing system for prospect management and tracking. If an institution's system is flexible, a means of flagging major prospects and the addition of a few fields may be all that is needed. However, it is not always feasible for institutions with very large master data bases to add the prospect management feature, since it focuses on such a small percentage of the file. Since it is a system tailored to an institution, the most important consideration is to provide the information that is essential to its development program. This will vary from institution to institution and may mean simply an alphabetical list of major prospects and a few details about them, something that can be managed easily on a word-processing system. If, on the other hand, it is important to be able to select prospects by geographic region, by staff or volunteer assignment, by rating, gift target, or a combination of elements, a more complex system will be required.

In setting up a system, an institution should plan for the kinds of routine reports needed as well as for the data it will need to call up at any given moment. Plan for growth, and, if possible, select a system that is flexible enough to allow for modifications and newly identified information needs. Include all important data fields, but do not clutter the system with unnecessary data. Remember, the more fields in the system, the more maintenance required. An elaborate system that has outdated information or empty data fields is almost worse than no system at all.

To ensure that the prospect management system is a useful tool, Baxter (1987) emphasizes that information must constantly be relayed to the person or department responsible for data entry and system maintenance. This means documenting all contact between the institution and prospects and forwarding the information to the system, submitting any additions or deletions, and keeping the system manager apprised of changes in a prospect's status. Regular reports from the system can identify any information gaps or highlight errors.

Baxter suggests the following list of possible data elements as a guide in setting up a prospect management system. Please note that these are suggestions rather than hard-and-fast requirements, as each institution has unique characteristics that influence system design.

Data Element	Comments
Identification	If possible, should be consistent with master file ID number.
Name	Prefix (title), last, first, middle, suffix.
Address, phone	Can allow for home, business, second home, and so on, but must keep in sync with master file.
Title	Business or professional position.
Salutation	Needed where prospect management system has word-processing capabilities.
Geographic region	Useful for institutions with constituents spread out over a large area, where location determines staff assignment, and for planning cultivation/solicitation trips and visits.
Source	Indicates type of prospect (alumnus, trustee, parent, corporation, foundation, and so on).
Wealth code	For those institutions whose lists have been screened by an outside vendor.
Class/degree	For educational institutions.
Gift rating	Prospect's capacity to give: usually a range of figures.
Interest rating	Prospect's involvement with the institution (readiness for solicitation).

Status	Where prospect is in solicitation cycle (cultivation, solicitation, donor relations, and so on).
Giving areas	The project, campaign, or type of gift the prospect is targeted for or given clearance (can be multiple occurrences).
Staff	Staff member assigned to manage the prospect.
Volunteer	Non-staff volunteer assigned to prospect.
Moves	Contact between institution and prospect, generally a date and brief description of the contact. Systems can be designed to accommodate numerous entries, to record last contact and next move, or [to have] comment fields that summarize past activity and future plans.
Solicitation	Request date, amount, purpose, solicitor (if other than volunteer); response date, amount, purpose.
Connections	Other ties to institution: spouse, family, classmates, business associates, and so on.
Identifiers	Institutional codes that identify special populations (sometimes called list or select codes).
Tickler	Date for staff or volunteer to conduct follow-up.
Comments	Free-form text to flag special circumstances or provide additional information.

Source: Baxter, 1987.

Whatever the choice of data elements and configuration of the system, fields should be set up to allow for swift and easy information searches.

The prospect management system is an integral part of a comprehensive approach for pursuing the extraordinary gift. It should be designed to ensure that an institution's best prospects are identified, cultivated, and solicited according to a master plan and that all activities are monitored. Used conscientiously, it can measurably help those who have responsibility for the success of major campaigns.

Five subsystems are usually found within most major donor prospect management systems: a rating system, a priority system, an approach system, an accountability system, and a report system.

Rating System. Step one in a program to obtain extraordinary gifts is identifying priority prospects. This system places a great deal of importance on the research function. Research and rating go hand in hand, and a solid records and research system is the foundation of any fundraising program. If not already in place, a research capability that will yield prospect ratings must be developed. The end result of a rating process should be not one but two rating codes: the prospect's giving capacity and the prospect's interest in the organization. A prospect's giving capacity is a collective best judgment (after a review of all the pertinent rating and file information about the prospect) of how much the prospect could contribute to an organization over three to five years if so inclined. The interest rating is a collective judgment of the prospect's interest in and concern for the organization based on personal information, the prospect's giving record, and file information on hand. Table 11 shows the numerical rating codes that might be used in a typical system.

Priority System. By adding the two numerical ratings (capacity and interest), an institution can determine each prospect's priority rating. The higher the rating, the higher priority the prospect is. The higher priority the prospect is, the more cultivation moves (structured contacts designed to bring a prospect closer to making a major gift) an institution will want make on the prospect in a given period of time, usually a calendar year.

To help guide an institution in determining how much

Table 11. Prospect Rating Codes.

Giving Capacity Code	Estimated Giving Capacity	Interest Code	Description
1	$ 2,500–4,999	1	Clearly turned off, no record of interest
2	5,000–9,999		
3	10,000–24,999	2	Minimal interest, occasional donor, attends meetings infrequently, and so on
4	25,000–49,999	3	Moderately active or formerly very active
5	50,000 and up	4	Very active, major donor, club member, committee person
		5	Member of governing board, other boards, or executive groups

cultivation a prospect gets, it is recommended that it use a cultivation quotient—the sum of the two numerical ratings multiplied by two. This represents the minimum number of cultivation moves an institution should hope to make on a prospect each year. For example, one prospect is rated 3/1 and another is rated 1/3, so both have cultivation quotients of eight (obtained by adding the two rating codes and multiplying by two). One is a rather unlikely prospect for a $10,000 gift at the moment, while the other one is a pretty likely prospect for a $2,500 gift. Their cultivation quotients tell the organization to plan for eight cultivation moves on each of these prospects in a year. But the institution may have to decide which prospect will get its attention first, because in one situation, a longer cultivation period may result in larger gift, while in the other, a smaller gift can be more readily realized.

Cultivation quotients are flexible guidelines. Staff and volunteers should have the authority to make more or fewer than the recommended number of contacts when circumstances dictate. Another important point is that ratings and, therefore, cultivation quotients can change during the year. Look at our previous example again. In the institution's opinion, the person rated 3/1 has a $10,000 to $24,999 gift potential but has not demonstrated much past interest in the organization. But a staff member or volunteer calling on the prospect discovers that the prospect has become much more interested. That changes the prospect's interest rating to 3, which increases the cultivation quotient to 12, thus calling for four more contact points during the year.

It should be clearly understood that ordinarily the campaign's top leadership should be assigned to cultivate and solicit those with the greatest ability to give and the greatest interest. It is equally important that the entire campaign stay focused on the best donor prospects throughout. Little time should be given to prospects rated 1/1. But what about prospects rated 5/1 or 5/2? Should time be spent on them? Yes, but it must be a measured amount of time and the effort disciplined. The cultivation of a prospect from one who is clearly not interested in an institution or has little interest to one who serves on the governing board usually takes a series of steps and is not accomplished in one leap. Hence, even though great ability to give exists, the proclivity to give needs to be developed, and that often takes more time than is available in a limited-term, movement-intensive campaign. Leave some time, give some effort to the long shots, but reserve the bulk of the effort for the already more involved prospects with major gift potential.

Accountability System. Each major gift prospect should be assigned to a member of the staff whose duty it is to see that a personalized campaign is waged to get the best gift possible. Each staff member becomes an account executive and acts as a catalyst providing the initiative and the strategy. The institution should attempt to assign most prospects to one or more volunteers for cultivation and solicitation and should strive to give its volunteers the feeling that they are responsible for their prospects. Every two to four weeks, staff should report on gift prospect assignments. The reports should list all prospects (individuals, foundations, and corporations) for whom the staff person is responsible; the volunteer or volunteers assisting with each prospect; the number of cultivation and/or solicitation contacts the campaign master plan indicates should be made with each prospect during the year; and the number of contacts made to date. By reviewing this report, each member of the staff will readily see which prospects need attention and can plan accordingly.

Approach System. Types of contacts include phone calls, letters, and personal visits by staff, the chief executive officer, or volunteers; attendance of prospects at institutional functions and leadership retreats; involvement in key issues and programs; publications; firsthand briefings and information on important events; and recognition events. In most systems, contacts are weighted according to significance, importance, and impact. A typical weighted system looks like this:

Cultivation Contact	*Contact Points*
Letter from a staff member	1
Phone call from a staff member	2
Letter from a volunteer	2
Invitation to a major event	3
Phone call from a volunteer	3
Phone call from chief executive officer	3
Visit by a staff member	4
Letter from chief executive officer	4
Attendance at an institutional activity (off site)	4
Visit by a volunteer	5
Attendance at an institutional event (on site)	5
Firsthand information on important events	6
Meeting with the chief executive officer	7
Personal recognition	7
Leadership retreat	7

Report System. Follow-through is absolutely necessary in making contacts with major donor prospects. There is no substitute for persistence and patience. A useful management technique is to require staff members to identify their top ten prospects. During regular staff meetings, each staff member assigned to these prospects should report on what is being done to move the prospect closer to making a major gift, who has the initiative, and what is the next step. Then, at the next staff meeting, the staff member should report any progress or difficulty in accomplishing the cultivation plan and discuss the next sequence of steps to be taken. A call report also should be filed after every phone call or visit.

The major donor solicitation guidance system with its five subsystems is a control mechanism that ensures that the big gift prospects are rated, given a priority, assigned to a member of the staff and to volunteers, cultivated and solicited according to a master plan, and reported on. The system should be designed to help get results, not to stimulate "making points for the purpose of making points." It should encourage well-thought-out, appropriate strategical moves that the institution feels will bring its prospects closer to making major gifts. Although no one knows for sure how many contacts it will take to bring a prospect to the point of making a gift (the average is generally thought to be seven to ten), the institution has to use something, such as the cultivation quotients, as a guide. It is appropriate to rely on the major donor solicitation guidance system as a tool to bring human factors into play because, after all, human factors are the most important elements in getting the prospect ready to give.

The prospect tracking and management system helps an organization manage its involvement with major prospects. Once someone is identified as a prospect, it is imperative that the institution involve that person in its life. Involvement precedes and often begets investment. And investment is the end game in the capital campaign.

Soliciting Major Gifts

Securing major gifts is the natural as well as the hoped-for end result of the cultivation process. Cultivation begins when the prospective donor first hears about a particular institution. It reaches its highest point when the donor asks, "How much will it cost?" Because tangible results are not usually obtained in a few weeks or months, cultivation demands a sensitive balance of patience and persistence.

Philanthropy is the act of expressing love for others, so major gifts are much more than money contributed to meet an institution's needs; they represent a person's opportunity for investment based on commitment. Solicitation is a delicate presentation of an opportunity to invest material assets that results in an intangible reward and sense of fulfillment. Solicitation is not begging but a high form of seeking investments. One advantage of the capital drive is that it necessitates asking for major gifts within a definite time frame. Occasionally, an institution can jump from identification of a prospect to immediately asking for an investment. But this does not often meet with success. On the other hand, waiting for the perfect time to seek a contribution has probably caused the loss of more gifts than has asking too soon. *It is better to act, albeit imperfectly, than to wait forever for the perfect move.* Some factors to consider in timing are length of cultivation, date of the prospect's last major gift, his or her age and health, and the urgency of the project for which funds are sought.

Preparing to Make the Major Gift Call. Each negotiation is a campaign in itself, says Campbell (1985). Do the necessary homework; know the prospect—his or her needs, wants, hopes, and ambitions. Get all the help available. Find out who the prospect's family members, friends, and advisers are and who at the institution the prospect knows and respects. Meet with those people and learn all they can tell about the prospect. Identify at least two possible projects that correspond to the prospect's interests. Document the need for each project and the benefits that will accrue if it is funded. Prepare a presentation—flip chart, proposal, or letter—to take to the meeting and perhaps leave with the prospect. Bring prospects to the institution regularly. Candidly discuss opportunities, issues, and problems. Ask for their council and advice. When possible, follow up, report back, and show appreciation.

Select solicitors who have made major gifts themselves. Teams of solicitors, most commonly two or three people, usually work better on major gift calls. Develop a strategy for the major gift prospects and review this strategy with the solicitors. If necessary, give them a script and rehearse it until it is internalized.

Use the phone or see the prospect in person and ask for a time to talk about the institution's capital campaign. Confirm the appointment in writing. It may be useful to send the prospect some easy-to-read information about the institution's plans along with the confirmation letter. Select a meeting site where the prospect is most comfortable. Avoid noisy and congested sites. Reconfirm the meeting by phone beforehand.

Large gifts from individuals sometimes result from personal conversation without the aid of a formal written presentation. This usually happens, however, only when the donor is very closely identified and involved with the institution. Even then, a follow-up presentation in writing often helps firm up the appeal. A written statement may be anything from a letter to a highly individualized—and usually quite extensive—published document. Ordinarily, however, a typewritten proposal with covering letter is adequate. The length may vary from one page to a major document with extensive supporting appendixes, but usually a statement from three to ten pages is all that is necessary. The written proposal should cover at least these four items: statement of the opportunity or need; proposed action for meeting the need or fulfilling the opportunity; financial data, including cost, other funds available, and how much is being requested; and summary statement of the benefits that the donor will derive.

Asking for large gifts should never be "hit or miss," nor should it be done in casual conversation. It is a serious mission requiring preparation and planning before visits, understanding of techniques to be employed during visits, and willingness to follow up after visits.

Making the Visit. During a visit, allow an initial period for conversation on topics of mutual interest, then introduce the reason for the visit. Present the background that has led to the presentation occasion. Do not let the conversation become a monologue; allow ample opportunity for the prospective donor to participate. Ask questions. Listen carefully to everything that is said. Finally, ask for participation, making clear how much the institution hopes for.

Be aware of "body language"—dress, actions, eye contact. First impressions are important. Consider objections and criticisms as opportunities for discussion and indications of interest. Deal with them as such, but never enter into an argument with a prospect!

Take ample time in a solicitation. Arouse interest to a point where the prospect asks, "How much do you want?" Remember, people give to help people. Sell the institution's programs and concepts, not the cost. Logic, emotion, and enthusiasm are the best motivators. Tax advantages seldom play a part in major gift decisions. They are most often a secondary benefit.

Ask for the gift! Keep the sights up and be specific about the amount. If possible, cite some other lead gifts in the major gifts range. It is not uncommon to ask for two to four times what it is thought a prospect will give. And there is no known case of a volunteer (or staff) being shot for asking for too much. A large request, if it is within the giving ability of the prospective donor, is usually flattering.

Should a "no" become evident, listen carefully to the reasons. Find out what must be done before a gift can be secured. Then leave the meeting without "closing" and plan a strategy for the next visit. Gifts made in haste or by an unconvinced donor tend to be minimal. Clearly establish the next move, including a date for a possible follow-up meeting. It is better not to leave the pledge card with the prospect, although some solicitors do this, and some prospects insist on it. If the pledge card is left with the prospect, the solicitor loses a primary reason to follow up, and it is possible that the prospect will either "file" it or make a minimum gift.

In discussing a major gift with a prospect, emphasize that the gift can be made not only as an outright gift but also in the form of securities and other property, and that a gift can return a lifetime income if the donor so desires. In most capital campaigns, unless solely for construction purposes, bequests are generally welcomed, too.

During many solicitations, the prospect will raise objections. Some objections are subliminal. For instance, some older donors who are alone or lonely will object to closing not because they have an objection to the case or reservations about investing but because they fear that the institution will cease giving them the attention inherent in the cultivation and solicitation process once the gift decision is announced. But most objections are more straightforward: "This is a bad time for us financially. All our assets are currently illiquid"; or "I do not agree with your CEO's priorities."

Whatever the objection, hear it out completely. In discussing the objection with the prospect, restate the objection and make sure it is understood in context. Explore ways that the objection might be overcome. Never let the objection lead into an argument, and do not make the objection bigger than it is. Respond to it with facts, and never make excuses. If the objection is weak, deal with it as quickly as possible and pass over it. It is perfectly legitimate to compromise on objections if in fact they will not be a hindrance to reaching the major goal.

Determine whether the prospect will donate if the objection can be overcome, and if so, do what reasonably can be done to remove the objection. Always remember that objections are really questions and that the prospect's investment in the project will help overcome the objections. This will help to convert the objections into reasons for giving. If the objection cannot be overcome, move along to another prospect. Do not waste time on prospects who absolutely are not going to give for whatever reason.

After the visit, write a short note of thanks for the prospect's time and interest. Where appropriate, draft a further note of thanks from the chief executive officer and, possibly, the board chair. Prepare a complete summary report on the visit, with particular attention to new information on the potential donor's special interests, background, and idiosyncrasies. Be sure to include at least the following information:

- Name of company, foundation, or individual visited, date visited, place of meeting
- If a foundation or corporation, names and positions of people visited
- Who went on the visit
- The purpose of the visit
- What points were highlighted or conveyed during the visit and whether this was done successfully
- As much detail as possible about what happened at the meeting (what comments were made by whom, and responses to those comments)
- Whether any materials were distributed during the meeting; if so, what they were, whether there are copies in the development office's research files, and whether there is any pre- or post-meeting correspondence that others should have copies of

- What concerns (if any) were voiced by the prospect and what positive comments were made
- Whether a request for funding or assistance was made and, if so, specific details
- Whether additional action or follow-up is needed and, if so, what types, by when, and by whom
- Whether other people should be alerted to the fact that this visit was made and, if so, who they are
- If appropriate, thoughts and recommendations on the best strategies or approaches for cultivating and soliciting the prospect

Errors to Avoid in Solicitation. In 1978, the Public Management Institute (Conrad, 1978) identified fourteen major errors that are most commonly made in solicitating gifts: (1) not asking for the gift; (2) not asking for a large enough gift: (3) not listening—talking too much; (4) not asking questions; (5) talking about the organization and its approach rather than the client benefits; (6) not being flexible and not having alternatives to offer the prospect; (7) not knowing enough about the prospect before the solicitation; (8) forgetting to summarize before moving on; (9) not having prearranged signals between solicitation team members; (10) asking for the gift too soon; (11) speaking rather than remaining silent after asking for the gift; (12) settling on the first offer that a prospect suggests, even if it is lower than expected; (13) not cultivating the donor before soliciting; and (14) not sending out trained solicitors. Study the list. These mistakes are all avoidable given proper preparation, approach, and presentation to the prospect.

Obtaining major gifts is a process—a cycle—open to all. Most of all, everyone must give this activity top priority in their day-to-day and week-to-week efforts. Nothing must be allowed to divert attention from the greatest source of support for an institution—major donors.

Acknowledgment and Recognition

Once a donor has made a significant gift, cultivation can move to a new and higher level. A sincere expression of gratitude can show the human quality of an institution. It goes without saying that every gift should be acknowledged when received; even the donor is expecting acknowledgment. If, in fact, the gift has a part in strengthening the institution, then the real opportunity to say "thanks" will come in six months or a year when the effect of the gift is more fully known. During that interim period, keep in close contact with the donor and never fail to follow up and provide the information that will tell the donor what the full positive effect of the gift has been.

Whether or not people say they want to be recognized, the plain fact is that 99 percent of all people love recognition. Since recognition is often a major motivation for giving, the campaign structure must provide a means for recognizing major donors. The opportunities should be established at the beginning of the campaign, with policy guidelines for naming facilities, providing endowments, and the many other kinds of activities that people will want to support in a comprehensive campaign. The use of events to dedicate buildings and open offices and wings and other such appropriate ceremonial activities are encouraged. The placing of plaques in buildings is always appropriate, as is the giving of distinguished service awards.

It is important that the right people thank those who have given. In each case, an individual determination of who should do the acknowledging should be made. There should also be continuing recognition for major donors. If they are properly handled in the recognition process, they likely will make even greater major gifts in the future.

Most of our discussion about major gifts has centered on individual donor prospects. About 90 percent of the money given to all campaigns comes from individuals, not foundations or corporations. But the process of identifying, cultivating, and soliciting major gift prospects can and should be used effectively for corporations and foundations, too, so long as it is remembered that foundations do not give support to buildings, nor do corporations make investments in programs—*people give to people*. In every instance where a corporate or foundation gift is made, it is a result of the representative of the institution asking a representative of the corporation or foundation to make a gift.

Securing major gifts, when all is said and done, is a relatively simple task—the right person, to ask the right prospect, for the right gift amount, in the right form, for the right reason, at the right time.

✳ 10 ✳

Managing Campaign Logistics and Day-to-Day Operations

This chapter addresses essential campaign operational matters, including the schedule for the campaign, campaign budget, gift reporting, and the use of professional counsel. Although campaigns have been known to be organized and conducted in very short periods of time (one campaign in Memphis, Tennessee, was conducted, from start to finish, in five months), it is more typical for campaigns to require from six to eighteen months of preparation and then two or three years, and sometimes longer, for the active phase. Once a campaign organizational chart (described in Chapter Seven) has been established, the next step is to develop the campaign timetable.

Typical Timetable

A capital campaign is an undertaking of great complexity. An organization's constituencies must be fully informed, prospective donors must be identified and classified as to giving potential, and prospects must be assigned carefully for solicitation. Various committees must launch their solicitation activities at appropriate intervals. And, finally, report meetings and the inevitable follow-up activities must be carried out in the closing weeks of each of the separate phases. All of these must be scheduled with careful regard for each volunteer's time.

It is sound campaign practice to seek the biggest gifts first. Early moves, therefore, have uncommon significance. And premature action can be dangerous. The simplified outline of activities that follows shows the timing of solicitation activities during a three-year "public phase" campaign. This calendar illustrates the principles of working from the top down and the fact that the larger the gift, the longer the period of time that may be required for consideration prior to the gift decision.

First Phase—Pre-Public Announcement
(twelve–fifteen months):

- Organize development and campaign office
- Retain counsel (if applicable)
- Draft plan and timetable
- Draft preliminary case statement
- Conduct market survey
- Enlist campaign chair
- Enlist other key campaign committee members
- Review campaign plan with committee
- Build prospect lists
- Identify, research, evaluate, and cultivate primary major prospective donors for early approach (lead gifts)
- Develop basic printed and audiovisual materials
- Seek lead gifts
- Enlist and educate major gifts committee(s)
- Solicit campaign committee members
- Begin enlisting and educating special gifts committee(s)
- Enlist general committee chair
- Publicly announce campaign (major event)
- *End first phase:* deadline for 50 percent of campaign dollar objective (no public announcement of a campaign should be made without having met a minimum of 30 percent of goal)

Second Phase—Major/Special Gifts
(eighteen–twenty-four months):

- Continue adding names to major and special gifts lists
- Continue prospective donor contact as required
- Continue major gifts solicitations
- Solicit special gifts committee

- Launch special gifts committee solicitations
- Continue distribution of campaign information to news media
- Enlist, organize, and train general campaign leadership
- *End second phase:* deadline for 80 percent of campaign dollar objective

Third Phase—General Gifts, Cleanup
(twelve-eighteen months):

- Formally launch general gifts solicitation
- Continue solicitation by major and special gifts committees
- Continue distribution of campaign information to news media
- Final campaign thrust followed by final report meeting for top volunteers
- Victory event
- *End third phase:* deadline for 100 percent of campaign dollar objective

The capital campaign is, of course, a collection of individual campaigns, each with its own leadership and timing. Once established, the time schedule must be respected. In some instances, the general campaign will need to be supplemented by area or regional campaigns. The following is a typical calendar for an area campaign (the length of time required will vary according to the area, the number of prospects to be solicited, and the size of the gifts to be solicited).

First Week:

1.   Chair and staff representative(s) meet to:
   a.   determine number of campaign workers needed to solicit prospects on the basis of completed prospect evaluation;
   b.   select names of prospective division leaders;
   c.   set up campaign calendar, including dates of all organizational meetings, the solicitation committee meeting, the announcement event, and the report and planning meetings;
   d.   determine and tentatively engage places for solicitation committee meeting and announcement event;

    e.   discuss arrangements for processing the necessary letters to be mailed over the chair's signature.

2.   Chair begins enlistment of division leaders.

Second Week:

1.   Chair, division leaders, and staff representative(s) meet to review the campaign program and begin enlistment of other volunteer workers.

2.   Chair's invitation to the announcement event is mailed to those on the guest list.

3.   Division leaders begin enlistment of team members.

Third Week:

1.   Letter announcing date of solicitation committee meeting is mailed to campaign workers as they are enlisted.

2.   Announcement of appointment of chair is released to appropriate news media.

3.   Area campaign goal is set.

Fourth Week:

1.   Chair calls division leaders to check on progress of enlistment of team members.

2.   Letters announcing date of solicitation committee meeting continue to be mailed.

Fifth Week:

1.   Campaign solicitation committee meets; training and information session is held; workers are assigned prospects.

2.   Workers call assigned prospects to remind them of the announcement event.

Sixth Week:

1.   Announcement event.

2.   On the day after announcement event, brochure and chair's letters are mailed to all constituents in the area who are not scheduled for personal solicitation.

3.   Solicitation of campaigners begins on the day following the

reception—chair should solicit division leaders, division leaders solicit team members.

4. Solicitation of all prospects begins.
5. Following the announcement event, weekly progress reports will be mailed to all solicitors through a campaign newsletter prepared by the area chair and the staff representative.

Seventh Week:

First report meeting is held.

Eighth Week:

Second report meeting is held.

Ninth Week:

Third report meeting is held.

Tenth Week:

Fourth report meeting is held.

Eleventh Week:

1. If necessary, a fifth report meeting is held.
2. Final check is made on outstanding pledge cards.
3. Chair sends letter of appreciation to all campaign workers.
4. Victory celebration with workers is held at final report meeting as goal is achieved.

Acknowledging and Reporting Gifts

From the beginning of the campaign, all gifts should be promptly acknowledged and each donor properly thanked. Each donor should receive a personal letter of appreciation from the institution as well as an official gift receipt. Think about the thank-you letter, too. Try to make it more than a thank-you; make it personal, informative, and meaty. Tell the donor what is happening, the amount raised, building project progress, amount of endowment money, and so forth. This is one of the details that needs advance thought. Who will sign the letters? At what minimum level will institutional administrators and campaign leadership sign—$100, $500, $1,000, or more? Does the plan call for the institution to ask each volunteer to thank each donor—and send the institution a copy? (It should.) For larger gifts, the chief executive officer should certainly provide a personal acknowledgment. The key volunteer working on the solicitation may also choose to communicate with the donor, as well as the chair of the board and the chair of the campaign. Gifts are made individually, and their acknowledgment should be considered individually. If more than one acknowledgment is to be sent, the staff should make certain that the acknowledgments complement and reinforce each other rather than being redundant.

Acknowledging gifts will be a time-consuming task, so there may be a need for additional secretarial staffing or word-processing capability to enable prompt preparation of letters. This is an important detail. Long delays in acknowledging and thanking donors for gifts leave a bad impression and are unprofessional. Be certain that everyone—donors and volunteers—is thanked as quickly as possible.

Another major consideration is reporting gifts, both internally and for volunteer and public information. As a part of the advance campaign planning, the institution must build internal recording and reporting systems that will enable it to handle gifts correctly and with dispatch. The system must be able to compile the gift data to formulate reports showing the number, source, and amount of gifts received and, more importantly, the purpose for which gifts were received. This is essential not only for practical reasons, such as reporting periodically to the campaign leadership and workers, but also for internal audit controls. Staff must be able to report daily where the campaign stands. The staff will almost certainly be asked daily for such information.

The staff should also consider preparing a weekly campaign report to be mailed to all volunteers and to others important to the success of the campaign. The format of such reports varies widely and can be determined by each institution. In some campaigns, a monthly report is all that is required. It helps to keep the focus on the campaign and can be used to build a fire under those volunteers not performing up to expectations. Each volunteer leader should review the division's or team's effort each report session. The bandwagon effect is important in a campaign.

Depending on the campaign's organization, the staff may want to be able to report in a number of ways—by division, by teams, by area, by class, by source, by amount, by fund, or all of these. Certainly, a breakdown of this nature will be desirable in the institution's final report of the campaign, so why not plan it in advance and have this capacity during the campaign? If an institution uses a computer, this is simple if it is programmed carefully. If it uses a manual system, multipart copies can do the trick.

Stewardship

An essential component of any follow-through program is the thoughtful, systematic organization of a stewardship effort. Stewardship effectively begins even before the first gift is received— when the board establishes policies regarding the acceptance, handling, management, and investment of gifts. Once a gift is received, stewardship encompasses a variety of activities, including recognition, appreciation, and reporting. It also obviously includes the wise and prudent financial management of the investment. It is the ongoing process whereby an institution continues contact with a donor to establish the basis for the next gift while exercising proper care and giving appropriate recognition for gifts already made.

Some individuals and many corporations and foundations will not pledge for a period of years but will give initially and will renew each year after that. This category of donors should be flagged and the donors asked to consider another gift near the anniversary date of their last gift. Even single-year donors who have not promised to continue giving should be asked on the anniversary of their gift. This also has proved to be productive in many campaigns.

Saving the Victory

If victory on schedule should elude an institution, it is important to do two things, says Russell R. Picton (1982). First, be candid. Announce the results to date and indicate that all gifts have not been received. Continue in a quiet, determined way to push for a successful conclusion as soon as possible. Second, have each leader call or visit each key prospect in the leader's division or team to ask the prospect to keep active until the work is finished and offer staff or other leadership assistance. Perhaps some reassignment of prospects is called for if a volunteer has not been effective. It does not take long for a campaign to die, so push harder than ever. This is where the campaign leadership must be aggressive. Here again, review the status of major prospects and look for new approaches if needed. Have the campaign cabinet consider going back to key prospects for a second gift. The initial gift rarely taps out the donor.

Campaign Budget

What does it cost to run a professionally managed campaign? Obviously, there is no single answer. There are several factors that will influence the cost of campaign fundraising: (1) the existing institutional resources already committed to the ongoing development program; (2) the size of the goal (there are certain fixed costs common to all campaigns that are more easily amortized in large campaign budgets than they are in small ones, such as preparation of a case statement, cost of professional counsel, major public announcement event, and victory celebration event); (3) the type of campaign model and asking methodology chosen; and (4) whether the campaign is a local or wide-area one. Very simply, campaign budgets can vary significantly. Information from recent efforts suggests that, in large campaigns, costs can be kept as low as 2 or 3 percent of the campaign goal. However, for the purposes of planning, the institution should assume that it will cost from 10 to 12 percent of the campaign goal to conduct the campaign.

Although there are several variable factors that must be considered before a final figure is arrived at, two fundamental points are of primary importance. The first is that it takes ample funding to ensure the success of a campaign. It is foolhardy when so much is at stake to overly restrict campaign expenses.

The second important thing to remember when preparing a budget is to consider all the campaign's needs and to include them at the outset. Most campaign budgets have lines for the following items: salary and benefits for the professional, administrative, clerical, and part-time personnel; fees for consultants; office supplies and printing; telephone and other communications networks; leased equipment; computer services; outside mailing service; clipping service; travel; publication; advertising; public announcement event (kickoff); entertainment; leadership workshops; area campaigns; special events; office furnishings; unclassifieds; campaign victory celebration; and an undistributed amount, usually 3 to 5 percent of the total budget, to meet inflationary and unforeseen factors.

The final important consideration regarding budget is to establish an internal procedure that provides for monitoring and scrutiny of budget expenditure at all times.

In addition to the costs of campaigning, there is also the little talked about loss called shrinkage—that is, the loss from pledges that are not paid. Some loss is uncontrollable, as in the case of a donor's death or business failure. However, some of the loss is caused by inadequate pledge reminder billing systems. The amount of income that short-term investments can earn these days makes it imperative that the organization collect its pledges on schedule, and earlier if possible. Normal shrinkage is usually 1 to 3 percent of the amount raised. The job of the professional staff member is to ensure that it stays as low as possible. An organization that does not have a responsive billing system that will enable it to bill accurately and on schedule may be headed for collection difficulty. The institution must check this system and make any corrections necessary before the campaign is begun. Including with the billing statement a status report on the campaign and information on what is being done with the funds raised can help the payment flow and is sound cultivation for later gifts.

Creating and Using Reporting Forms

The various printed forms and computer programs needed to record, retain, retrieve, and reproduce the information associated with the wide variety of campaign tasks should be created by the institution before the campaign begins. There are two types of basic reports for which the professional staff is responsible—financial and people (volunteers and prospects). The number and level of sophistication of financial progress reports will vary depending on the size and complexity of the campaign. Of course, a great deal of operational procedure, particularly pertaining to fiduciary matters but also pertaining to the wider scope of development office activities, probably will already be in place in the established development office. Two examples of the kinds of forms that are routinely generated in support of the capital campaign effort are provided here. Exhibit 1 shows a sample weekly campaign progress report. A typical prospect status summary can be formulated as shown in Exhibit 2. For both types of form, the information may be maintained and conveyed through hard copy or computer production procedures.

For the institution interested in a complete library of the variety of materials and tables used in a typical campaign, there is a logical, chronological, comprehensive manual, *The Campaign Manuals* (Builta, 1984a, 1984b), a two-volume scrapbook of a particular campaign. The first volume, *The Campaign,* includes in chronological order the most important communications between the campaign headquarters and volunteers. The second volume, *Steps and Procedures,* is a procedures manual that deals directly with record-keeping systems. It also contains an index to simplify finding a particular form or set of instructions. Another excellent publication is the *Capital Campaign Resource Guide* published by the Public Management Institute (1984). An easy-to-use, complete workbook, it contains a comprehensive array of forms and worksheets.

Outside Professional Counsel

A successful capital campaign will generally adhere to the principles stated in this book. However, the simple memorization of these principles will not guarantee a successful campaign. Capital campaign success is more likely when the mechanics are supplemented by experienced human insights, strategies, sensitivities, and judgments of the kind that transcend the prescriptions of

Exhibit 1. Campaign Progress Report.

Week ending _____

I. Campaign goal $
II. New gifts and pledges
III. Total previous gifts and pledges

　　　　Grand total gifts and pledges

IV. Amount needed to reach goal
V. Recent campaign activities

VI. Appointments scheduled

Donor Category	Campaign Goal	Received to Date	Balance Needed
Board	$	$	$
Individuals			
Corporations			
Foundations			
Other			
TOTALS			

any written document. These added ingredients are often provided by outside professional counsel.

An institution with a sizable and experienced fundraising staff may decide to proceed without aid from outside counsel. But the majority of institutions find such aid both advisable and necessary. Outside counsel is most often employed when the organization feels that it must supplement its staff's ability to handle a campaign, the institution feels that it needs expert advice, or the development office feels that it needs objective advice.

When considering the use of outside counsel, it is important to understand that the role of professional counsel is not to raise money but rather to help the institution raise it. Use of professional counsel does not relieve the institution's board and administration of their responsibilities for the success of the campaign. In most

Major Prospects	Researched	Prospect	Assigned to Staff	Possible Volunteer(s)	Assigned to Volunteer	Meeting Held	Letter and/or Proposal Submitted	Gift/Pledge Made; Seek More	Refused; Try Again	Gift/Pledge Made Adequate	Firm Refusal	Comments

cases, professional counsel is used to supplement in-house capabilities. Professional counsel enables institutions to draw on the breadth and depth of experience not generally possessed by a single institution. It is usually retained for one or more of the following purposes: to conduct an internal audit; to conduct a market survey; to prepare the campaign case and other case-stating materials; to provide full-time (resident) campaign management; or to provide part-time counseling. Counsel can be uniquely helpful in providing third-party objectivity in analyzing such areas as internal organization, staffing, and short- and long-term planning.

Most professional firms subscribe to the strict code of professional ethics promulgated by the American Association of Fund-Raising Counsel (AAFRC) (1986). This code states:

(1) Members of the Association are firms which are exclusively or primarily organized to provide fund-raising counseling services, feasibility studies, campaign management and related public relations, to nonprofit institutions and agencies seeking philanthropic support. They will not knowingly be used by an organization to induce philanthropically inclined persons to give their money to unworthy causes.

(2) While the Association does not prescribe any particular method of calculating fees for its members, the organization should base its fees on services provided and avoid contracts providing for contingency, commissions or a percentage of funds raised for the client.

The organization should base its fees on high standards of service, and should not profit, directly or indirectly, from materials or services billed to the client by a third party. Member firms will not offer or provide the services of professional solicitors.

(3) The executive head of a member organization must demonstrate at least a six-year record of continuous experience as a professional in the

fundraising field. This helps to protect the public from those who enter the profession without sufficient competence, experience, or devotion to ideals of public service.

(4)   The Association looks with disfavor upon firms which use methods harmful to the public, such as making exaggerated claims of past achievements, guaranteeing results, and promising to raise unobtainable sums.

(5)   No payment in cash or kind shall be made by a member to an officer, director, trustee or advisor of a philanthropic agency or institution as compensation for using his influence for the engaging of a member of fundraising counsel.

(6)   In fairness to all clients, member firms should charge equitable fees for all services with the exception that initial meetings with prospective clients are not usually construed as services.

AAFRC member firms charge on a fixed-fee basis, and the costs are governed by the amount of time spent, not the size of the campaign goal. Any contractual agreement should carry a cancellation clause applicable both to the client and to the firm. There are other consulting firms that are not members of AAFRC. Professional organizations such as CASE, NSFRE, the National Association of Hospital Development (NAHD), the Association of Governing Boards (AGB), and similar national and regional organizations can provide leads on firms and individual consultants who are not members of AAFRC but who have nevertheless established a reputation for reputable service. Also available are individual, free-lance consultants, senior advancement officers from all third-sector areas, retired chief executive officers, vice-presidents, and other administrators of institutions, and other specialists in specific fields and disciplines that may be applicable to an institution's campaign needs.

An organization should always try to engage an individual or consulting firm with experience, background, and particular talent to provide the assistance needed. It is important to check with the consultant's past clients and others who know the firm or individual. Ask whether the consultant is familiar with similar kinds of institutions or has undertaken comparable assignments. Determine whether the individual or firm is respected in the profession and delivers promised performance and results on time.

In selecting counsel, an institution should not only check the references but also make certain that it meets the individual with whom it will be working. With the larger firms, the person who meets with the institution's board and administration to make a presentation before counsel is engaged often is not the person who will be working actively on the institutional account.

E. Burr Gibson (1983) outlines the advantages and disadvantages of using outside counsel. Among the advantages:

- Counsel can provide an objective viewpoint to the institution, and it often has more credibility with the chief executive officer and board members, thereby allowing it to be tougher in circumstances where that is called for and "to absorb heat" when that is called for.
- Counsel also brings credibility because it can call on a broad range of experience and share this experience with the institution.
- Consultants are paid fees high enough to motivate the chief executive officer and board to work effectively and efficiently.
- Counsel can apply the brakes to ensure that sufficient cultivation and solicitation time is spent with the critical top 10 percent of prospects while at the same time keeping an eye on the entire campaign—anticipating needs, prodding to get things done, giving support to the staff, and suggesting systems and strategies to be used.
- Counsel also offers a sounding board to experienced development directors who have no other knowledgeable people close at hand.

Among the disadvantages, Gibson lists these:

- Outside counsel may be too cautious in the goal-setting process—this may happen because counsel wants to ensure a makeable goal for the client.
- The best person in a firm, the one who matches with the institutional needs and chemistry, may not be available at the right time from the firm. The consultant assigned to the client may prove incompatible and difficult to work with, and the firm may find it difficult to provide the correct person to serve the client's needs in the time frame needed. There also exists the possibility of an excessive disparity between the firm's top management representative and the day-to-day contact person when a firm is utilized.
- Because counsel's function is to show an institution how to raise money but not necessarily to raise money for it, the consultant, therefore, may provide good strategic counsel but limited operational help, and many campaigns are as much in need of operational assistance as they are of strategic guidance.
- If counsel is used on a full-time residence basis, much information may not be captured in the files at the end of the campaign and may leave when the campaign director leaves.
- The utilization of counsel also may mean a missed opportunity to train staff at the institution.
- The use of counsel can be costly even though it may, in fact, be very cost effective.

Almost every institution that undertakes an ambitious campaign generally concludes that counsel can be of value. In fact, almost all major institutions conducting successful capital campaigns over the past quarter century have used counsel in one way or another. How and when to use counsel are individual questions to be asked and answered by each institution as it considers its campaign.

The Critical Difference

Most senior fund raisers contend that the capital campaign is both a science and an art. It is the science, the methodology and the mechanics, that is generally first learned and applied by less experienced professionals. However, it is often the individual's ability to rise above the scientific application and mechanical knowledge that distinguishes a successful campaign director and, indeed, a successful capital campaign. The ability to go beyond what is commonly known and universally applied, to bring a special human touch, a liberal measure of common sense, and an insightful, experienced perspective to a campaign is of vital importance. Unfortunately, these values cannot be learned entirely through reading, nor can they be practically taught in the classroom. They are generally the result of on-line experience in the natural environment of the marketplace. This point must be stressed to anyone who is interested in working in a capital campaign. It simply is not enough to understand and to apply the science of fundraising. The process must be lifted above science and brought to a state of art. An analysis of successful development programs and successful capital campaigns over a long period of time and throughout a variety of organizations makes it clear that the ability to transcend to a higher level—to a level of uncommon human understanding and motivation—is a trademark of almost every campaign that has been conducted successfully.

✳ 11 ✳

Successful Publications, Promotion, and Public Relations

Designing Campaign Publications

Just how much value literature has to a campaign is hard to quantify. Publications and publicity alone do not raise money, but funds cannot be raised without them. Interestingly, they are especially helpful with those that are not "insiders"; and they give confidence and provide support and security to both volunteers and staff. So campaign literature must be planned in light of its specific purpose and with the belief that it will be read and heeded.

Types of Campaign Publications. The case statement and its derivatives are clearly the most important single pieces of campaign literature. However, in addition to the case statement, the program brochure, and the question-and-answer folder, the campaign will also need several other written pieces: (1) a pledge or contribution card or form; (2) a brochure on tax information and estate planning in making major gifts; (3) instructions to workers; (4) a fact booklet on the institution; (5) an impact-of-institution brochure or financial impact study; (6) a campaign or program newsletter; (7) campaign reports; and (8) transcript materials (major gift presentations and foundation and corporate proposals). The resources provide samples of selected pieces used in four separate campaigns.

A brochure on tax information and estate planning and a companion piece on memorial or named gift opportunities are

139

important pieces of campaign literature. Both are intended to raise sights and encourage larger gifts by pointing out tax advantages and offering an opportunity for personalizing gifts in a permanent and appealing way. These brochures will take a variety of forms depending on the circumstances of an individual campaign.

Another vital piece of campaign literature is an instruction booklet for workers. Such a volunteer's guide should provide a step-by-step program designed to educate volunteer solicitors and make them feel at ease and should describe the suggested procedure for cultivating prospects and securing major gifts.

A facts sheet about the institution need not be elaborate, but it should be comprehensive and provide a variety of important general reference information that will be educational to the volunteers and provide answers to many of the routine questions that might be asked by prospects, especially those not intimately familiar with the institution.

The campaign newsletter is another piece of literature that takes infinite shapes and forms. It is important that the campaign newsletter appear regularly. It should make liberal use of pictures of individuals involved with the campaign, volunteers and donors, and include as many names of people as is legitimately possible. The best campaign newsletters also have a well-thought-out purpose. They serve not only to provide recognition and reward for volunteers and donors but also to set the tone for the campaign and to move the fundraising effort forward in an organized, effective, efficient manner.

Another important part of campaign literature is pledge documentation. The first form of this documentation is a campaign pledge card. The typical pledge card for any campaign will provide a space for typing or printing the name and address of the prospect, a statement indicating that the donor's pledge is made "in consideration of the gifts of others and toward the campaign goal," a place to record the amount of the pledge, how it will be paid if other than in cash, the payment period, and the frequency of payments to be made during the pledge, including the starting date, and a place for the donor's signature. The card should also provide a space for indicating the amount paid, if any, at the time the pledge was made and the balance remaining. It is important that a statement appear on the face of the pledge card indicating that "contributions are deductible for federal and state income tax purposes as provided by law." There should also be instructions on how to make checks payable.

Also to be included, usually on the back of the card, is a statement indicating whether the soliciting institution intends to treat the pledge as a legally binding obligation. (The majority of campaigns do not treat pledges as legal obligations.) There should also be ample space for the donor to indicate a gift designation if the gift is to be restricted, any commemorative gift wording that the donor might wish to have used, and a place for other information. The pledge card should also include a place for the volunteer's name and the date of the solicitation.

In addition to the basic pledge card, most pledge card instruments have two perforated, detachable pieces referred to as "ears." The first ear is used for a confidential statement indicating the gift rating of the prospect to guide the solicitor in making the call. The information included on this stub is highly confidential, and the volunteer should detach it before seeing the prospect. It should never be shown to a prospect.

The other ear is a temporary acknowledgment form. It should be separated from the pledge card at the time the commitment is made if its use is required. These forms usually include places to write the name of the donor, the total amount of the gift, and the amount paid at the time of the pledge, if any, and for the volunteer to sign and date the temporary acknowledgment. Usually, the temporary acknowledgment indicates that an official gift receipt will be mailed in the near future.

The second instrument used to record pledges is a letter of intent. A sample letter of intent is shown in Exhibit 3. The third form of pledge commitment is a letter written by the donor on personal or corporate stationery indicating the same information as would be recorded on a pledge card or included in a letter of intent.

The number, quantity, and costs of the publications needed to support a given campaign can and will vary. However, never skimp on quality. In addition to the various printed documents, appropriate audiovisual materials should routinely be prepared,

Exhibit 3. Sample Letter of Intent.

Date _____

Name, Chief Executive Officer
XYZ Institution
Everytown, N.Y. 00000

Dear _____ :

To assist (name of institution) in fulfilling its important responsibilities and in consideration of the gifts of others, I intend and expect to contribute the sum of $ _____ to (name of institution and title of campaign).

My gift is:
    1. Designated for the following purpose(s):

_____

or

    2. To be used at the discretion of the Board of Governors of
       (name of institution).

I expect to make this gift over a period of _____ years as follows:

$ _____ Herewith
$ _____ on or before _____ 19__
$ _____ on or before _____ 19__

or

_____

_____

This statement of intention and expectation shall not constitute a legal obligation and shall not be legally binding in any way on me or my estate. While I consider that I have a moral obligation to make this gift, I reserve the right to adjust or to cancel it in the event of unforeseen circumstances.

Sincerely yours,

/s/ _____

including a synchronized sound/slide show, motion picture, cassette, and/or portable presentation, and flip charts, graphs, posters, and building models.

It is also important to design the presentation of the case so that it can be easily interpreted differently for various market segments. The same information about the organization may be viewed differently from the perspective of a corporate executive, a wealthy philanthropist, a vendor, or a neighborhood group. In designing literature and institutional approaches to various constituencies, it is important to remain flexible so that the approach can be specifically tailored to produce optimal results.

No function of the campaign literature and audiovisual material can be more important than supporting and sustaining a mood of importance, relevance, and urgency and an atmosphere of optimism and institutional community. This function becomes more and more important as campaign goals go higher and higher and schedules have to cover more and more time. As solicitation moves from the inside out, from one group of potential givers to another, and as the limited number of traveling teams of official advocates go from group to group—and in wide-area campaigns from city to city—the risk of having the campaign die on the vine becomes real indeed.

The key to avoiding this problem is for the campaign chair, chief executive officer, and others to keep telling the message of the campaign, to actively, continuously be engaged in the case-stating process. After their original statements, these leaders can never let up until the task has been completed. Never should they make a speech or write a report without referring to the unfinished task with all the gravity due its importance and with the confidence of certain and complete success. What they and the campaign publications say, and keep saying, is important in itself; almost equally important is that everything and everyone say it again and again and carry the same message, even if stated with different emphasis for different constituencies. Continuity is the business of all institutional publications, including magazines and newsletters. It is the main business of campaign bulletins or newsletters, which sometimes make the mistake of dealing almost solely with progressive statistics. These bulletins deserve careful planning so that every issue deliberately plays up attainment of higher standards, involvement of respected people, outside praise, significant campaign growth, quotations worthy of repetition, and every good thing to be thought of that can make for confidence.

Preparing Campaign Publications. If an institution does not have a top-quality publications department, it should seriously consider hiring outside help to produce campaign publications, especially the major ones. If outside help is used, do not relinquish control over the finished product. Monitor progress and require periodic checks with the campaign leaders. Do not scrimp on campaign publications. Prestige pieces are a necessity, and they will pay for themselves. In creating the communications package for a campaign, review the purposed strategy, audience message, and goal for each piece. If necessary, restate the message as it should appear in each communication, remembering that different communications are written to address and to reach different audiences.

Always develop logic to support the request or message in each publication. Analyze what the audience has indicated it would like to hear; make sure to use the process of feedback to secure important information. Write, dictate, or design the first draft of a communication and then edit to eliminate triteness, fuzziness, and pet phrasing. Then test the communication with a segment of its target audience and listen for a response from that audience. It may be necessary to revise after audience feedback and review.

It is also important to offer a word about style. The principles of clear, concise, idiomatic writing that apply to other nonfiction can be the guide for brochures as well. Campaign literature too often contains a good deal of specialized language— professional jargon that is familiar to educators, medical staff, or seminary scholars but a deep mystery to almost everyone else. Try to avoid it. Keep in mind that most donors, and all major ones, will be lay people who respond best to plain language, short sentences, and familiar usage. One rule of good writing that particularly applies to fundraising brochures is to avoid generalities and look for specifics. Every institution has its own history, achievements, and vital statistics. Know them and include them in the writing.

David W. Barton, Jr., is fond of reminding people that in *Huckleberry Finn*, Mark Twain's characters speak in five distinctive dialects. Barton specifically mentions that Twain pointed to this in the book's introduction, because he had taken pains to get the dialects right. The characters speak authentically, and Twain wanted the reader to appreciate what he had accomplished. What he accomplished is a masterpiece because he respects his characters enough to get their languages right. Twain put in Huck Finn's mouth the words Huck would use in real life. Every institution speaks in a different voice with a different tone and emphasis in style. If an institution can capture its own flavor and essence in its campaign literature, its constituents will respond to it. Twain said the difference between the right word and the nearly right word is the difference between lightning and a lightning bug; the right word and the right image, aimed at the right person at the right time, in the right way, can produce lightning.

The institution must also be concerned about layout and design of its publications. Graphics should be done by a professional designer, but it is the writer's responsibility to gather the material needed and guide the designer on tone and style. It is helpful to give the designer a few samples of the institution's recent literature as a guide to its taste, unless the pieces are particularly poor and the institution wants to start over. Try to give the designer more illustration material than can be used so that the designer will have a range of choice. Avoid extremes in either direction— conservative or modern. The institution is interested in raising money, not winning graphic awards or arts awards. Clean, readable, attractive campaign literature is the goal.

Photographs are generally favored over artwork because of their immediacy. They should be informal, candid, unposed. Use pictures that add warmth to the story and bring the institution to the donors. In today's publications, larger pictures are generally favored over smaller ones. An uncluttered look is preferred to a cluttered look. Institutions occasionally have orderly, up-to-date picture files and can simply provide a selection for the designer. If that is not the case, hire a professional photographer to take a fresh set of pictures for the campaign.

Architectural drawings are essential when an objective of the campaign is a new building. Nobody would contract for a building without some idea of what it would look like, and the same applies to those who put up the funds. Further, an attractive rendering dramatizes the building, and floor plans help to explain the named and memorial gift opportunities. Sometimes there is a problem getting renderings for the brochure because of delays in making decisions about the components. The architects thoroughly understand this problem and are usually willing to cooperate. Blueprints are not essential. Most people cannot "read" them. Thus, they tend to confuse rather than clarify.

In preparing materials for campaign workers, package the materials conveniently and compactly; summarize key information and do not overload the volunteer with unnecessary facts; and provide sample questions and answers as well as simple charts and graphs to aid them in their understanding and acceptance of the campaign.

Developing a Realistic Marketing and Public Relations Plan

Effective campaign literature is not enough; for a campaign to succeed, a comprehensive public relations and marketing plan is also required. The objective of any public relations plan in support of a capital campaign should be to increase awareness, understanding, and appreciation on the part of targeted audiences in selected geographical areas with the aim of motivating support for the campaign. Target audiences will vary depending on the size and kind of institution conducting the campaign. The ultimate public relations challenge in a capital campaign is to bring into sharp focus for these targeted audiences the past achievements of the institution that have contributed to its current high stature, its current achievements in its area of interest, and its future hopes and aspirations as it seeks to maintain and enhance its reputation.

Donors on all levels and from all sources are more inclined to contribute to institutions that can make this part of their case. Effective public relations programs produce a climate for fundraising but should not be expected to directly attract gifts or volunteers. As is the case with every other phase of the capital campaign, it is paramount that those involved with developing and implementing a public relations plan learn the organization and its cause very well.

Once the institution has done its homework—defined its mission and priorities—and a fundraising strategy has been established; it becomes a task of the public relations program to identify audiences to be informed and cultivated; to state the campaign's message, understanding what response is being sought from each target audience; and to identify potential methods for communicating the message to the audiences selected. Among the methods available for communicating the message are personal visits, open houses, speeches, slide presentations, letters (personal or mass mail), brochures, leaflets, graphs or charts and other visual displays, special press conferences to announce significant gifts, films, radio and television public service announcements or purchased time, groundbreaking or dedication events, regional campaign announcement events (in wide-area campaigns), news and feature stories in newspapers or magazines, and newsletter, magazine, or newspaper advertisements.

It is not enough simply to block out the period of time when the capital campaign will be conducted and say that during that time the institution is going to have a good public relations program. Good public relations should precede the fundraising activity, accompany the fundraising activity, and go on after the active fundraising period has passed. And that includes good internal as well as external public relations.

The Campaign Should Be Named. Whatever name is used for the campaign, it should have dramatic impact and meaning for both the institution and its constituents. Symbols, logos, titles, themes, and other identifiable marks should be developed for and used throughout the campaign. A communications advisory committee can often be extremely helpful here.

After the campaign has been thoroughly planned—and a significant portion (30 to 50 percent) of the campaign goal should have been achieved before the formal announcement—it should be formally announced through a major media event, such as a formal dinner or a major press conference, or both. The media should be used to keep the campaign's progress before the public. In addition to cultivating newspaper and broadcast media coverage, the institution should use its publications to provide continuing publicity for the campaign. Printed materials, such as the chief executive officer's report and other external magazines and bulletins, and announcements for athletic events all should be used to keep the campaign before the institution's publics.

When the campaign has been completed, a victory dinner

should be held, and a final report should be issued to everyone involved in the campaign.

It is important that community leaders be involved in decision making about the public relations program. To this end, a communications advisory committee should be established, says Donald R. Perkins (1985). This committee is of great importance in any well-planned and professionally administered campaign. Committee members should be experts—public relations executives, marketing experts, media professionals, and senior members of advertising firms. This group should review and recommend program materials, media coverage, and special events. Not only can the members of this committee give professional advice but they can also offer active assistance in working with the media. They can publicize the institution's efforts in areas where it is not known, accompany representatives of the institution on visits to the media, and make phone calls to say a story or an idea for one is on its way.

In establishing such a committee, the institution should select members for specific purposes—areas to be reached or the kinds of stories the institution is apt to produce more abundantly. Bring them to the institution if at all possible, to orient them to the institution as it is now, not as it was when they last visited. Be professional and do not ask members of the committee to help sell what is not legitimate news; keep the committee informed about successes and give credit to those who helped. Make sure the committee members know that they are appreciated—send letters from the chief executive officer welcoming them to the committee and at the end of the first year thanking them for their time and effort and noting their success; note their efforts in institutional publications; and invite them to institutional events.

Generally stated, the basic steps in a public relations program for a capital campaign are to (1) gain support for the campaign from all the organization's constituencies, beginning with members of the institutional family (and be sure to keep all constituencies adequately informed about campaign progress); (2) secure broad agreement on the plan from all major parties involved in the campaign; and (3) work closely with all elements of the development or advancement structure within the organization to secure their support and cooperation. If all advancement efforts are not already combined, it is highly recommended that the organization seriously consider combining them in preparation for a capital campaign, at least temporarily. If this is not possible, at least secure a pledge of complete cooperation in working toward the campaign goal from all members of the institutional advancement program. There should be enough incentive to overcome any future territorial conflicts about who is going to call the shots.

Public relations in a capital campaign cannot operate in a vacuum. The person responsible for campaign public relations must be considered an important and integral part of the campaign team. The campaign public relations director should attend all meetings and special events connected with the campaign— especially meetings held at the highest levels. The director should be allocated time, when appropriate, to discuss campaign public relations plans and report on progress. This person must be thoroughly familiar with the master fundraising plan and know when, where, and how funds are to be raised. Also important is to know what strata of the population are expected to make contributions. This is extremely important so that the public relations director can determine what those people read, watch, and listen to and develop strategies for reaching them effectively.

Above all, every public relations effort connected to a capital campaign must be planned and carried out with the dignity and sophistication the institution merits. Well done, a campaign public relations effort will pay dividends far into the future.

✳ 12 ✳

Concluding the Campaign and Building on the Momentum

Perhaps the greatest enemy in a capital campaign is volunteer procrastination. Maintaining volunteer effort can be frustrating, especially during the "dog days" of the campaign, after the public announcement and the initial excitement and enthusiasm of the campaign have long since passed, the arduous, detailed work of concluding the campaign is at hand, and everything seems to have come to a halt. Procedures for maintaining momentum should be planned well in advance. The following suggestions from Picton (1982) should prove helpful:

- Use the campaign organizational structure. Require all chairs to keep in touch with the volunteer leaders [in] their part of the organization, and [those leaders to keep] in touch with their workers, by visit or by phone on a regular basis. Push for the successful completion of each prospective gift. Each chair, co-chair, and worker is responsible for regularly reviewing the assignments of each volunteer under them. Caution: do not push volunteers for gifts per se. Keep volunteers aware that the suggested level of giving or rating of each prospect much be asked for and received if the campaign is to be successful.
- Try to keep everyone aware of deadlines—whether it is a regular, scheduled report meeting or the

final report meeting, push constantly so that each person will complete assignments on schedule. Most people need deadlines. Arrange to have each worker called and reminded of report meetings a day or so in advance and ask if they will have a report. If not, when?

- Particular attention should be given to uncompleted assignments which are of significant importance to the campaign's success . . . the top 10 to 20 percent of the prospects expected to give the majority of the campaign objective. Although it is rare when all major gift assignments are completed by the deadline, every effort should be extended to push for this conclusion. Major gifts sometimes take a long time to gel. However, careful, thoughtful follow-up is essential. [No matter how often they are reminded of] the importance of the top few prospects to the success of the campaign, staff and volunteers are still inclined to spend an undue amount of time and effort on the smaller donors. Do not neglect them, but concentrate efforts where the returns can be greatest. Remember Seymour's theory of thirds (discussed in Chapter Six).

- . . . A major gifts committee composed of the chief executive officer, chief development officer, campaign chair, and selected key volunteers already committed should be included as a part of the campaign cabinet to concentrate on these key problems and other major obstacles which will arise. Having a troubleshooting committee should make it easier to enlist the campaign chair, since that individual can accept the position knowing there will be someone to turn to, if necessary. And this committee is a good vehicle to have available when attempting to enlist a powerful individual who may not want or be able to accept major campaign responsibilities.

- Regular reports indicating the status of the program will, of course, be given at report meetings.
  Be certain the official report is mailed to all
  volunteers immediately as a follow-up. Showing
  comparative results by division or teams can be a
  helpful tool to help overcome procrastination.
  Keep deadlines before volunteers. Most people
  work better when under pressure. Also send
  reports to major donors and prospects. It keeps
  them attuned to the campaign. And remember that
  many a major donor has increased an original gift,
  so continued cultivation of donors as well as
  prospects is essential during the campaign.
- If media attend key report meetings it will be
  helpful, especially if there is something eventful to
  report. If the media will not come, see that a report
  is filed with them. Widespread word of success
  adds momentum. Any announcement of a significant gift for a special purpose, like a portion of
  a building, or for some other major objective
  should be carefully planned so that it is featured
  properly.

Even the best leaders and volunteers, those well trained and
committed to the cause, will sometimes find fundraising challenging and difficult. It is the job of the staff to help everyone fight
through these periods, to maintain momentum, to encourage and
lift those who are flagging, and to express the right mixture of
confidence and enthusiasm, tempered by sober reality, to carry the
campaign through to victory.

Victory on Schedule

Picton (1982) shares the following thoughts on celebrating a
victory. Ideally, success on schedule will be the campaign's good
fortune. If so, it is important to plan the victory celebration
carefully. Continue to feature the campaign's leadership. All the
credit and limelight should be theirs, not the staff's. Be certain that

each person who has had a major campaign responsibility or who did an outstanding job is appropriately recognized. Encourage the attendance of major donors who really made success possible. Be certain that all volunteers are invited and recognized, too. The celebration should be a well-organized, happy occasion.

Recognize those major donors who will agree to be recognized. How an institution recognizes them depends on the institution and each individual donor. Being recognized from the dais is enough for some, while others like certificates, plaques, or some other imaginative, tangible symbol of their generosity. The institution may want to honor some donors at other, smaller occasions—private affairs. Campaigns also provide chances to provide recognition while in progress—the naming of a facility after a donor, the placing of plaques and the offering of citations, the presentation of distinguished service awards or, in the case of colleges and universities, honorary degrees, and the election to advisory groups or governing boards. Each situation should be examined separately. But by all means, no matter how the institution chooses to provide recognition, do it. Maintain friendly contact with donors and report on what the gifts have accomplished. Use direct mail, the telephone, and face-to-face opportunities to accomplish this. This will reinforce the donor's appreciation and will also give the institution an opportunity to keep the donor aware of continuing needs. Additional gifts often result from the pleasure derived from recognition and information received.

In addition to honoring the donors, it is equally important to honor the workers. Praise volunteers for their efforts in all campaign announcements, reports, and news releases and invite workers as well as donors and prospects to special events. Maintain contact with and seek advice from important workers as well as major donors.

Prepare media handouts concerning what the capital campaign gifts have accomplished and will accomplish, and recap the highlights of the campaign. Once again, feature leadership and major donors if they will permit it. If media representatives will attend the victory event, a greater audience will be informed of the triumph of the campaign, and that will help develop public relations for the institution. Whatever the celebration program, it should be done in a thorough but light and entertaining way, leaving everyone feeling good about what has been accomplished. Go first class! Everyone wants to be recognized for their accomplishments, and everyone wants to be on a winning team. Recognition of these factors in planning the victory celebration means that volunteers will be more likely to accept when the organization asks for their assistance in future fundraising activities, whether a campaign for annual support, another capital campaign, or other specific programs.

Donors should not be forgotten after the victory is celebrated. They should be invited to special occasions at the institution, lectures, research symposiums, special luncheons or dinners, plays or musical productions, or gallery openings. Whatever will bring them on site is sound cultivation. If the capital campaign was for a specific construction or renovation project, be certain to invite all donors to the dedication or opening. If a donor gives a scholarship, it is nice to have the donor meet the student recipient. This is just common sense, but sometimes institutions get so involved in daily activities that they overlook these possibilities for continued cultivation.

Never ask volunteers to do something today, then forget them tomorrow. Every worker and donor has a right to expect to be remembered forever for what they have done. Responsibility for remembering them belongs to the public relations and development departments. All good deeds in the past should be regarded as promises for the future. The best way to "remember your people" is to give them further opportunities to serve the institution. Never write anyone off as a future prospect—at least not until the day the will is probated.

Campaign Final Reports

At the conclusion of the campaign, two types of final reports should be prepared. The first is an internal report. It should include a cover letter from the campaign director to the general chair of the campaign, with a copy to the chair of the board, summarizing the major accomplishments achieved within the campaign and problems encountered. It should also include any recommendations or suggestions the campaign director would like to make. The document should also provide a plan for stewardship, describing activities that can be developed to both recognize the donors and keep them informed about the benefits being derived from their contributions. It may also include other suggestions for preparing the institution for a more fruitful long-range development program. This report should contain a list of prospects who have not yet committed themselves to the campaign, a brief plan for approaching prospects who can still be seen and solicited, and a report on the volunteers indicating the assignments taken, assignments completed, and assignments yet to be completed. It should also include a suggested collections procedure for any outstanding pledges to the campaign, along with a cash flow projection indicating the amount already received and income projections for each of the next years during which pledge payments are scheduled. It may also provide a list of named and memorial gift opportunities that were recorded during the campaign.

One part of the report should be a statistical review of the campaign, listing the campaign goal, the total subscribed by donor group (corporations, foundations, individuals), the total number of donors, the total cash received to date, and the number of volunteers involved with the project. In larger and more complex campaigns, there may also be an analysis of the prospects by campaign division. The report should also contain an expense summary showing the expense accounts, the budget allocation, and the expenditures made against the budget allocation.

One of the most important parts of the final report is a scrapbook that will serve as a visual record of the campaign activity. It should be organized chronologically and should show how the campaign and all its aspects were built. Early in the preparation for the campaign, the institution should prepare a file folder so that as materials are generated, they can be automatically collected in the scrapbook file. The responsibility for preparing the scrapbook is usually assigned to a member of the office staff. It is important to understand that the compilation of this scrapbook should begin as the campaign goes along, rather than trying to reconstruct and assemble all the materials at the end of the campaign.

The second final report is a public document. It is circulated widely to donors, workers, key constituents, and, depending on circumstances, to prospective donors and workers, too. If this is done, the document can become a designed part of the transition from the current campaign to the ongoing, continuous development effort. This final report, which can take infinite shapes and formats, should include a listing of all donors, unless it is a comprehensive campaign where all annual gifts have been counted in the campaign goal, too. In this case, the organization may opt to list only donors of a certain amount, say, $1,000 or more. It is equally important to consider segregating listings of donors, especially if the campaign has encompassed several separate objectives under a total goal, and to provide recognition according to the size of the donation: obviously, more attention will be given to $100,000 donors than to $1,000 donors. Give recognition to key volunteers and workers as well as donors. A campaign cannot succeed without both groups. The report should also provide an adequate amount of financial detail—amounts pledged, amounts collected to date, and plans for expenditure—to satisfy donors and volunteers alike that their efforts are indeed providing the benefits the campaign aimed to provide.

There is sometimes a temptation to eliminate this report, with the rationale that the campaign is already over, and the report represents an additional expense that could be avoided. Do not be rationalized out of doing it! Whatever the institutional investment required, it assuredly will be returned in full and plentiful measure in the future.

Postcampaign Audit

At the end of the campaign, the institution should analyze its effort. Grenzebach (1986d) says that this analysis should be geared to answer the following questions:

- Was the campaign on the whole well received?
- [Which expenditures] proved the most beneficial and [which] the least effective?
- What promotional materials and events were the most effective?
- What was the best method of solicitation?

- What procedures should be repeated, and what ones should be abandoned?
- What key leadership developed during the campaign?
- What key prospects appeared?
- Has the institution recorded all the data that turned up during the solicitations?
- Should it publish a final report on the effort?
- How well did the campaign, volunteers, staff, and consultants, if used, perform?
- Did any individuals identify themselves as prospective board members during the campaign?
- Did others who might serve on important institutional committees surface?
- Was the goal met, but did some of the objectives of the campaign fail to be fully funded?
- Did the efforts of the campaign bring about a need for increased staff and greater budget to undergird the development effort in the future?

The institution may think that the conclusion of its campaign marks the conclusion of its intensive work. Actually, its work should just be beginning. The end of the campaign is the time to capitalize on its success and to move the institution's development efforts to a new and higher level for the future. It is the time to establish and to begin to sustain an ongoing major gifts program. Conducting an audit to find answers to the important questions listed above is a vital step in this process. But even more vital is taking action once the answers have been obtained.

Only the Beginning

In almost every campaign with more than one objective included in the overall fundraising goal, not all of the objectives are fully funded during the campaign. This provides the opportunity at the end of the announced campaign period to carry over the funding of an important facility or other unmet needs into an ongoing development program or to develop a short-term campaign separate from the original one. It also presents an excellent opportunity to reconstitute a new, smaller working group of volunteers who are specifically dedicated to completing the task at hand, thus giving the institution an opportunity to begin to integrate people who emerged during the campaign as major donors or able workers into the working group of key volunteers. This transition period is the time to clean up old business and establish the basis for new, future relationships.

Even as an institution concludes the current campaign, it is planning the next campaign. The ongoing major gifts development program never truly ends. The methods and contacts developed must sustain the institution and prepare it for the next campaign or special effort. Workers developed in one campaign are the leaders of the next. They need to be continually developed through active, meaningful, appropriate, increasingly responsible involvement from the time one effort ends until the next one begins. Ask volunteers to continue to serve by involving them in the ongoing annual giving program. Many will now be ready and able to solicit top gifts either face to face or through telephone solicitation programs during the annual campaign. Ask them to continue to work as volunteers in single-purpose capital campaigns that may be undertaken after the comprehensive or historical effort is completed. And ask them to continue to work as a part of the planned and deferred gifts program. Find a niche for each and every one and use them, or the risk is run of losing them, possibly to the organization down the street! The cultivation of prospects needs to continue and weaknesses of the campaign need to be identified and corrected as a part of the continuing development effort. It is also important to maintain staff capabilities beyond the campaign period as the institution looks to the future.

The fact that in most cases 90 percent of the dollar objective will come from 10 percent of the constituency makes it vitally important that the institution treat its potential and actual major donors with extreme care. When the campaign is successful and celebration is at hand, it is time to begin a new period of cultivation of present donors and to continue cultivation of prospective major donors to future campaigns. Chances are that the institution will have found new top prospects for continued support because of their gifts to the campaign, and there will be a number of major disappointments that will need special attention. However, what will emerge is a new listing of the top 10 to 20 percent of an institution's constituency, and they are the key to future fundraising success and a major source for future institutional leadership.

How this new list is treated is important. First, it must be acted on, not just made. Second, room must be made within the organization to accommodate these people. It is often hard to effect the succession of leadership or to make room for new faces. But it is important that it be done and that it be done in creative, enthusiastic, energetic ways that make everyone, old and new, feel wanted and welcome.

The key is involvement; that begets investment. The secret to involving volunteers and donors, old and new alike, is simple, well known, and timeless—give them something meaningful to do; earnestly seek their counsel, advice, or support. What is most important is that the institution proactively and systematically goes about involving its key donors and volunteers. *Do not leave involvement to chance.* There should always be a place in the organization for someone who is willing to work and who agrees to give. Further, during the campaign, outstanding volunteers will have come to light because of their excellent performance. Do not overlook or forget them. Be certain they are brought into an institution's planning and have a voice in its future activities, and do this as soon as possible. Name them to committees; nominate them for positions on the board. By tying up all the loose ends, by following through, the institution will have prepared a neat package for future activities.

✳ 13 ✳

Trends Affecting the Future
of Capital Campaigns

It is impossible to know the future, but many of the most experienced and forward-looking people in the fundraising profession have been pondering it for some time. The heads of some of the largest, most prestigious consulting firms in America as well as senior practitioners actively involved in NSFRE have offered various observations about the future. Some of the most probable scenarios being discussed include:

- There will be increased competition for private dollars and less federal, state, and local support, hence greater pressure on philanthropists. This is already occurring. Fortunately, the response by Americans is heartening. Giving reaches record levels year after year.
- Fundraising techniques will become more sophisticated. This is already in evidence. Personal solicitation techniques are being improved, and widespread use of computers is greatly elevating overall sophistication of the process.
- More frequent, more numerous capital fundraising efforts and plans will be conducted, with greater emphasis placed on institutional structure. While there are more campaigns today, unfortunately they do not regularly emphasize planning.
- "Capital"/building campaigns will launched to underwrite such things as equipment, salaries, expanded endowment, and operating expenses. The comprehensive campaign model described in Chapter One is growing in popularity, particularly

with large colleges and universities and with many other third-sector institutions as well.

- Buildings will continue to be attractive to donors. Bricks and mortar seem a timeless attraction. Today, renovation, especially when it is cost-effective, is often as popular with donors as new construction.

- Larger gifts will continue to constitute the greater share of capital goals. All the trends and campaign results now being reported confirm this.

- More capital campaigns will seek planned gifts. Planned gifts often constitute more than 50 percent of the major gift total in modern campaigns.

- Funds will be borrowed for construction and the money to pay back the loans raised later. This is very risky, but hard-pressed institutions will reluctantly be forced to do this.

- There will be growing presence of women at all levels—as major donors, top volunteer leaders, chief executive officers, and chief development officers. Women own the majority of the personal wealth in America.

- Tax laws will continue to change, and recent events suggest that these changes will not provide incentives to donors. This is a disturbing trend. The only solace is that tax incentives are not the dominant motivating factor in major gift giving. Nevertheless, work needs to be done to reverse the trend, because it represents a sense that there is a diminished need for and role of philanthropy in our society. Nothing could be further from the truth.

- There will be an increase in direct-mail, mass-marketing approaches to fundraising, especially for issue-related causes. There is already, however, early evidence that this technique is being overused and the saturation point being reached. How effective it will continue to be is open to question.

- Ninety percent of giving to campaigns will come from individuals. There is a need to put corporate and foundation giving in proper perspective as compared to individual giving.

- There will be an increasing use of "charitable" dollars as a marketing tool by major corporations, not to mention consultants specializing in this strategy. The American Express effort for the Statue of Liberty is one of the best examples of this new phenomenon. This falls outside traditional philanthropic motivation and thus justifies and requires closer scrutiny.

- There is a noticeable lengthening of the gestation period of larger gifts (twenty-four to thirty-six months is now considered average), as well as lengthened pledge payout periods and major gifts that are more complicated in a technical sense (not straight cash or property, but complex combinations based on financial planning techniques—for example, a life insurance policy may be bought to cover the children's inheritance, making a larger gift to the charity possible). These facts are now being widely reported. The 1986 corporate report of Brakeley, John Price Jones, Inc., addresses all three.

- Corporate involvement in philanthropy will continue to decrease, with less understanding of both philanthropy and volunteerism in the corporate world. Many attribute this at least in part to the merger mania that has swept corporate America. But the changes, unfortunately, seem to be more fundamental. Involvement in philanthropy generally is not as important to or as rewarded by corporations as it once was.

- There will be more knowledgeable top volunteers, but, correspondingly, individuals of top leadership caliber will become increasingly overcommitted. This is the result of more and more institutions turning to campaigns as a method of last resort to address financial concerns while the pool of available volunteer talent is not growing rapidly enough to keep pace with demand.

- Debt-retirement campaigns, while not desirable, will increase. These traditionally have been very tough campaigns to conduct. That is not expected to change, but the desperate need of some organizations will force them to run this type of campaign anyway.

- Computers will be increasingly used to track prospects, build donor information, and process gifts. This is the unmistakable direction philanthropy is taking.

- Capital campaign goals will become more realistic, although increasingly larger. This is a necessity. In 1987 in Houston, Texas, in a depressed economy, there reportedly were campaigns with $100 million in total goals being conducted, both locally and by organizations outside Houston but with Houston goals established. At some point, something has to give.

• Staff members will become more involved in complex situations, even soliciting in some areas. This is controversial, but it is happening and will continue to happen increasingly in the future.

• The nature of wealth is changing. Better research will be a necessity to identify and track the new sources of wealth. Young, upwardly mobile professionals are making a significant mark on society. Entrepreneurial enterprises proliferate at record rates.

• The importance of professional organizations such as NSFRE, CASE, and NAHD will grow, because fund raisers must help one another as professionals to forecast trends. It is now imperative that these organizations gear themselves to serve this need.

Essential Areas of Development

In 1986, John P. Butler III, president of Barnes & Roche, Inc., a national consulting firm, spoke before a group of professional fund raisers about a few areas of the development profession that he believes to be essential to the future of capital fundraising. Butler made the following observations regarding the case, prospects, leadership, and staffing.

Case. The demand for dollars from third-sector organizations seems to be without limit. Despite the fact that more philanthropic dollars than ever are going to support nonprofit institutions, money is not being raised fast enough, nor—all too frequently—for the right purposes. Board members and administrators must recognize that there are limits to fundraising income for third-sector institutions. They cannot look to fundraising as the sole solution to the fundamental issue of financing these institutions in the 1980s and 1990s and into the future.

The institutional planning process that delineates the "demands" must become more thorough and precise in projecting the needs. This involves questioning not only new or contemplated activities but also existing programs. Within the confines of sound policy guidelines, calculated decisions on the relevancy, productivity, and accountability of each institution and its activities must be made. Is more endowment needed, or should existing endowment funds be used more efficiently? Is a new building required, or should existing facilities be redesigned and reallocated to a more necessary function? These are not easy questions to answer; unfortunately, they are even tougher questions to ask at many institutions. Development officers have a responsibility to raise these questions and to press for answers to them. If the answers are not forthcoming, today's increasingly sophisticated donors cannot be expected to respond as they must if each institution is to meet the real "demands."

The day of the purely "emotional" case is rapidly drawing to a close. To be successful now and in the future, each institutional case and the related package of needs must deal with the realities of today and tomorrow; it must be well documented and delineated; it must have a procedure for measuring its performance; and it must relate specific institutions to the world at large. The institutions that are willing to take this more pragmatic approach are the ones that will weather the problems of the last half of this decade and, more importantly, be in a position to meet the 1990s and beyond.

Prospects. Prospects in the 1990s will be better educated and less passive about institutional efforts. Despite growing tendencies to look to the vast resources of corporations, foundations, and other funding sources, particularly for the quick fix, individuals will continue to be the primary source of support. But these individual prospects are an evolving breed. The third sector is dealing with a rapidly changing population and is faced with equally rapid changes in demands and interests. Dual and even triple alliances to a conflicting variety of interests are commonplace today, with a resultant weakening of institutional ties with and support for a single organization. And running through all of this is the accelerating redistribution of wealth among old-line families and the broader distribution of newly acquired wealth among entirely new constituencies. The latter case presents several challenges in terms of the liquidity of the wealth and the lack of a philanthropic tradition, as well as limited knowledge of the most advantageous methods of giving.

Research and evaluation have become recognized as absolute

necessities in fundraising. Significant progress has been made both in the scope and variety of research and in the use of electronic technology of the 1980s to maintain the available data and to track donors through the evolution from a first-time donor to one of the "chosen few" who will make the "pacesetting" gift of the future. But much remains to be done in terms of extrapolating from this data base the right information on which to base decisions about capital gifts. Institutions need quality control of their data or they run a risk of drowning in a sea of superfluous "nice to know" garbage about their prospects. Each institution needs to provide meaningful education and cultivation experiences to its prospects, even those who appear to be knowledgeable and sophisticated supporters. Loyalties need to be nurtured from the beginning of an association, or institutions will lose their prospects to organizations that are more farsighted and aggressive in their cultivation and involvement work. Each institution must give its prospects a sense of value in what they do for the institution and a feeling of partnership, not merely contributorship.

Approaches to individuals for gifts must be more creatively planned and must recognize the changing character of wealth. Planned gifts (estates and income-producing gifts) will be an increasingly important vehicle of individual giving. Gifts of real property will be more prevalent than gifts of cash, and there is every reason to project that the payment of commitments will be extended beyond the currently accepted three to five years. Creative giving techniques involving business considerations as well as pure philanthropy must be more in the forefront of institutional thinking. The movement toward "quid pro quo" in all giving must be managed carefully to ensure that a gift is in an institution's best interests. Philanthropy is still far removed from "mechanized" solicitation of gifts, particularly in the upper ranges, but each institution needs to be creative in its use of electronic technology to communicate the institutional story and must be alert as to how cassettes, television, videophones, and other electronic media can be employed. But each institution must also recognize that technological advances are tools to be used in fundraising, not answers in themselves.

Leadership. Every institution must be most concerned about volunteer leadership in the 1980s and 1990s. The American tradition of philanthropy is built on the foundation of volunteerism, and that tradition must not be lost. Recent years have seen a trend toward professional staff filling the role of volunteers, particularly in the cultivation and solicitation of major prospects. This is a great mistake! Institutions must generate a sense of institutional responsibility in their volunteers and maintain their participation by maximizing the productivity of the time and energy they give. Involvement precedes and begets investment. Each institution needs to work with volunteers as experts, not replace them.

Institutions will find important and effective leadership emerging from new sources. Tomorrow's leaders will be younger, more aggressive, less bound to family and societal ties, more demanding of effective staff support, and less willing to involve themselves in nitty-gritty matters of procedures and operations. They will bring new and sometimes controversial views to cultivation and solicitation, and they will reflect a recognition of professionalism among volunteers and staff. They will be a volunteer group less moved by nostalgia than by goal achievements; easily attracted by a more potentially satisfying challenge; and less willing to live with mediocrity. It may be that the volunteers of the 1980s and 1990s will be a substantial drain on staff energy and morale, but with a potential return well worth the effort.

Staffing. Future development staffs will be better trained in areas of management and administration, computers, marketing, financial management, and psychology. They will be less institutionally oriented and more professionally mobile. They will be more involved in non-fundraising areas of management and institutional planning, as well as productivity evaluation, cost accounting, and so forth. They will be a "tougher" group who demand more of themselves, their colleagues—both professional and volunteer—and their institutions.

Those who are practicing in the field as professionals must be alert to the ever increasing danger of government control of the profession. Fundraising needs regulation, but if it fails to regulate itself, the government will provide, and has provided, regulation for the protection of the populace. Professional fund raisers need to require their organizations, CASE, AAFRC, NSFRE, NAHD, and others, to be constructive in proposing rather than reacting to regulations, tax law revisions, and related matters. While the proliferation of these professional groups has advantages in terms of accommodating a variety of special interests, all professionals are affected by certain broad issues of common concern, and the professional fraternity should recognize the need for close cooperation on those issues and for decreased parochialism.

The Capital Campaign—Pro and Con

In 1980, Joel P. Smith led a thought-provoking seminar for senior development professionals that included a discussion of the capital campaign. In the essay developed from the ideas he presented there (Smith, 1981), he makes the following points.

For twenty-five years, it has been an almost unchallenged axiom of fundraising that capital campaigns are a good idea. They are the centerpiece of fundraising programs in most institutions, and many institutions judge the success of fundraising programs by the magnitude and frequency of the campaigns they conduct. There is quite a persuasive case to be made for capital campaigns, but there are some skeptical observations to offer about them, too.

Pros. Capital campaigns provide valuable discipline in terms of planning, setting a schedule, establishing goals, and providing an opportunity to manage by objective, which in fundraising is a rare opportunity.

Campaigns inspire donors to make larger commitments than they otherwise would—commitments, to be sure, that may be spread over some period of time, but nevertheless larger than they would be in the ordinary course of events.

Campaigns produce results with long-term effects. The institution enjoys the results not just during the campaign period itself; because standards have been raised during the effort, it is reasonable to expect a higher level of giving after the campaign than was experienced beforehand.

Campaigns provide valuable intensive experience for the development staff. Because so much is going on, and with such intensity, there is an opportunity for dramatic professional growth that would not otherwise occur. There is so much to do that, one way or another, staff learn how to do it and get it done, and emerge as more experienced professionals.

Campaigns provide not only a discipline but also an esprit. They create a climate in which a team comes together emotionally joined to accomplish some mutual objective, and, because fundraising is a human, emotional activity, that spirit is a very valuable component in getting it done.

These arguments amount to a really quite persuasive case, and it is not at all surprising that so many institutions have accepted them and have gone forward with campaigns. Indeed, some have gone forward with several campaigns within the last few decades.

But there are some other considerations, rarely ventilated.

Cons. When it comes down to the day of decision, lots and lots of institutions are forced to reluctantly conclude that they simply do not have staff with the requisite competence and experience to get a campaign done. Consequently, they turn to consultants or to short-term contract employees to conduct a campaign. This is not to denigrate consultants or contract professionals. There are many honorable, able people who help a lot of institutions in those roles. Nevertheless, turning to temporary help does have serious drawbacks. First, the consultants and contract professionals are going to leave after the campaign. Therefore, the opportunity for professional growth, which is one of the most forceful arguments in favor of the campaign, is forfeited to some degree. Instead of building a professional staff that will be in place in order to conduct a refined fundraising program when the campaign is over, the institution has set up a situation in which some of the key players will leave, taking with them valuable knowledge and experience, no matter how conscientious they are about recording their knowledge in the institutional files. Furthermore, no matter how sophisticated the consultants and contract professionals, they may not be able to represent an institution with the same understanding, conviction, and depth of experience and local knowledge that the institution's professional staff can. And if there is a sine qua non of being a first-rate fund raiser, it is to have conviction and understanding about the place being represented.

Almost by definition, campaigns put a terrific emphasis on

current results. The point of a campaign is to force as many gifts as possible in a prescribed period of time in order to achieve a goal that is often a terrific stretch. Really sophisticated fundraising is patient, and campaigns do not permit patience. Campaign deadlines, while they provide discipline, sometimes also cause impatience. The emphasis on getting gifts now in order to reach the goal may cause an institution to accept, for example, a $50,000 gift when a larger gift would be available if the institution were more patient. There is a definite risk of haste and waste in campaigns.

It is difficult during a campaign to maintain an appropriate focus on an institutional agenda, because there is so much attention directed to the bottom line and such enthusiasm, eagerness, and determination to make the number on the bottom as large as it can possibly be made. But what is more important than amount is utility—not just to bring gifts to the institution, but to bring gifts that underwrite the institution's most important purposes. It is ironic that institutions lose that focus during campaigns, because campaigns are almost always preceded by months of discussion and planning about what it is important to raise money for. But the product of that discussion often is a comprehensive wish list rather than a rigorous evaluation of whether it is more important to have gifts to improve facilities or to expand services. Assuming that an institution cannot have both, how is it to make an institutional choice? Campaigns rarely force that kind of trade-off thinking but instead encourage the optimistic attitude that the longer the laundry list of desirable objectives, the more probable it is that the institution will achieve the vast dollar amount that represents the total objective.

Campaigns make fundraising episodic. The institution pulls out the throttle and really goes for it for two, three, or four years, and then there comes a respite in which it falls back, gives the volunteers and others some time off, then regroups to think about another campaign. Most refined fundraising programs are not episodic. They are patient and sustained, they look to the long term, and they resist the temptation to be proud of immediate accomplishments.

Then there is the matter of taking time off when a campaign is over. The conventional wisdom is that campaigns are so intensive and call for such effort, not only from the institutional team but also from volunteers, that everybody needs a rest. Furthermore, the argument runs, if the institution is successful in a really ambitious campaign, it will have picked all the pears that there are on that tree and is going to have to take some time off to let new pears grow. This is a really dangerous fallacy. It assumes that the body of prospects with whom the institution works is finite, that there is a certain number of interested people, loyal to an institution, from whom it is reasonable to expect a gift, and that during the campaign the institution will go to them and get an answer, yea or nay, so that when the campaign ends, it is important to take time off to give those loyal supporters a rest and to renew and to regroup.

But that is not what happens during a campaign. What happens is that a significant portion of the prospects give the institution an ambiguous answer, and when the institution concludes its campaign and takes time off, it is forfeiting the opportunity both to follow through with those people and to work systematically with the people who have become interested in the institution during the campaign. Three years is a long time. The body of prospects is not some fixed constellation of individuals that remains static over that time. It changes by 20, 30, or 40 percent during the campaign, and during that time there is an emerging of alliances with people who become interested in an institution for the first time, who become enthusiastic. To let down immediately after a campaign is to forfeit the opportunity to nurture those alliances with people who have the potential to become important prospects over the next several years.

In addition, campaign goals are getting terribly large. The list of needs in a capital campaign today will add up to a number that is likely to startle most people who care about an institution. For those who are understanding and who are really close to the institution, an explanation of those needs will be received sympathetically. But with many, many people, the institution has the burden of making a persuasive case that is awfully difficult to make convincingly. How much credibility can there be in a claim that an unusually large goal is a realistic reflection of what an institution needs, that it has done the kind of institutional soul-searching that warrants the assertion that these really are worthy objectives that are critical to the quality of the institution? Is the institution coming across as grasping, as reaching for some dramatically large amount hoping that somehow it might get it but willing to settle for less?

Clearly, whether to have a capital campaign is not the only issue. Another very significant question is, if a capital campaign will not be conducted, what the alternatives are. Surely no one can be satisfied with less than the most ambitious fundraising program that is appropriate for the institution's situation. The quality of all institutions is in jeopardy, and most have reached a point where their health can no longer be improved by reducing expenditures. The road to survival is not to sacrifice the quality of the organizations that constitute the third sector through radical cost cutting. The road to survival—for some, literal survival, and for most, survival with a respectable level of quality—is somehow to bring to the institution enough funds to underwrite critically important objectives, the objectives that define quality for each institution and its mission. Smith left those he was addressing with two final questions: Is a capital campaign the right way to do it? If not, how will it get done?

A Proposed Solution

The best answer, and one that addresses many of Smith's concerns, is the continuing major gifts program, conducted as an integrated part of a planned, ongoing development program. This approach requires that many of the essential components of any successful campaign be incorporated into the everyday life of the organization. It presupposes that an organization's administrative leaders have done careful, thoughtful analysis and planning and that the resulting capital objectives fit into the overall long-range strategic plan. It mandates that the board approve plans and, through that process, accept leadership responsibility. It requires that the needs be real and compelling and the case for them articulate and stimulating. It directs that the case and goal be tested and validated in the market prior to a campaign, insists that proper internal preparation take place, and, finally, appreciates that there must be a prospect pool able and willing to subscribe the goal.

In the past, too many organizations have succumbed to the temptation to proceed with a campaign even though the signals warned against it. In the future, more discipline needs to be exercised by boards and by institutional managers. Facts, not whims, must set an institution's fundraising course. This is true whether the campaign is conducted in Jackson Hole, Wyoming, Peru, Indiana, or New York City; it is true whether the goal is $250,000 or $50 million; and it is true for colleges and universities, hospitals, social, community, and health and welfare organizations, and churches and synagogues alike.

Resources

A. Communications Materials Checklist

B. Sample Case Statements

C. Sample Program Brochure

D. Sample Question- and-Answer Sheet

E. Sample Campaign Plan of Action/ Volunteer Handbook

F. Sample Pledge Forms

G. Sample Newsletters

H. Sample Letterhead and Envelopes

Included in the resources is a selected, representative sample of the most important campaign literature from four separate campaigns. The materials presented here demonstrate the importance of using publications to create a "look" and "feel" for the campaign, to provide a unifying and binding element, and to convey a tone for and sense of the campaign. The medium becomes a part of the message when materials are carefully thought out and crafted. It is essential to the case-stating process that a campaign's many voices spread the same message. It is equally important that all campaign literature be harmoniously coordinated and integrated into the campaign itself.

Owing to space and reproduction limitations, I have not included examples of four-color brochures and other complex pieces I had hoped to present. My thanks to all those who labored so intensively to create these materials.

Resource A.
Communications Materials Checklist

Communications Materials

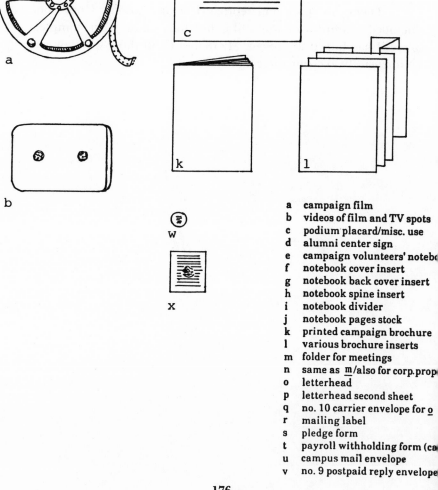

a campaign film
b videos of film and TV spots
c podium placard/misc. use
d alumni center sign
e campaign volunteers' noteb
f notebook cover insert
g notebook back cover insert
h notebook spine insert
i notebook divider
j notebook pages stock
k printed campaign brochure
l various brochure inserts
m folder for meetings
n same as m/also for corp.prop
o letterhead
p letterhead second sheet
q no. 10 carrier envelope for o
r mailing label
s pledge form
t payroll withholding form (ca
u campus mail envelope
v no. 9 postpaid reply envelope

Iowa Endowment 2000: A Covenant with Quality

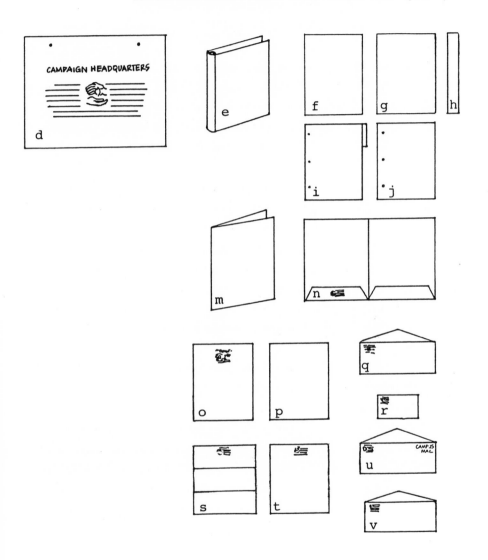

w   pin of the symbol, for volunteers
x   symbol/logo decals for all givers

Resource B.
Sample Case Statements

The St. Louis YMCA

The mission of the St. Louis YMCA is to provide quality programs in fitness, family activities and positive personal values for youth - all at a price to encourage participation across the broadest possible spectrum of economic levels of our society.

The YMCA of Greater St. Louis is serving people - all kinds of people - children of all ages, teens, adults, seniors, and handicapped, every race and religion, every income level, male and female alike. As we seek to improve and expand our considerable array of programs for youth and adults, our basic goal remains ever-constant ... "to assist each individual to grow in body, mind and spirit".

This is the YMCA of Greater St. Louis.

Milestones Along the Way

1853

October 20, 1853. Referring to the founding of the St. Louis YMCA, the Missouri Republican says, "It is our privilege to record the beginnings of an enterprise, which contains in it the germs of more good to St. Louis than any undertaking which has ever been entered upon here".

178

- 2 -

1877   Supported by community business firms, the YMCA
            organizes to find jobs for the unemployed.

1905   The YMCA initiates the first resident summer camp
            for St. Louis area youth.

1926   The St. Louis YMCA begins the national movement of
            Y Indian Guides, a program directed to cement
            father/son relationships.

1964   Amid the turmoil of the civil rights movement, the
            St. Louis Y pioneers a detached street worker program
            for inner-city youth.

1967   To meet the exercise needs of a growing office-bound
            workforce, the YMCA emphasizes cardio-vascular fitness
            as a way to prolong active, productive lives.

1977   The St. Louis YMCA successfully completes a major capital
            campaign for needed expansion.

1983   Resulting from the dramatic rise in both single-parent
            families and homes with two working parents, the St. Louis
            YMCA becomes the leader in before-and-after-school child
            care based in elementary school facilities.

- 3 -

The Path of Progress   In 1853, the St. Louis YMCA consisted of a couple
                          dozen men in a city of 74,000 people. Today, the
                          metropolitan area contains over two million people
                          and the Y serves nearly 150,000 women, men, girls
                          and boys.

                          In 1977, the City of St. Louis launched a vigorous
                          program of growth and development. That same year,
                          catapulted by a ten million dollar capital campaign
                          adding three new Program centers, the YMCA of Greater
                          St. Louis entered a period of unparalleled growth.

                *   Total attendance has nearly doubled.
                          The St. Louis Y ranks third in attendance
                          in a comparison of St. Louis leisure time
                          organizations.

          ARCH   6,369,640

          CARDINALS (baseball)   2,559,709

          YMCA   1,986,143

          ZOO   1,903,000

          BLUES   596,000

          BOTANICAL GARDEN   ˙ 550,000

          GRANT'S FARM   515,298

          ART MUSEUM   500,000

          THE MUNY   387,826

          SYMPHONY ORCHESTRA   336,330

          STEAMERS   335,805

          CARDINALS (football)   309,612

- 4 -

*   Y participatns represent one sixth
     of the people served by United Way
     agencies.

*   48.7% of YMCA memberships are women
     and girls.

*   There are more youth involved in YMCA
     programs than are enrolled in the St.
     Louis City Schools.

*   A 160% increase in participant-generated
     income has created greater self-reliance
     and financial stability.

The YMCA of Greater St. Louis ... Today

Visible   Twelve neighborhood program centers, a branch
                         serving Washington University students and a
                         youth and family camp.

"Of" the Community   475 civic and business leaders serve on YMCA
                         Corporate and Branch Boards of Directors.

Well-attended   149,118 individuals actively participate in
                         Y programs and services annually.

- 5 -

Current Program

Fitness

The YMCA provides much more than quality fitness
facilities. Fitness testing, nutritional counseling
and many other services support the Y's entire
approach to physical conditioning and good health.
Over 65 St. Louis corporations recognize the important
relationship between physical health and employee
productivity. These employers look to the Y to
deliver fitness programming to their people.
Reduced health costs, lowered absenteeism and employee
satisfaction are the valuable by-products of corporate
fitness.

Aquatics

The YMCA teaches more people to swim than any other
organization in our community. Aquatic enrollments
total 39,968.

Youth Sports

Nearly 21,000 girls and boys learn the fundamentals of
basketball, gymnastics, T-ball, soccer, hockey and other
sports in the YMCA Y-Winners program. Although winning
is fun, Y-Winners emphasizes learning the game and giving
every kid the chance to participate. Parents are
developed as coaches. Kids have fun. Everyone becomes
a winner.

- 6 -

Camp Lakewood:

Resident Summer Camp

Values development, new experiences and recreation ... this is summer camp for over a thousand girls and boys at Camp Lakewood. Building self-reliance and responsibility in children requires a variety of learning experiences. Swimming, canoeing, nature exploration, horseback riding, crafts, campouts and many other activities allow kids to lead, to work independently and to test their abilities. Scholarships are available for children unable to pay full fee.

Trout Lodge

Occupying the same grounds as Camp Lakewood, Trout Lodge offers nearly 14,000 people a beautiful setting for family retreats and outdoor educational experiences. Religious, Educational and business groups are booked throughout the year. Trout Lodge is a nationally approved site for Elderhostel and offers seniors a variety of non-traditional educational programs.

Child Care and Development

Over 9,000 children and their parents realize the benefits of YMCA preschools, day care centers, latchkey programs, day camps and summer fun clubs. Far from a baby-sitting service, Y programs instruct, nurture and enhance child development through positive learning experiences.

- 7 -

Leadership Development	782 teenagers develop leadership skills and enjoy responsible involvement in Youth In Government, Camp Lakewood's Counselor-In-Training program and in a variety of Branch volunteer activities.
Adult Sports	19,801 adults enroll in league team sports.
Handicapped Classes	553 handicapped individuals utilize Y facilities for physical therapy, group exercise classes and swim classes.
Youth Employment	In partnership with the business community, the YMCA employs over 2,000 young people, ages 16 to 21.

A Plan For The Future   The YMCA has always followed the philosophy that
as long as its core programs meet high standards and attract
sufficient volume, they remain. However, new approaches
and new programs are being continuously developed in response
to constantly emerging needs in an ever-changing society.
That is why, after six years of rapid growth, the Y instituted
an intensive planning process:

    1. The Department of Urban Affairs at St. Louis
       University provided information on the changing
       demographic nature of Branch service areas.

- 8 -

2. Y officials interviewed six or more "community knowledge-
    ables" in each of the 12 geographic areas in which YMCA
    program units are situated asking each person to comment
    on how changes are impacting lives and how the "Y" might
    best respond. Y workers were particularly interested in
    the ramifications of factors affecting family life, the
    value-developing needs of youth, and the degree to which
    Y fitness programs meet modern needs.

3. Based on this data plus questionnaire results from
    members, YMCA staff and board members:

    a. Examined current programs for relevance and projected
        program design changes appropriate to the findings.

    b. Projected participation levels of redesigned programs
        in five year and ten year intervals.

    c. Determined the personnel, facility and operating
        revenue changes required in order to achieve projected
        program levels.

4. A planning committee commissioned by the Metropolitan
    Board conducted extensive review meetings to determine
    the validity of the conclusions each contained.

5. In November, 1984, the YMCA's Metropolitan Board adopted
    the master plan, established general priorities for
    facility development and engaged the national Y's
    Buildings and Furnishings Service to provide construction
    cost estimates.

- 9 -

Points In Plannings: Some major demographic and lifestyle changes that influenced
                              program and facility decisions were:

* Married couples' share of all households plunged sharply
  in the '70s indicating that families will face increasing disruptions and breakdowns.

* The rapid rise of women in the workforce (approaching
  50 percent) signals a continuing rate of growth of female
  participation in the YMCA (now at 48.7 percent). Other
  "Y" programs that will be in increased demand as a result
  are after-school youth programs, day care and, teen-age and
  grade school-age programs with a strong values component.

* The "baby boom" generation has reached child-bearing age
  increasing the need for activities for young families,
  fitness and recreation facilities designed for family use,
  and the expansion of facilities and programs for pre-
  schoolers.

* Those constituting the "empty nest" family cycle and senior
  citizens make up an increasing proportion of the population
  For most St. Louisans, one-third of life will occur after
  the eldest child leaves home. Greater need for active and
  vigorous lifestyles means added pressure on the YMCA to
  respond with programs and facilities tailored to that age.
  Adult fitness, camping and social activities are but a few
  Y programs already experiencing this demand.

* The increase in disadvantaged persons - the physically and
  culturally handicapped and the economically deprived calls
  for creative approaches to the needs of these special
  populations.

- 10 -

YMCA Responds:

The dramatic expansion of YMCA program brought about by the highly successful "Path of Progress" capital development program of 1977 is poignant testamony to the impact the YMCA can have on the quality of life in St. Louis given the needed tools. Recent experience indicates that an equally dramatic growth rate will be achieved in the decade ahead with the commitment of all top community leaders. The payoff in enriched lives will be as significant as in any project in recent memory.

A Objectives:

Fitness for Living: Expand enrollment in fitness activities from 92,701 youth and adults to 154,000 - a 66 percent increase in participation in sports and cardio-vascular programs! New levels will be accomplished through the development of a new fitness center in West County, a leased fitness facility for working youth adults in Downtown St. Louis, and expansion of fitness facilities in several existing centers.

Family Programs: Mount a concerted effort to increase enrollments in family-related activities from 19,848 to 36,000. In order to provide values education and family enrichment experiences to greater numbers of people, a comprehensive new building designed to serve all ages will be built. Extensive family camping facilities are planned at the YMCA of the Ozarks.

Aquatic and Water Safety: A new pool and expanded locker rooms that will increase the number who can use existing pools will result in a broadening of aquatic and water safety services from 31,850 to 41,000 further strengthening the Y's title as "swim teacher for St. Louis".

- 11 -

Combined Impact: What is planned is a quantum leap in the
positive impact of YMCA programs on the lives of St. Louisans
By combining the upgrading and expansion of existing faciliti
with new construction limited only in areas in which no YMCA
buildings now exist, significant growth will be accomplished
a considerable saving over other alternatives. Participation
in YMCA activities will increase an impressive 66 percent.

New and Improved   To achieve planned objectives, YMCA and community
Facilities   leaders must act now to establish new Y facilities and renove
                         others.

WEST COUNTY CENTER $ 4,000,000
Construct a new family program and fitness
center accessible to the youth and families
of the Parkway and Rockwood school districts.

YMCA OF THE OZARKS   5,000,000
Build a new lodge and family program center,
remodel youth camp cabins and build new program
areas for resident camping at Sunnen Lake.

NORTH COUNTY CENTER   1,050,000
Completion of the Emerson Fitness Center will
expand fitness programs for all ages. The
addition will include a gymnasium, indoor track
and expanded locker rooms.

- 12 -

DOWNTOWN FITNESS CENTERS	2,600,000

This includes two projects: major renovation
of the existing Downtown Y which was constructed
in 1962 and the leasing and remodelling of space
for a 2nd cardio-vascular fitness center for men
and women located closer to the River.

MID-COUNTY FITNESS AND FAMILY CENTER	2,000,000

Renovate and upgrade locker rooms, the gymnasium,
the pool, exercise areas, and public use areas to
expand capacity and increase service to Brentwood
and to those employed in the Clayton Area.

KIRKWOOD/WEBSTER GROVES	1,050,000

Replace older portions of the Kirkwood building
to house a gymnasium, indoor track, expanded
locker rooms and exercise areas.

SOUTHSIDE & CARONDELET CENTERS	654,000

Renovate these two old but busy buildings in order
to extend their useful lives by ten years or longer.
Both facilities serve areas whose stability and
gradual revitalization are crucial to the further
renaissance of the City. Replacement now would
cost many times planned expenditures.

- 13 -

MONSANTO   250,000

This program center was built in 1980 and has far
exceeded planned participation levels. It is so
successful that it has become a national model of
what can be done by non-profit organizations to
address the family recreation needs of the inner
city. Additional space is needed for more fitness
areas and for day care facilities.

JEFFERSON COUNTY AND WEST ST. CHARLES COUNTY   700,000

Property acquisition and outreach facilities
are needed in these two remaining major
population growth areas. Modest facilities
are planned to serve day care needs and provide
a command post for community-based Y programs.

WESTPORT FITNESS CENTER   500,000

Plans involve leasing and renovating existing
space for a cardio-vascular fitness center for
the apartment dwellers and the young adults
working in the Westport Area.

WASHINGTON UNIVERSITY - CAMPUS Y   90,000

This Branch addresses the needs of college
students to develop socially and to relate
meaningfully to the larger community through
service projects. An expanded endowment will
supplement a budget that is modest in comparison
to the impact on values and the broad community
service this Center provides.

TOTAL IMMEDIATE PROJECTS: $17,894,000

- 14 -

<u>Call For Action</u>:   The need is now at hand to build upon an earlier investment
and a rich legacy, to build for today's needs and for tomorrow's.
The goal is challenging but not unreasonably so. Eight years
ago, the task of achieving a smaller goal must have seemed much
more formidable. Yet, the goal was reached.

While much has been achieved, much remains to be done.
Large concentrations of St. Louis families who need and would
respond to YMCA programs live too far from existing facilities
to participate regularly. Several YMCA buildings reflect heavy
use over long periods of time. The quality-seeking people of
modern society are not attracted to institutions with buildings
that have seen better days and call into question the leadership's ability to either understand the present or anticipate
the future. Other YMCA buildings are incomplete due to phased
construction and now are ready for completion as earlier planned.

This important bridge on the YMCA's and St. Louis'
continuing path of progress needs the generous support of all
those who see in the programs of The YMCA of Greater St. Louis
an enduring asset in the ongoing life of this community and its
people.

457b

/11/85

**THE YMCA OF THE
GREATER HOUSTON AREA**

Second Century Development Program

YMCA OF THE GREATER HOUSTON AREA
Second Century Development Program

W. J. Bowen
eral Chairman   2700 So. Post Oak   Room 1550   Houston, Texas 77056   (713) 961-5092

THE YMCA & THE CITY OF HOUSTON
"PEOPLE HELPING PEOPLE"

The YMCA of the Greater Houston Area provides young people with an opportunity to realize their full potential, to develop a positive image of self and others, to appreciate good health and fitness, and to acquire a value system and a spiritual awareness.

The YMCA began its service to Houston nearly a century ago with one small downtown facility and a first-year membership of 421. This year, the YMCA of the Greater Houston Area will serve more than 137,000 members through 23 operating units. Between 1972 and 1976, YMCA participants multiplied by 59%. This increase is largely attributable to the fact that the YMCA took its programs out to the community, to 2,500 different locations — schools, churches, parks and other neighborhood areas. Programs for young people are emphasized — 75% of YMCA participants are under 18 years of age. Forty percent of them are women and girls.

The YMCA has demonstrated a capacity for innovation and flexibility in responding to rapid and significant changes in Houston's social, cultural and economic conditions. It plans to maintain and expand services to all members of the community, to people of every age, ethnic or income group, at every level of fitness. It will continue to bring together those who care to teach and those who seek to learn.

As the YMCA nears its second century of continuous service to Houston, its programs and facilities must improve and expand to meet the needs of our growing population. The purpose of this campaign is to provide the funds which will directly address those needs, thus ensuring that the YMCA remains a major force for spiritual, mental and physical enrichment.

Towards a Second Century of Service to the Greater Houston Area

PROGRAMS &
SERVICES

Health & Physical Fitness

The 23 operating units of the YMCA
located throughout the Greater
Houston Area all provide for the
development of fitness of body and
lifetime skills in sporting activities, with
opportunities for team play and
competition with peers. Last year, the
YMCA arranged and supervised
thousands of teams for basketball,
baseball, soccer, tennis, football and
swimming.

In the area of aquatics, the YMCA has
the most comprehensive program in
Houston today. It has 21 swimming
pools, and classes for everyone from
Mom and tot (six months and up) to
senior citizens. In 1976, 18,000 people
participaed in organized YMCA
aquatic programs.

The Houston YMCA provides personalized, planned physical fitness
programs based on a series of tests.
Its programs address fitness,
cardiovascular disease prevention,
cardivascular rehabilitation, stress
reduction and education.

The downtown Houston YMCA, used
by more than 1,000 Houstonians daily,
is considered one of the finest fitness
centers in the country. Its health
facilities, complete under one roof,
have made a significant impact on the
good health and productivity of the
Houston business community.

Community Services

In the area of community service, the
YMCA is striving to keep pace with a
growing suburban community while
working diligently to meet the needs
of the inner city. Neighborhood
community services keep the Y in the
middle of the community — physically,
mentally and spiritually.

● Day care is a pressing need
everywhere in Houston. Divided
families and working parents create a
pressing need for YMCA's pre-school
child care and before- and after-
school services, including pickup and
delivery from the classroom. Many of
th YMCA branches have qualified as
state licensed day care centers in
order to meet the growing demand.

● The YMCA of the Greater Houston
Area, in conjunction with HISD, is
pioneering the community school
concept of using HISD facilities as
community recreation centers in the
afternoon and evening, providing
recreation, skill development and
special interest classes for all ages.

● YMCA programs are reaching out
to teens in hopes of offering young
men and women positive solutions to
the pressures of today's society.
Tutoring, drug assistance and dropout
programs are all attempts of the Y to
offer an alternative to delinquency.

● Recognizing the need for
community services for the elderly, the
YMCA will begin to expand programs
throughout the Greater Houston Area
to serve retired and senior adults.

Outdoor and Environmental Education

The YMCA cultivates a new and first-hand appreciation for our environment in Houston's young people. YMCA Camp Cullen has been proclaimed one of the finest camping facilities in the Southwest. It is operated year-round for weekend use and traditional one- and two-week sessions are held during the summer.

In order to give more outdoor exposure to Houston youth, 18 of the 23 YMCA centers offer day camp programs. Day camp is an opportunity for fun, outdoor education, group living and skill development. It differs from Camp Cullen only in that participants return home at night.

Specialty camps, such as fitness camps, gymnastic camps, family camps and parent-child weekends, all provide different types of retreat atmospheres at remote locations.

The Y outdoor education program does not end with camping. In cooperation with HISD, the YMCA provides outdoor educational experiences to an average of 120 boys and girls daily for 102 days of the school year. These young people spend two or three days at Camp Cullen, studying nature — through investigating ponds and rock formations, learning to identify trees and flowers — achieving a deeper appreciation for God's creation and the environment in which they live.

Education and Training

The YMCA has always responded to identified needs within the Houston community, especially in the area of education. The Y founded the South Texas College of Law in 1923, the South Texas College of Commerce in 1928, and the South Texas Junior College in 1948. The '70s have seen the Y continue to have an impact on the educational and training field in Houston. Informal educational opportunities include classes in foreign languages, speed reading, art, bridge, ballroom dancing, automotive repair and such other leisure-time learning experiences as interest of students and availability of instructors make feasible.

Club programs and group work are traditional in the Houston Y. Junior and senior high school clubs provide young people with the opportunity to affiliate with wholesome groups, experience leadership training and have social and recreational outlets. "Youth and Government," a mock legislative event held annually at the State Capitol in Austin, offers them a positive exposure to the democratic process as they elect a governor, pass laws and carry out the affairs of state.

Human Relations

The YMCA places a strong emphasis on serving the family. There are programs for all members and specific parent-child programs, including thousands of participants in the Indian Guides and Indian Princesses and single parent-child programs. *All* YMCA activities are aimed at strengthening the family and promoting better understanding of people with different backgrounds and cultural heritages.

The YMCA operates in 84 countries throughout the world, and the Houston YMCA is a vital part of this worldwide fellowship. Houston has become an international city, and the Y plays an important role in assisting individuals from all over the world.

Local branches provide assistance and hospitality to foreign students studying and visiting in Houston. Lay leaders from Houston have visited Mexico, Canada and the USSR as part of the YMCA exchange and leadership development programs.

Residence Services

The YMCA of Greater Houston has 405 rooms at three locations to meet the needs of young men who come to the urban community in search of employment. The resident finds more than a room at the Y. He is provided with information about the city, employment counseling, a gym and related facilities, personal and religious counseling, and a complete auxiliary service program which includes food and laundry.

Many of Houston's corporate leaders spent their first few nights at the YMCA enjoying a warm welcome and a Christian environment. Last year, 146,436 resident nights were registered, with the downtown facility operating at 99% capacity.

THE YMCA OF THE GREATER HOUSTON AREA'S
SECOND CENTURY DEVELOPMENT PROGRAM

HOW THE YMCA IS FINANCED

Roughly 85% of the YMCA of the Greater Houston
Area's $6 million operating budget comes from
fees and dues charged for programs and services.

Sound management has accounted for the
Houston Area YMCA's outstanding record in
budget balancing, but fiscal success is at best a
tool for measurement and a means to an end.
Our business is people ... enriching their lives.
The YMCA is open to all and adheres to the
philosophy

> "that those able to pay for all or part of their
> YMCA program and fees should do so, but that
> no youngster will ever be denied a YMCA
> program or service because of a lack of funds."

**The participation of the YMCA as a
member of the United Fund is for partial
annual operating costs only and does not
help in any way to offset the Y's capital need.**

Income That Supports the YMCA Budget

GROWTH OF PARTICIPATION 1971 - 1981

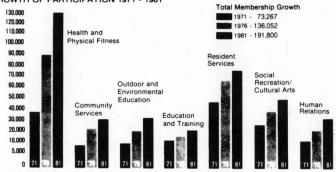

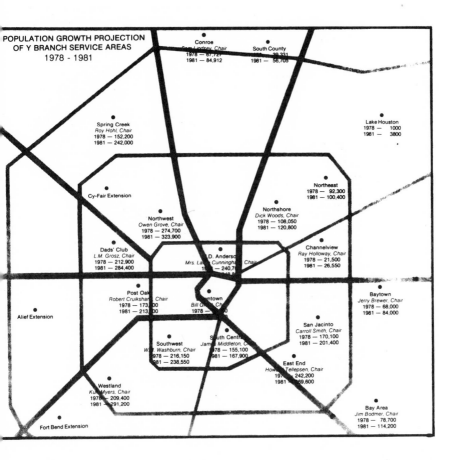

POPULATION GROWTH PROJECTION
OF Y BRANCH SERVICE AREAS
1978 - 1981

Conroe
Sam Lindsey, Chair
1978 — 67,727
1981 — 84,912

South County
1981 — 56,705

Spring Creek
Roy Hohl, Chair
1978 — 152,200
1981 — 242,000

Lake Houston
1978 — 1000
1981 — 3800

Cy-Fair Extension

Northeast
1978 — 92,300
1981 — 100,400

Northwest
Owen Grove, Chair
1978 — 274,700
1981 — 323,900

Northshore
Dick Woods, Chair
1978 — 108,050
1981 — 120,800

Dads' Club
L.M. Grosz, Chair
1978 — 212,900
1981 — 284,400

J.D. Anderson
Mrs. La... Cunningham, Chair
1... — 240,7...

Channelview
Ray Holloway, Chair
1978 — 21,500
1981 — 26,550

Post Oak
Robert Cruikshank, Chair
1978 — 173,00
1981 — 213,00

...ntown
Bill G... Ch...
1978 — ...

Baytown
Jerry Brewer, Chair
1978 — 68,000
1981 — 84,000

Alief Extension

San Jacinto
Carroll Smith, Chair
1978 — 170,100
1981 — 201,400

Southwest
W... Washburn, Chair
...978 — 216,150
...981 — 238,550

S...uth Centr...
Jam... Middleton, C...
...78 — 155,100
...81 — 167,900

East End
How... Tellepsen, Chair
19... 242,200
1981 ...9,600

Westland
Ku... Myers, Chair
197... 209,400
1981 ... 291,200

Fort Bend Extension

Bay Area
Jim Bodmer, Chair
1978 — 78,700
1981 — 114,200

FINANCIAL OPERATIONS SUMMAR
YMCA OF THE GREATER HOUSTON ARE

	1976		1975	
	Amount	Percent	Amount	Percent
OPERATING REVENUE				
Contributions	$ 223,030	4.9%	$ 174,031	4.5%
Membership Dues	1,611,832	34.9%	1,460,996	38.1%
Program Fees & Services	2,021,440	43.6%	1,570,139	41.0%
Investment Income	14,379	0.3%	24,926	0.7%
Miscellaneous Revenue	130,369	2.8%	23,742	0.6%
United Way Allocations	620,459	13.5%	578,337	15.1%
Total Operating Revenue	$4,612,509	100.0%	$3,832,171	100.0%
OPERATING EXPENSES				
Program Activities				
Camping	$ 166,660	3.8%	$ 236,317	6.2%
Physical Education & Athletics	810,574	18.2%	829,385	21.8%
Youth Development	427,647	9.6%	159,239	4.2%
Residence	322,357	7.2%	268,635	7.1%
Health Club	293,603	6.6%	235,760	6.2%
All Other	40,637	0.9%	31,326	0.8%
Building Maintenance	1,022,122	23.0%	992,003	26.1%
General Administration	1,270,743	28.6%	967,491	25.4%
National Support	48,850	1.1%	42,434	1.1%
Deferred Renovation Charges	42,085	1.0%	40,763	1.1%
Total Operating Expenses	$4,445,278	100.0%	$3,803,353	100.0%

YMCA OF THE GREATER HOUSTON AREA
COMPARATIVE BALANCE SHEET
ALL FUNDS DECEMBER 31, 1976

ASSETS

	1976	1975
Current Assets:		
Time and Demand Deposits	$ 304,093	$ 291,900
Accounts Receivable	53,745	40,749
Pledges Receivable	39,448	22,414
Accrued Interest Receivable	3,360	155
Inventories	56,678	26,340
Investments:		
Capital Stock	88,479	1,465
Undivided Part in Land Investment	305,500	50,000
Notes Receivable	41,702	-0-
Fixed Assets:		
Land	1,865,200	1,877,145
Buildings	5,536,846	7,032,766
Site Improvements	909,102	1,083,570
Furniture and Equipment	439,522	697,740
Other Assets:		
Prepaid Expenses	56,383	1,231
Carrying Value of Assigned Royalties	-0-	2
Total Assets	$ 9,700,058	$11,125,477

LIABILITIES

	1976	1975
Current Liabilities:		
Accounts Payable	$ 246,422	$ 151,921
Accrued Interest Payable	7,114	6,392
Accrued Wages Payable	-0-	60,007
Deferred Revenue	37,577	19,034
Notes Payable ... $1,332,195 $1,294,278		
Less Assigned Joining Fees ... (89,456) (151,555)	1,242,739	1,142,723
Custody Fund	3,747	9,388
World Service	(7,588)	4,249
	1,530,011	1,393,714
Fund Equity	8,170,047	9,731,763
Total Liabilities	$ 9,700,058	$11,125,477

The YMCA will enter its second century of service to the Greater Houston Area at the beginning of 1985. It will continue to provide leadership to our community, particularly to our youth, as it has throughout its first hundred years.

In order to carry on its tradition of service through the provision of healthful social programs for the whole community and to keep pace with the continually increasing population of the Greater Houston Area, the YMCA has embarked on a campaign to raise funds for physical facility and program needs.

In June of 1977, following more than a year of research and deliberation, the Metropolitan Board of Directors of the YMCA approved a list of needs totalling $4 million. The board carefully researched high-density population build-ups before approving a capital development plan that will impact the total Greater Houston Area. Analysis of the current scope of YMCA services and the patterns of population growth show a crucial need for expansion of the YMCA branches. The Board accordingly has allocated the entire $4 million to these decentralized facilities. A portion of the goal will be directed into existing facilities in order to keep them fully operative and relevant to ongoing needs in their respective communities.

In sum, the Board of Directors has committed the Y to bringing its programs and services directly to families where they live.

Following is a general breakdown of
the $4 million need as determined
and approved by the Board of
Directors:

**FOR CONSTRUCTION OF PERMANENT
BRANCH PHYSICAL FACILITIES:**
In order to provide permanent Branch Cen-
ters for expanded programs and services:

Amount Needed **$2,480,000**

FOR ACQUISITION OF LAND:
Needed to support the continuous growth of
YMCA service areas and programs:

Amount Needed **$ 270,000**

**FOR MODERNIZATION OF SERVICE-
ABLE, EXISTING PHYSICAL FACILITIES:**
In order to make maximum use of basically
sound structures in a fiscally responsible
manner:

Amount Needed **$ 450,000**

**FOR EXPANSION AND IMPROVEMENT
OF BASIC SOCIAL SERVICE
PROGRAMS:**
Thus widening the scope of YMCA activities
throughout the branches and throughout the
Greater Houston Area:

Amount Needed **$ 500,000**

**FOR CONSTRUCTION TO PROVIDE
ADDITIONAL ATHLETIC AND
RECREATIONAL PROGRAMS:**
To widen the availability of outside activities
at the Branch centers:

Amount Needed **$ 300,000**

**THE YMCA OF THE GREATER HOUSTON
AREA'S SECOND CENTURY
DEVELOPMENT PROGRAM:**

TOTAL **$4,000,000**

HOW YOU CAN PARTICIPATE

Successful attainment of our $4 million goal will ensure that the YMCA will be able to keep pace with the growing needs of the Greater Houston Area.

The campaign for funds is purposely structured to concentrate on gifts from the private sector: individuals, corporations and foundations.

All gifts to the YMCA are tax-deductible and may be paid over a period of several years for maximum financial advantage. The YMCA campaign is equipped to correctly process gifts of securities and real property as well as outright cash pledges.

A named or memorial gift will perpetuate a donor's expression of esteem and respect — a wide range of these opportunities is available at significant gift levels. Some examples of available named or memorial giving opportunities are listed on the last page of this Statement.

It is hoped that maximum advantage will be taken of these opportunities to permanently recognize individuals, corporations and foundations. In all instances, the YMCA will follow the intentions of the donor regarding the style of recognition given.

To make your pledge or contribution to the YMCA of the Greater Houston Area's Second Century Development Program, please contact:

Mr. W. J. Bowen
General Chairman
c/o The YMCA Campaign Office
2700 South Post Oak Road, Suite 1550
Houston, Texas 77056

Pledges should be made payable to the YMCA of the Greater Houston Area.

SOME SUGGESTED NAMED OR MEMORIAL GIFT OPPORTUNITIES

$1,000,000 RANGE
Westland YMCA Branch	$1,000,000
Spring Creek YMCA Branch	1,000,000

$250,000 to $500,000 RANGE
Westland Branch Physical & Social Service Facility	$ 500,000
Spring Creek Branch Physical Facility	250,000
Channelview Branch Social Service Facility	250,000

$150,000 to $200,000 RANGE
Spring Creek Branch Gymnasium	$ 200,000
Westland Branch Gymnasium	200,000
Southwest Fitness Center	200,000
Bay Area Physical Facility	150,000
San Jacinto Branch Social Service Facility	150,000
Bay Area Site	150,000

$75,000 to $125,000 RANGE
Camp Cullen Program Pavilion	$ 125,000
Northshore Branch Program Building	100,000
Northwest Branch Program Building	100,000
Spring Creek Branch Swimming Pool	75,000
Bay Area Swimming Pool	75,000

$25,000 to $50,000 RANGE
Westland Branch Teen Center	$ 50,000
Camp Cullen Program Director's Residence	25,000
Camp Cullen Caretaker's Home	25,000

CAMPAIGN STEERING COMMITTEE

Daniel C. Arnold
James A. Baker III
Jack S. Blanton
Josephine A. Bryan
Hugh Q. Buck
George Bush
John T. Cater
Ernest Cockrell, Jr.
John H. Duncan
C. Pharr Duson, Jr.
Margaret Elkins
Walter W. Fondren III
Joe H. Foy
James H. Galloway
James W. Hargrove
John W. Hazard
Jackson C. Hinds
Gerald D. Hines
Ford Hubbard, Jr.
John Wilson Kelsey
Wendel D. Ley
Ben F. Love
Alexander K. McLanahan
Robert Mosbacher
Edward J. Mosher
Joseph Rice Neuhaus
R. A. "Al" Parker
F. Max Schuette
Edgar A. Smith
Henry J. N. Taub
Howard T. Tellepsen

METROPOLITAN BOARD OF DIRECTORS
EDGAR A. SMITH, PRESIDENT
President, Alamo Barge Lines

DAVID D. ALLEN
Reynolds, Allen and Cook

KARL AMELANG
Amelang/Gilchrist
Investment Builders

DANIEL C. ARNOLD
Vinson, Elkins, Searls,
Connally & Smith

HARRY S. BADGER
Lockwood, Andrews & Newman

W. JACK BOWEN
Transco

JAMES T. COX
Hoover, Cox & Miller

MRS. LAREE CUNNINGHAM
Northside Bank

JACK B. DALE
C.S.D. Inc.

FORREST M. DARROUGH
Life Member

JOE T. DICKERSON
Life Member

LOUIS I. DIETZ
Life Member

JERRY DOMINY
Dominy-Ford Assoc.

SETH DORBANDT
First Nat'l Bank, Conroe

JOHN H. DUNCAN
Gulf Consolidated Ser.

RON EMBERG
Advalorem Records, Inc.

MRS. WALTER W. FONDREN
Life Member

ARTHUR M. GAINES, JR.
HISD

A. J. GALLERANO
Foley's

JAMES H. GALLOWAY
Life Member

EDWARD GAYLORD
Robertson Tank Lines Inc.

DR. VOORIS W. GLASPER
Dentist

ROBERT GREER
Cullen Bank

GEORGE W. HANSEN
Armco Steel Corp.

JOHN W. HAZARD
Northside Bank

JOHN G. HOLLAND, SR.
Rolligon Corp.

DON D. JORDON
HL&P

ALLAN C. KING
Goldking Productions

GILBERT LEACH
Marathon-Metallic Bldg. Co.

WENDEL D. LEY
Life Member

JOHN L. LOFTIS
Exxon USA

JOE A. MC DERMOTT
Joe McDermott, Inc.

ROY H. MOORE
Southwestern Bell

EDWARD J. MOSHER
Life Member

DEE S. OSBORNE
Quintana Petroleum

LOUIS PAINE
Butler, Binion, Rice,
Cook & Knapp

R.A. "AL" PARKER
Life Member

MARIO QUINONES
Houston Tile

BILLY REAGAN
HISD

JUDSON ROBINSON, SR.
Life Member

NAT S. ROGERS
First City National Bank

TED ROGERS
National Supply Co.

F. MAX SCHUETTE
Southern Nat'l Bank

EDDY C. SCURLOCK
Life Member

CHESTER L. STRUNK
Champlin Petroleum

HENRY J.N. TAUB
J.N. Taub & Sons

HOWARD T. TELLEPSEN
Tellepsen Construction

GRAY WAKEFIELD
Peat, Marwick, Mitchell and Co.

CARL WALKER, JR.
Assistant District Attorney

LOWEL WESTERMAN
Exxon Inc.

BEV R. LAWS
General Director, YMCA

Resource C.
Sample Program Brochure

EXCELLENCE
WITH
CARING

Lutheran Hospital Foundation   1910 South Avenue   La Crosse, Wisconsin 54601-5467   (608) 785-0530 Ext. 3045

Dear Friends:

In the 85 years since it was founded, La Crosse Lutheran Hospital has touched, in some way, so many families in the Tri-state Region. At times of medical crisis, we almost take for granted this outstanding center of health care excellence — it was here when we arrived and we expect it always will be. We expect, too, that it will be equipped and staffed to provide the very latest and most complete medical care available anywhere.

Our expectations of La Crosse Lutheran are based on past performance and on a record of constant planning for the future medical needs of our communities. This unceasing effort to keep abreast of ever changing medical knowledge and technology is achieved, of course, by the devotion and dedication of people.

We all recognize the contributions of the medical staff and hospital and clinic personnel, but let me emphasize the voluntary contributions made by the people of the Tri-state Region. From its founding in 1899, volunteers have served La Crosse Lutheran Hospital with their time and resources — without this abiding community support, the record of our hospital's performance would be limited indeed.

Now, this year, we are needed to give our tangible support to La Crosse Lutheran Hospital by pledging to the capital improvement campaign. It's our turn to help this center for health care excellence meet our expectations, to be here when we need it, to be equipped and staffed to provide Excellence With Caring.

Your thoughtful consideration of our program and request for support is sincerely appreciated.

James O. Ash

James O. Ash
General Chairman

La Crosse Lutheran Hospital - 1987

THE CHALLENGE

Our challenge at La Crosse Lutheran Hospital for over 85 years has been the challenge of medicine — to provide superior, cost-effective medical care to our patients while keeping pace with rapidly advancing medical knowledge and technology. Together with Gundersen Clinic, Lutheran maintains its leadership role in providing consistently excellent care without compromise.

"Quality health care requires investment — time, effort, and money— by all of us. This project helps ensure continued health care quality."

John H. Shuey

While the horizon of medicine is infinite, those practicing medicine want to be sure that quality health care is not jeopardized by cost containment guidelines. At La Crosse Lutheran, like hospitals everywhere, we are acutely aware of quality vs. cost. Our hospital's Board of Trustees and management continuously address this issue.

The average patient bill at Lutheran is about $350 less than at other similar Wisconsin hospitals. This results in a savings to our community of more than $5 million a year.

In 1977 Lutheran was the first hospital in the community to offer a structured Same-Day Surgery service. Today, Same-Day Surgery accounts for 25 percent of all surgeries performed here, and a 30 to 50 percent savings on our patients' hospital surgical bills.

And our innovative 21-day residential treatment program for chemical dependency, charging $1,300 per client treated as compared to traditional hospital inpatient 21-day programs that cost $4,000 to $6,000, has saved our government, our insurance carriers and our patients nearly $3 million dollars over the last three years.

Through energy conservation programs, $110,000 is saved each year. Group purchasing of supplies through Shared Health Services, has saved another $154,000 during the past year.

These cost containment policies and philosophies of La Crosse Lutheran make it a leader among hospitals.

Our commitment is real. Commitment not only to do our part to keep health care costs under control, but to maintain a modern medical facility committed to Excellence With Caring.

COMMITMENT TO THE FUTURE

"Dramatic changes are occurring in the delivery of health care in this country. With this project, the La Crosse Lutheran Hospital and Gundersen Clinic will be better equipped to supply the needs of this area for the demands on the health care system of the future."

Sigurd B. Gundersen, Jr. M. D.

It is in this same spirit that we confront the next challenge facing La Crosse Lutheran Hospital. In providing the most efficient and effective medical care, the time is right for us to further our commitment to the future and to Excellence with Caring. This takes the form of a $25.35 million Capital Improvement Project. Selected from 35 alternative proposals — assessed, evaluated, and approved under the closest scrutiny — the project is designed with cost containment, increased efficiency, and the latest patient care advances in mind. It will position La Crosse Lutheran, patients and staff alike, to greet the 1990s, and beyond with confidence.

Focusing primarily on medical programs and services, building improvements are concentrated in four distinct areas within the hospital.

REPLACING AGING FACILITIES AND SAVING BEDS

"With a 'kick-off' pledge of $300,000 by the La Crosse Lutheran Hospital Auxiliary, how can the campaign not succeed."

Robert T. Frise

La Crosse Lutheran Hospital's new construction will add three additional floors to the 1979 and 1973 wings. Designed to replace the obstetrics, cardiology and laboratory services, this new construction will reduce the hospital's overall capacity by 67 beds. In addition, it will bring greater space efficiencies permitting the aging south wings to be used for a number of the hospital's growing support and ancillary services. These units, almost 60 years old, cannot continue to meet the space, safety and comfort needs of our patients and modern medical practices.

In spite of this inpatient bed reduction, La Crosse Lutheran remains the largest hospital and maintains the highest occupancy rate in the Tri-state Region. By reducing the bed count and encouraging shorter hospital stays, we continue the trend toward maximum efficiency.

An added benefit of the new construction is the reconfiguration of the main lobby area into a highly efficient area designed to expedite the patient admitting process. To accommodate our growing outpatient services, the registration department for these patients will be expanded and located conveniently near the Trauma & Emergency Center and the main lobby. Relocation of the Auxiliary Gift Shop and Flower Mart, will provide for expansion of the Outpatient Physical Therapy Department.

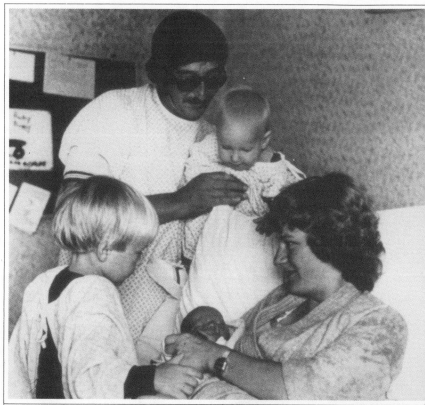

Births at La Crosse Lutheran Hospital
1964 to 1983

OBSTETRICS:
THE NEW LIFE FAMILY CENTER

All obstetrical services at La Crosse Lutheran Hospital and Gundersen Clinic, Ltd. are collectively grouped under the New Life Family Center. This collection truly makes Lutheran and Gundersen leaders in providing maternity care that meets the needs and desires of mothers and their families.

"La Crosse Lutheran Hospital and Gundersen Clinic can always be proud of the service that they provide to the mother and her newborn. With the facilities planned for the new addition, the finest service and caring for families will be available in the Tri-state Region."

Thomas N. Roberts M. D.

Acknowledging the tremendous growth in the number of births at Lutheran (over 350 percent in the last 20 years) and the changing demands for delivery alternatives, the building project will provide the special environment essential to outstanding family-centered maternal and newborn care. The new obstetrical unit will have six attractively decorated, homelike "birthing rooms" which enable the family to stay in one room throughout the birth experience. One of the birthing rooms is designed as a high risk labor, delivery and recovery room. In addition, there will be two delivery rooms for Cesarean births associated with a high risk labor room and two-bed recovery room.

Besides providing additional and more efficient space for labor and delivery, the new obstetrical unit will include a special area for patient and family education.

Critical to the care of the high risk infant, the neonatal intensive care unit and a four-bed pediatric special care unit, now located on two different floors of the hospital, is scheduled for relocation adjacent to the new obstetrical unit. La Crosse Lutheran's New Life Family Center provides this region with two neonatologists and one of Wisconsin's few perinatologists. This specialized obstetrical care makes it possible for mother and infant to remain together during their hospital stay.

This area's only pediatric cardiac surgery and infant neurosurgery is also available at La Crosse Lutheran Hospital.

La Crosse Lutheran Hospital continues to serve this region as a major medical referral center and, through supportive efforts in programs as well as services, aids the Region's hospitals in providing critical care to mothers and their newborns.

FIFTH FLOOR NEEDS:

Neonatal Intensive Care Unit
$585,000

NICU/Peds/ICU
Family Waiting Room
$38,000

NICU Nursery Area
$180,000

Maternal Contact Area
$37,400

Peds ICU Rooms (4)
$20,000

Delivery Room
$47,000

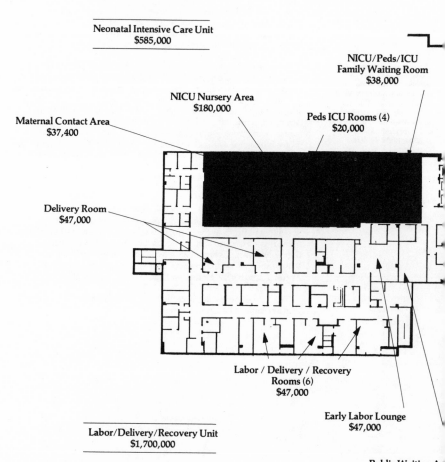

Labor / Delivery / Recovery
Rooms (6)
$47,000

Early Labor Lounge
$47,000

Labor/Delivery/Recovery Unit
$1,700,000

Public Waiting Ar
$63,000

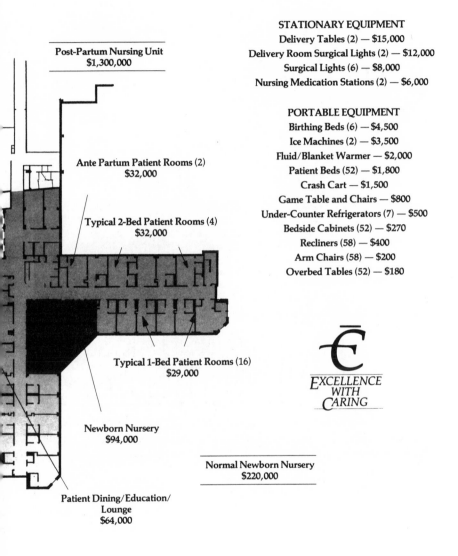

Post-Partum Nursing Unit
$1,300,000

Ante Partum Patient Rooms (2)
$32,000

Typical 2-Bed Patient Rooms (4)
$32,000

Typical 1-Bed Patient Rooms (16)
$29,000

Newborn Nursery
$94,000

Patient Dining/Education/
Lounge
$64,000

Normal Newborn Nursery
$220,000

STATIONARY EQUIPMENT
Delivery Tables (2) — $15,000
Delivery Room Surgical Lights (2) — $12,000
Surgical Lights (6) — $8,000
Nursing Medication Stations (2) — $6,000

PORTABLE EQUIPMENT
Birthing Beds (6) — $4,500
Ice Machines (2) — $3,500
Fluid/Blanket Warmer — $2,000
Patient Beds (52) — $1,800
Crash Cart — $1,500
Game Table and Chairs — $800
Under-Counter Refrigerators (7) — $500
Bedside Cabinets (52) — $270
Recliners (58) — $400
Arm Chairs (58) — $200
Overbed Tables (52) — $180

E̅C
EXCELLENCE
WITH
CARING

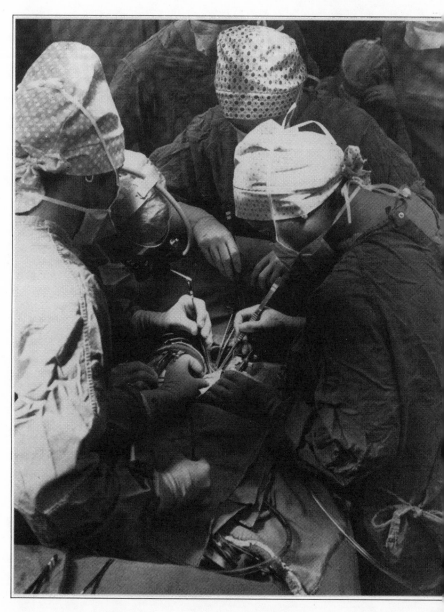

HEART CARE:

THE WISCONSIN HEART INSTITUTE

"The Excellence with Caring campaign is vital to adequately provide the needed facilities to respond to future demands in the health care field for La Crosse Lutheran Hospital's service area."

Elaine Bakken

The Wisconsin Heart Institute was organized just two years ago but our commitment to heart care began over 20 years ago with one cardiologist and one cardiac surgeon. The Institute consolidated community cardiology services with those of Gundersen Clinic and La Crosse Lutheran Hospital and, today, offers sophisticated and comprehensive heart care.

The number of heart disease deaths in this country is greater than auto accident and cancer deaths. In addition to being America's number one killer, heart disease can have disabling effects on the individual's, as well as the family's, quality of life.

However, the first symptom of heart disease does not have to be a person's last. Over 60 percent of heart disease is preventable. And surgery is one of the last options considered for a patient. In fact, through efforts of prevention, diagnosis, and treatment, actual open heart surgeries declined slightly last year.

In 1978, 879 patients were treated in our Coronary Care Unit; a brief five years later, 1,294 patients were treated. These statistics continue to climb because of the hospital-clinic commitment to the prompt care of all cardiac conditions using the most modern techniques and equipment available. There has been dramatic growth in the treatment of patients utilizing angioplasty, electrophysiology, nuclear cardiology, and graded exercise testing (GXT).

The building project will consolidate the Institute services on one floor and create a new 'intermediate care area' — a much-needed transfer point for patients from the Coronary Care Unit and the Cardiac Rehabilitation Unit as well as for other medical/surgical patients requiring intermediate care services.

The Wisconsin Heart Institute, committed to providing quality heart care to residents of the Tri-state Region, offers services to area physicians enabling their patients to continue to be active and to lead rewarding lives while receiving their care close to home.

*S*IXTH FLOOR NEEDS:

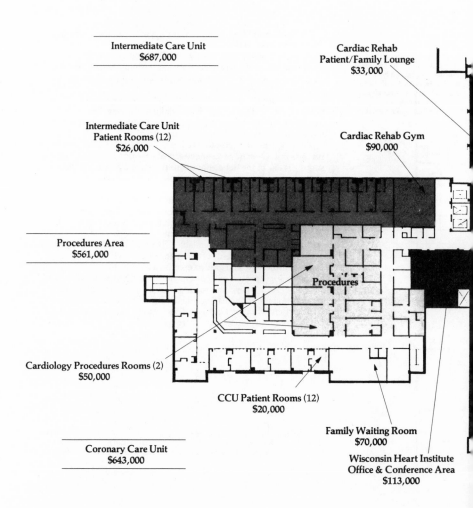

Intermediate Care Unit
$687,000

Cardiac Rehab
Patient/Family Lounge
$33,000

Intermediate Care Unit
Patient Rooms (12)
$26,000

Cardiac Rehab Gym
$90,000

Procedures Area
$561,000

Procedures

Cardiology Procedures Rooms (2)
$50,000

CCU Patient Rooms (12)
$20,000

Family Waiting Room
$70,000

Coronary Care Unit
$643,000

Wisconsin Heart Institute
Office & Conference Area
$113,000

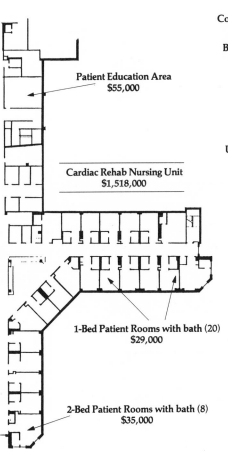

Patient Education Area
$55,000

Cardiac Rehab Nursing Unit
$1,518,000

1-Bed Patient Rooms with bath (20)
$29,000

2-Bed Patient Rooms with bath (8)
$35,000

STATIONARY EQUIPMENT
Critical Care Fluoroscopy — $200,000
Monitoring Equipment:
Computerized Control Stations (2) — $45,000
ICU Monitors (12) — $15,000
Bedside Monitors/Terminals (12) — $8,500
Arrhythmia Computers (3) — $35,000

PORTABLE EQUIPMENT
Portable Fluoroscope — $85,000
ICU Beds (33) — $4,000
Conference Table — $1,500
Under-Counter Blanket Warmer — $1,500
Crash Cart — $1,500
Refrigerators (3) — $750
Arm Chairs (33) — $200
Recliners (33) — $200

EXCELLENCE
WITH
CARING

THE LABORATORY:
THE CRITICAL CONSOLIDATION

The requests for tests critical in diagnosing and treating patients
continue to increase, resulting in over 355,000 tests performed in 1983
alone. We voluntarily postponed the laboratory services expansion,
approved by the State of Wisconsin three years ago, so that it could
become a part of the current proposal and be built as a centralized unit
on one floor instead of multiple laboratories on three floors.

The new laboratory, containing less square feet than the existing
quarters, will bring histology, pathology, bacteriology, blood bank,
immunology and all laboratory offices into one consolidated efficient
area. La Crosse Lutheran Hospital's modern, new laboratory, located
closer to patient care areas, will perform its vital role in the consistent
provision of quality, cost-effective patient care.

Laboratory Offices (8)
$16,500

Conference Room
$43,000

Clerical

Immunology

Immunology Lab
$52,000

Histology

Accessioning

Media
Prep

Laboratory

Blood
Bank

Virology

Balance
Reagent

Pathology

Urinalysis

Fluoroscopy

Decontamination

TB &
Fungus

Hematology

Laboratory Wing
$1,900,000

Microbiology

Chemistry

Anerobe

Hazard
Storage

Hazard
Storage

Electron Microscopy
$16,000

FOURTH FLOOR NEEDS:

STATIONARY EQUIPMENT:
Pass Through Sterilizer — $10,000
RO5 Water Still (2) — $6,000
6' Fume Hood — $5,000
RO Still — $5,000
5' Hood w/sink — $5,000
5' Hood w/gas — $4,500
4' Fume Hood — $4,000
Microscope Table — $500

PORTABLE EQUIPMENT:
Tissue Processor — $15,000
Double Door Refrigerator — $6,500
Steam Autoclave — $3,000
Crash Cart — $1,500
Refrigerator/Freezer — $750
Recliners (8) — $350

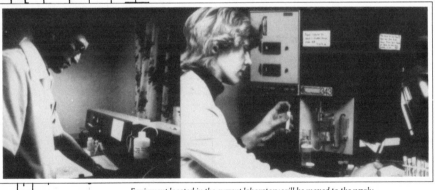

Equipment located in the current laboratory will be moved to the newly constructed laboratory.

MEETING THE CHALLENGE:
THE *T*RI-STATE AREA

La Crosse Lutheran is the largest hospital in the Tri-state Region. Most of the 17,000 inpatients served each year come from an 18-county area. While 36 percent (6,300) of all patients are from La Crosse County, another 6,000 patients annually come from other Wisconsin counties surrounding La Crosse; 2,500 come from the Minnesota counties of Winona, Fillmore and Houston; and, more than 2,000 come from Iowa counties.

In addition to our commitment to Excellence With Caring for the patients who come to La Crosse Lutheran Hospital, our commitment to technology, information and treatment support for the Tri-state Region's hospitals with fewer beds, physicians and their patients is strong.

"The needs have been identified. We now must marshall our resources to meet these needs. This capital campaign, to me, represents a commitment to quality, a commitment to community, and a commitment to caring."

Dorothy Dedo

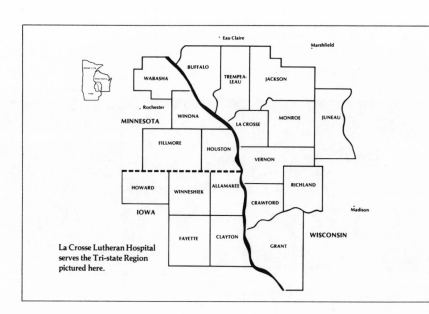

La Crosse Lutheran Hospital serves the Tri-state Region pictured here.

HEALTH CARE:
CONTAINING THE COSTS

"At Lutheran we are very aware of the public concern about the cost of health care. Our commitment is to optimize the use of resources available and to constantly look for less costly ways to provide quality service."

Jack Schwem

In 1984, the average increase in U. S. hospital prices was six percent. La Crosse Lutheran Hospital prices increased by only five percent. Included in this increase was $1 million to help reduce our future borrowing for this building project, making our actual price increase only about three percent.

Traditionally, Lutheran's capital and equipment costs have comprised only a small percentage of our total financial requirements, even during periods of major construction. We are committed to this cost-containment philosophy once again.

We have initiated an extensive fund raising campaign in an attempt to further reduce the need for borrowing. Each dollar contributed during the campaign will result in a savings of $4.50 in future debt expense.

La Crosse Lutheran believes that this unique building project addresses identified services and technological needs within the cost-containment commitment of the hospital.

Personal and community support will assure us that the quality of care we receive today will be available for our children and our children's children.

CAMPAIGN LEADERSHIP

James O. Ash
GENERAL CHAIRMAN

Terry Gillette
CHAIRMAN, BUSINESS AND
PROFESSIONAL DIVISION

Roland L. Solberg
CHAIRMAN, INDIVIDUALS AND
FOUNDATIONS DIVISION

Kenneth O. Blanchard
CHAIRMAN, TRI-STATE DIVISION

Stefan T. Guttormsson
CHAIRMAN, STEERING COMMITTEE

Sigurd B. Gundersen, Jr. M. D.
CHAIRMAN, MEDICAL STAFF DIVISION

Peter Koukola
CHAIRMAN, EMPLOYEE DIVISION

Walter F. Baltz, Jr.
VICE CHAIRMAN

Jack Glendenning
VICE CHAIRMAN

A. Erik Gundersen M. D.
VICE CHAIRMAN

Adolf Gundersen M. D.
VICE CHAIRMAN

Richard T. Lommen
VICE CHAIRMAN

Donald Zietlow
VICE CHAIRMAN

James O. Heinecke
TREASURER, FIDUCIARY COMMITTEE

Edward Carlsson, Ph. D.
FIDUCIARY COMMITTEE

Grace Hanson
IMMEDIATE PAST PRESIDENT,
LA CROSSE LUTHERAN HOSPITAL AUXILIARY

John H. Shuey
PRESIDENT,
LUTHERAN HOSPITAL FOUNDATION

Robert T. Frise
CHAIRMAN OF BOARD,
LA CROSSE LUTHERAN HOSPITAL

Jack Schwem
PRESIDENT,
LA CROSSE LUTHERAN HOSPITAL

Nora A. Starcher, CFRE
EXECUTIVE DIRECTOR,
LUTHERAN HOSPITAL FOUNDATION

EXCELLENCE
WITH
CARING

HOW YOU CAN HELP

Excellence with Caring is a shared responsibility beginning with each and every one of us. Personal and community support is vital to the success of the capital fund drive for La Crosse Lutheran Hospital. We ask you to consider financial support of this project, sharing in the hospital's investment to assure continued quality health care for you and your neighbors.

There are several opportunities available to you to help Lutheran while gaining tax and income benefits for yourself. To make your gift effective, carefully consider one of the following:

"As visitor and patient at La Crosse Lutheran Hospital, I am always impressed with the high quality medical care and the warmth and compassion of the staff."

Barbara Frank

Cash: Cash gifts are the most common campaign gifts and may be pledged over a three- to five-year period. A pledge often enables you, as a donor, to contribute a larger gift if it is spread over a longer period of time.

Stocks and Bonds: Stocks, bonds, or other forms of securities which have appreciated in value are the next most common form of gift. The tax advantages to the individual make them highly attractive. Money market funds also make excellent gifts.

Real Estate: A gift of real estate is another convenient way to contribute. If you are hesitating to sell some real estate due to potential large capital gains taxes, you may transfer the property to Lutheran Hospital Foundation and derive substantial benefits.

Life Insurance: This may provide an easy way to make a substantial gift. You may be one of the fortunate people whose life insurance policy has outlived its original purpose. A policy can be assigned to Lutheran Hospital Foundation whether it is paid up, partially paid up, or is a new policy.

Gifts Through Your Will: While current gifts are needed, you are not limited to this form of giving. By making a bequest to the Foundation in your Will you can help ensure the future of quality health care at Lutheran Hospital. Or, you may consider leaving your assets in Trust, assigning the income to one or two beneficiaries and the Trust principal to Lutheran Hospital Foundation.

Other Forms of Giving: These include life income plans and trusts, family business gifts, and commemorative or memorial gifts. There are a variety of plans which can bring immediate benefits to you. We urge you to consult your own legal or financial counsel to determine which plan is best for you. Appropriately, you'll be able to receive the maximum benefit for your objectives, while supporting La Crosse Lutheran Hospital at the same time.

*T*IME ENOUGH TO *G*IVE ENOUGH

Systematic giving over three to five years makes possible substantial gifts. Depending on the donor's tax bracket, the net cost to the donor can be substantially decreased. Seemingly small amounts paid regularly over 36 months add up to a significant total:

"I heartily endorse financial support of the Lutheran Hospital's "Excellence With Caring" Campaign.
   It is extremely comforting t me to know that my family h available medical service available and that it is easily accessible and convenient."

J. O. Heine

THREE-YEAR PLEDGE	MONTHLY	QUARTERLY	SEMI-ANNUALLY	ANNUALLY
$1,000.00	27.78	83.33	166.67	333.33
$1,800.00	50.00	150.00	300.00	600.00
$3,000.00	83.33	250.00	500.00	1,000.00
$3,600.00	100.00	300.00	600.00	1,200.00
$5,000.00	138.89	416.67	833.34	1,666.67
$7,500.00	208.33	625.00	1,250.00	2,500.00
$9,000.00	250.00	750.00	1,500.00	3,000.00
$10,000.00	277.78	833.34	1,666.67	3,333.33
$15,000.00	416.67	1,250.00	2,500.00	5,000.00
$25,000.00	694.44	2,083.34	4,166.67	8,333.33
$36,000.00	1,000.00	3,000.00	6,000.00	12,000.00

*E*XCELLENCE
   WITH
*C*ARING

Questions & Answers
regarding the
YMCA of Greater St. Louis
Capital Campaign

Making a World of Difference

231

What is "Making a World of Difference," and what does it mean to the people of St. Louis?
"Making a World of Difference" is the long range plan of the YMCA of Greater St. Louis which defines the programs the YMCA must provide to be effective in meeting the needs of the youth and families of each of its service areas. And since many of these programs require special facilities such as pools and gyms, securing the financial resources to fund these facilities is the first step of the plan.

Is this development program authorized by the United Way?
Yes. The United Way has approved the plan and authorized this campaign to raise the necessary funds.

How will the funds be used?
Estimated construction costs for planned projects is 17.8 million dollars. This includes: constructing a Family and Program Center as a part of a $5 million building and renovation program at our YMCA camps on Sunnen Lake near Potosi, Missouri; constructing a new Family Program Center on Clayton Road in West St. Louis County; adding gymnasiums and/or other fitness facilities to the Downtown, Kirkwood, Mid-County and North County buildings; purchasing and developing extension sites near Wentzville, West Port Plaza and Jefferson County; adding day care facilities at the Monsanto Branch; renovating the South Side and Carondelet buildings; and supplementing the Washington University Campus Y endowment fund.

As a United Way agency, why does the YMCA need capital financing?
The United Way provides assistance to its member agencies for operating expenses only, not for the capital expenditures the YMCA needs to make to acquire and upgrade facilities. These facilities, in turn, are needed to house the programs the Y has planned to meet the needs of a changing St. Louis community.

Why doesn't the YMCA amortize the cost of new construction or renovation by charging additional fees to those who directly benefit from its programs?
In the case of some facilities that are used almost exclusively by healthy adults, we do. However, since nearly 80% of YMCA operating costs are now borne by participants, loading on additional fees for construction of facilities that serve youth and young families would make Y programs unaffordable to those who need them most.

Is there more than one way for me and/or my company to make a contribution?
Yes. You may schedule your tax deductible contribution over a three to five year period by one or more of the following methods.

• in response to reminder notices sent by the YMCA on a quarterly, semi-annually or annual basis.

• by donating securities, stock, bonds or property.

How much should I give?
From time to time our volunteers may offer an amount for you to consider, but no one can tell what amount you should give to this campaign. You are encouraged to plan a gift over a period of three years to enable you to make a more substantial pledge.

Will I be notified when my pledge payment is due?
Yes. Unless you request otherwise, the YMCA will send you a reminder at intervals specified by you.

In case of my death will my pledge be binding on my estate?
Payment of such a pledge often results in substantial inheritance tax savings, but payment is optional with the administrator of an estate.

Are memorial opportunities available?
Yes. Memorials and designated gifts of $25,000 and above will be permanently identified in an area designated by the donor. The naming of entire areas of a Y building, such as "THE JOHN AND MARY SMITH GYMNASIUM" can also be accommodated when the amount of the gift approaches 50 per cent of the cost of construction of that room. For more details on special memorials, contact the campaign office at 436-1177.

How will the successful conclusion of this campaign affect the St. Louis community?
Each of the twelve program centers on the Missouri side of the St. Louis metropolitan area, plus our youth and family camps near Potosi will benefit from this campaign. Their programs will be enhanced for both current participants and the estimated 60,000 additional participants these expanded facilities will accommodate.

If I have a specific project in mind, how can I be certain my gift will go there?
Checks should be made out to "The YMCA of Greater St. Louis Capital Campaign." However, you may further designate your gift for a specific branch or camp by indicating so elsewhere on the check or on the accompanying pledge card. It is the policy of the YMCA that funds raised by a branch are for the exclusive use of that branch.

All gifts and pledges will be promptly acknowledged.

If I require additional information, whom do I call?
• Call your nearest branch and ask to speak with the executive director, or . . .

• Call Dick Stoll
  Campaign Director
  YMCA of Greater St. Louis
  1528 Locust St.
  St. Louis, Missouri 63103
  Telephone: (314) 436-1177

When will we see the results of this campaign?
We expect to complete gift solicitation by June 30, 1986. Construction planning will begin immediately thereafter. Actual construction will be initiated on a priority basis as funds become available.

Resource E.
Sample Campaign Plan of Action/Volunteer Handbook

PLAN OF ACTION

AND

VOLUNTEER HANDBOOK

LUTHERAN HOSPITAL FOUNDATION

"EXCELLENCE WITH CARING"

Campaign Headquarters
1910 South Avenue
La Crosse, WI 54601

(608) 785-0530 Ext 3748

Adopted by
Steering Committee
February 15, 1985

TABLE OF CONTENTS

Page

I. INTRODUCTION 1

II. TYPE OF CAMPAIGN--A THREE-STEP APPROACH 2

III. BASIC PRINCIPLES. 4

IV. CAMPAIGN GOAL 8

V. LEADERSHIP 8

VI. ORGANIZATION OF COMMITTEES 8

VII. ENLISTMENT PROCESS 17

VIII. ORGANIZATIONAL MEETINGS 17

IX. SOLICITATION MACHINERY 18

X. THE VOLUNTARY WAY 18

APPENDICES

ORIENTATION HANDBOOK SECTION

PROJECT DESCRIPTIION

-1-

I.   INTRODUCTION

The purpose of this Plan of Action is to serve as a blueprint
for the intensive campaign phase of the 2.5 Million Capital program
of Lutheran Hospital Foundation for the benefit of La Crosse
Lutheran Hospital.

Based upon experience gained in planning and directing
campaigns over a period of years, this Plan of Action is designed
specifically to meet the circumstances and requirements of the
La Crosse Lutheran Hospital Project. It is prepared for the Leaders
who will assist in the attainment of our goal.

A realistic, experienced-based Plan of Action is vital to a
successful appeal--just as a blueprint is to successful construction.

Professional fund-raising counsel has been engaged to direct
the campaign. The function of the firm's director is:

1.   To provide experienced day-to-day guidance to the
campaign's volunteer leaders.

2.   To acquaint the volunteers with proven methods,
techniques and procedures.

3.   To plan and carry out the marketing of the campaign,
including preparing printed and audio-visual marketing
communications tools and coordinating fund-raising
publicity and public relations activities.

4.   To establish and maintain the detailed records necessary
for the campaign and for follow-up.

5.   To serve as the "insistent voice" to see that a successful
Plan of Action is followed.

-2-

The Plan of Action for this campaign sets forth the function of solicitation of funds to be carried out entirely by volunteers.

Welch Associates, Inc. is retained on the basis of a fixed fee and does not receive a commission on the funds raised.

The Plan, when approved for implementation, will provide the sightline for all campaign activity. Measurements against its fulfillment will be made at frequent intervals. Review and course-corrections will be made as appropriate to achieve the goal.

II. TYPE OF CAMPAIGN--A THREE-STEP APPROACH

A. The Preparatory Step: Research

A base of research data is necessary to mount a campaign. Lutheran Hospital Foundation has devoted major attention to developing information on prospective donors. The first step both for near-term fund-raising and long-range development is the continuation and enhancement of this research.

B. The Pre-Campaign Step: Awareness Program

There are three thrusts in an Awareness Program:

1. Developing a Steering Committee of the Boards of the La Crosse Lutheran Hospital and the Lutheran Hospital Foundation, the Gundersen Clinic and the La Crosse Lutheran Hospital Medical Staff in order to include

-3-

wider volunteer participation in both the planning
and implementation of the Capital program.

2.   Development of a Campaign Cabinet of Members of both
Boards and business people of the community.

3.   Development of the "Think Tank" Committee of La Crosse
Lutheran Hospital and Gundersen Clinic Employees to
involve them in the plans of the Capital program.

C.   The Capital Campaign: Intensive Phase

The initial phase of the Capital Campaign will be
comprised of the "in house" solicitation of: the Board of
Trustees of La Crosse Lutheran Hospital, the Board of
Directors of the Lutheran Hospital Foundation, the Board
of La Crosse Lutheran Health Services, Inc. (where
applicable), the Medical Staff, Hospital Administration and
employees, and Gundersen Clinic employees.   Once the "in
house" solicitation is completed, the Campaign will go public.
At that time the leadership will solicit community business and
industry, individuals, Foundations, as well as Tri-State
businesses and residents of La Crosse Lutheran Hospital's
service area.

To organize volunteers into teams and committees to see
personally these prospects will require extraordinary effort
on the part of many leaders, starting with the Campaign
Steering Committee and Campaign Cabinet.

-4-

The success of this campaign is related directly to the effectiveness with which the right volunteers are enlisted to visit, present the case, and solicit the right prospects.

Subscriptions payable over three years (four tax years) will be sought. Longer periods will be made available when necessary to obtain larger commitments.

III. BASIC PRINCIPLES

First, four criteria which we use to predict a successful campaign are provided; we constantly measure this campaign against these Four Indicators of Success. They are followed by other principles of effective campaigning.

A. Caliber of Volunteers

The enlistment of people of stature as active members of the campaign organization is a prerequisite to a successful campaign.

B. Pace-Setting Giving

Once enlisted, members of the campaign organization will "create the campaign" by the example they set in terms of contributing early and at levels which will inspire others to follow. In this manner, a solicitor then can ask another to follow by his or her example rather than by advice.

-5-

C. Meeting Attendance

To be effective, volunteers must have information and perspective. A direct connection exists between a person's attendance at meetings and his or her success in further enlistments and solicitations.

D. Campaign Schedule

A campaign can be judged successful only if it is on schedule. Each Division must, therefore, be on schedule--to the day--so that the next Division can be on schedule. Future volunteers will adhere to their schedules only as well as their leaders do.

E. Personal Solicitation

There is no substitute for the face-to-face solicitation. The pledge card--the primary means of <u>recording</u> the intention of the contributor--is <u>not</u> given or mailed to a potential contributor to fill out at leisure. Contributors should not see a pledge card until ready to subscribe.

Effective campaign control requires that solicitors keep the pledge card in their possession until signed. Following signing, the solicitor re-obtains the card and personally sees that it reaches the campaign office.

Solicitations are not carried out by telephone--such solicitations almost always result in sub-standard contributions. Sub-standard contributions result in failing campaigns.

-6-

F.   Subscription Period

Prospects will make larger commitments when they
recognize the flexibility provided by the pledge period.
A person or company that can write a check for $30,000
at one time can usually pledge $90,000 over a three-year
period if asked to do so.

It should be noted that seeking average contributions leads to failure. Assume $1,500,000 is the goal and
there are 300 prospects. Some will want to proceed by
asking each prospect to give $5,000 and will expect to
reach the goal by 100 per cent participation at that level.

The effect, however, is to set a ceiling on any one
contribution, and when this is added to the fact that not
all potential prospects will participate, failure is bound
to be the result. Those who are able to give $50,000 or
$100,000 or more will only give the $5,000 since it is the
suggested amount. Others, not as capable, will give less
than $5,000. Still others will refuse to give anything.
At best, only a small fraction of the $1,500,000 will be
obtained.

Instead of seeking an average commitment, solicitors
use the suggested "target figures" to secure the largest
possible investments, proportionate to the commitments of
others.

-7-

G. Named Commemorative Opportunities Program

Most large contributions in a campaign are made through a commemorative opportunity program. The program is used to suggest particular levels of giving to appropriate prospects. For example, instead of Mr. X being asked for a contribution of $150,000, it is suggested to him that a particular opportunity valued at $150,000, such as a room, or a wing, can be named to honor someone or an enterprise.

H. One Step at a Time

A successful campaign results from a series of steps-- taken one at a time--each done in correct sequence according to the plans and schedule.

At any one time, there is normally only one step with which each volunteer is to be concerned.

When a step is improperly taken, the next will be more difficult; when a step is correctly made, the next will be easier and more effective.

-8-

IV. CAMPAIGN GOAL

On December 18, 1984 the Lutheran Hospital Foundation Directors adopted "The Campaign", a 2.5 million Capital program. From the first solicitation of the first member of the Board of Directors to the last solicitation, the plan will require nine months of active organization and solicitation. Pledged contributions will be accepted for payment over three years (four tax years).

V. LEADERSHIP

People give money to a program presented to them with enthusiam and conviction by persons honored and respected. Members of the Board must take the initiative to ensure that leading citizens, themselves included, accept responsible roles in the life of La Crosse Lutheran Hospital and in the campaign. They must work by encouraging and enlisting friends, colleagues and fellow community-minded citizens to work and to give. This point must be stressed: leadership will make the difference between success and failure.

VI. ORGANIZATION OF COMMITTEES

Position Descriptions: Two broad, general categories comprise a basic campaign organization:

A. Service Divisions:

-- the divisions or committees organized for support or service functions, and

B. Soliciting Divisions:

-- the divisions organized for the solicitation function.

-9-

In some cases, volunteers work within both categories in the campaign, e.g., a member of the Steering Committee might very likely be enlisted as a solicitor (team member) in one of the soliciting divisions as well. Other than this overlap of responsibilities, volunteers will be asked to assume only one post in the campaign.

A.   SERVICE DIVISIONS AND COMMITTEES

1.   Campaign Cabinet

The Cabinet is responsible to (and under the leadership of) the Campaign General Chairman.

It is comprised of the Campaign General Chairman, the Chairmen of each Soliciting Division and each Service Division, the Executive Director of the Foundation, the President of the Hospital, the Campaign Director, and any others the General Chairman may want to include at his discretion.

The Cabinet will be expanded to include additional chairmen enlisted throughout the campaign as the General Chairman sees fit.

The Cabinet will normally meet at least monthly at a time and place to be determined by the General Chairman. At certain times, weekly meetings may be advisable.

-10-

2. Steering Committee

The purpose of the Steering Committee is to provide advice and counsel and to serve as a sounding board for the program. Other purposes include helping to assemble lists of prospects, and assist in determing the assignment of prospects to various soliciting divisions and, at times, to individual solicitors within each division.

The committee consists of a Chairman and a number of members of the Lutheran Hospital Foundation Board, La Crosse Lutheran Hospital Board, Medical Staff and certain members of the Gundersen Clinic.

The Campaign Director, the Executive Director of the Lutheran Hospital Foundation and staff will assist the work of this committee and help coordinate their activities.

Membership on the Steering Committee does not necessarily preclude other campaign assignments.

3. Fiduciary Committee

This Committee can consist of as few as two individuals, though in many circumstances more are desirable. These members will be selected from the membership of the Steering Committee.

The campaign treasurer is one of these people. It is usually desirable that the treasurer for the campaign be a

-11-

volunteer, though it is not necessary. The treasurer is responsible for receiving and keeping during the course of the campaign the two primary documents that result when a pledge is made: the original, signed pledge card and an audited copy of the transmittal of the original pledge card.

At least one auditor is required for the campaign. The auditor receives from the campaign office the original, signed pledge card, four copies of the Transmittals, and tapes corresponding to the totals on these. On receiving the cards and transmittals, the auditor is responsible for verifying the accuracy of all items received, signing all copies of the transmittals, passing the pledge cards and deposit slips to the campaign treasurer with one copy of the transmittals, keeping his appropriate copy, and returning to the campaign office the appropriate copies.

Full details of this procedure will be supplied to both the auditor and treasurer separate from the campaign plan.

B.   SOLICITING DIVISIONS

1.   Official Family Divisions

A.   Board of Directors and Board of Trustees

This Division will be charged with the solicitation of members of both Boards and, where applicable, the members of the Board of La Crosse Lutheran Health Services, Inc.

-12-

In all campaigns, support from the "family" is secured before others are asked. While some individual Board member's giving ability will be limited, others have a much greater potential. It is vitally important that each Board member demonstrate commitment to the program through a personal gift.

It is very important to the overall success of the campaign that the personal giving of the Board members set the pattern for all other prospective contributors to the program. It is most desirable that this support be demonstrated as early as possible in the campaign so that solicitors who follow will have established guidelines with which to measure.

It is recognized that quite a large percentage of business or corporate affiliations of Board members would be top prospects without any Board relationship. These business or corporate affiliations of Board members will be selected for solicitation in the Public phase of the campaign.

While membership as a solicitor in this Division is very important, it may be necessary that some, if not all, members of the Board also be available for solicitation of other top prospective contributors as well.

-13-

B. Medical Staff

This Division will be charged with the solicitation of the Medical Staff of La Crosse Lutheran Hospital.

The giving ability in this Division is the strongest and the depth and breadth of support will be a very important factor in demonstrating to the community the commitment of the family.

Because the majority of prospects of this Division are all concentrated at the hospital, it will be easier to hold information meetings and to make individual contacts; therefore, we will enlist volunteers on the basis of one solicitor for each five prospects.

C. Employee

This Division will be charged with the solicitation of the Administrative Staff and Employees of La Crosse Lutheran Hospital and Gundersen Clinic.

While the giving ability in this Division will be varied, the breadth of support will be an important factor in demonstrating to the Community the commitment of the family.

-14-

Because the prospects of this Division are all
concentrated at the hospital, it will be easier to hold
information meetings and to make individual contacts;
therefore, we will enlist volunteers on the basis of one
solicitor for each five prospects.

2. Public Division

A. Campaign Cabinet

The Campaign Cabinet will have the responsibility of
soliciting the pace-setters of the community or the Top 40
prospects. These are the prospects who are considered to be
the most likely to make the largest financial commitments to
the program.

Their actions will serve, along with the Boards,
Medical Staff and Employees, to set the pattern for others
who will follow.

B. Business and Professional Division

The Business/Professional Division will be led by a
Division Chairman who will have as many volunteer
solicitors as he needs to effectively solicit the prospects
in this division. In some cases a solicitor may have only
one prospect--ensuring that the right solicitor is calling
on the right prospect. Also, in many cases more than
one solicitor will be calling on a particular prospect.

-15-

The criteria for selection of volunteer solicitors will be to enlist for each prospect the one person (or team) that can best obtain the greatest possible participation from that prospect.

C.   Individuals/Foundations Division

This division will have the responsibility of soliciting the next 100 prospects (Individuals, including Family Foundations and other community Foundations). These are the next best prospects (following those prospects that are in the Business/Professional Division).

As will be the case with each subsequent division, a chairman will be enlisted for this division and one volunteer solicitor for each five prospects.

As with other divisions, it is expected that most, if not all, of the volunteers in this division will come from the list of prospects for solicitation by this division.

D.   Tri-State Division

This division will solicit the next 250 prospects (individuals, corporations and foundations).

-16-

3. General Division

The remaining prospects will form this division; this is the only division in which some of the prospective donors may not be solicited in person. All persons who have not been solicited in one of the other divisions would be provided an opportunity to participate in the campaign through this division.

4. Regional Division

This division will be designed through the consultation with leadership in the area.

-17-

VII.   ENLISTMENT PROCESS

The enlistment process for the soliciting committees will follow a scheduled and ordered pattern from the General Chairman through division chairmen, through vice chairmen, through team captains, through team members. As a general rule, no one should have to enlist more than five others. In every instance on enlistment, a leader will be asking those who he or she is enlisting to do no less than he or she has already agreed to do.

VIII.   ORGANIZATIONAL MEETINGS

Organizational meetings will be scheduled for every level of each soliciting division--a separate meeting will be held for the chairman of the division through the team member level. These meetings will follow in successive order as each level of volunteers is enlisted. Each person enlisted will be asked to attend the meeting or meetings scheduled for his or her level, before being asked to make his or her own pledge and prior to doing any enlisting or soliciting. An orientation meeting will address the case, campaign methods, schedules and responsibilities. A kick-off meeting will address solicitation techniques and will be the time for assignments to be accepted. Between the two meetings, the volunteer will make his or her own financial commitment.

-18-

IX. SOLICITATION MACHINERY

The duties of leaders--chairmen, vice-chairmen and team
captains--include the responsibility to solicit those they've
enlisted. But, as noted above, such solicitation will take place
only after the newly-enlisted members attend the orientation
meeting. The solicitation of leaders and members will be carried
out through the "chain of command" in the committee organization.
(The General Chairman will ask his division chairmen to make their
pledges--in turn, the division chairmen will solicit their vice-
chairmen; vice-chairmen will solicit their team captains; each
team captain will solicit his or her team members.) The end result
is that all members of the soliciting committee will have made their
own pledges before asking others to do the same.

X. THE VOLUNTARY WAY

Most institutions that have come to have a significance in our
history, such as La Crosse Lutheran Hospital, have utilized the
principle of voluntarism--in preference to a system of coercion and
compulsion. The tendency of our people to form voluntary groups
to overcome pressing problems and to take advantage of special
opportunities is a vital part of American life. Now--even more than
before--voluntarism and private initiative are taking positions of
prominence in our nation.

WORKER'S HANDBOOK

Welcome Aboard!   La Crosse Lutheran Hospital is embarking upon the most exciting phase of construction and remodeling in its 85 year history and you have volunteered to help. The "Excellence With Caring" campaign, of which you are a part, is going to be successful because everyone will get the opportunity to participate.

This handbook is intended to outline the campaign for you, and to be a guide in the basic fundamentals of solicitation. Please peruse it thoroughly, along with other printed materials, until you have a full grasp of the program.

Yours is a job of great importance. The final decision of the prospect will be based, to a very large extent, upon your presentation, knowledge and enthusiasm for the project as well as for the future of La Crosse Lutheran Hospital.

Why?

Why? This is the question that many no doubt will ask when requested to consider their gift to the "Excellence With Caring" campaign for La Crosse Lutheran Hospital.

From its incorporation in 1899 by a group of Lutheran pastors, the mission of La Crosse Lutheran Hospital has been to care for the health needs of the people of our Tri-State Region. In these more than 85 years of faithful service, the Hospital has been changing and growing into a strong, vital, health care facility. Various expansion programs, the development of modern technology, acquisition of up-to-date medical equipment and its active teaching program have made the hospital a truly significant institution within our community.

Fine facilities and modern equipment are essential, but it is the people of La Crosse Lutheran Hospital -- employees, medical staff, board members, volunteers, benefactors and friends -- who have been the major force in continuing the tradition of our founding fathers: People Helping People.

In a period of time when profound changes are occurring in the health care system, it is important that La Crosse Lutheran Hospital be prepared to provide quality health care for future generations of patients who will depend upon it -- as well as those of today.

Designed with cost containment, increased efficiency, and the latest advances in patient care in mind, the plan will position Lutheran, medical staff and patients alike, to greet the 1990s and beyond with confidence. When all phases of the project are completed, every service and area of the hospital will share the benefits, which, of course, translates into the La Crosse Lutheran Hospital's continuing commitment of "Excellence With Caring" for our patients.

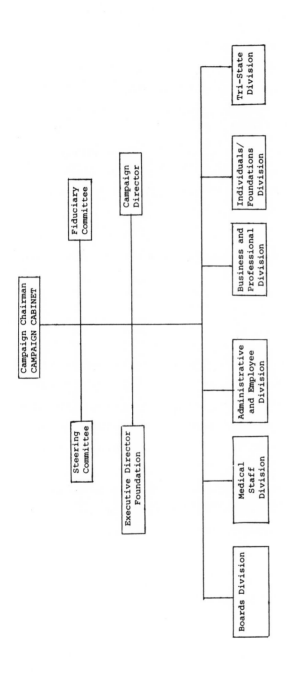

Campaign Chairman
CAMPAIGN CABINET

Steering Committee

Fiduciary Committee

Executive Director Foundation

Campaign Director

Boards Division

Medical Staff Division

Administrative and Employee Division

Business and Professional Division

Individuals/ Foundations Division

Tri-State Division

Subsequent Divisions (To Follow Tri-State Division):

General

Regional

LUTHERAN HOSPITAL FOUNDATION
"THE CAMPAIGN"

Business and Professional Division

Organization

Chairman

2 Vice Chairmen

4 Team Captains

20 Team Members

Individuals and Foundations Division

Organization

Chairman

2 Vice Chairmen

4 Team Captains

20 Team Members

Tri-state Division

Organization

Chairman

3 Vice Chairmen

9 Team Captains

45 Team Members

Total Organization

= 112 Volunteers

= 537 Prospects (including volunteers)

6/14/85

LUTHERAN HOSPITAL FOUNDATION
"THE CAMPAIGN"

Business and Professional Division
Individuals and Foundations Division
Tri-State Division

1. Enlistment of Chairmen of Divisions	April 24
2. Pledges from Chairmen	May 6
3. Enlistment of Vice Chairmen for the three Divisions	May 31
4. Enlistment of Team Captains for the three Divisions	June 12
5. Orientation of Vice Chairmen and Team Captains	June 14
6. Pledges from Vice Chairmen and Team Captains	by June 14
7. Enlistment of Team Members	by June 21
8. Orientation of Team Members	
A. Business/Professional Team	June 24
B. Individuals/Foundations Team	June 25
C. Tri-State Team	June 26
9. Pledges from Team Members	by June 26
10. Introduction Letters to Prospects	June 26-27
11. Team Member Meetings for Selection of Prospects	
A. Business/Professional Team	July 2
B. Individuals/Foundations Team	July 8
C. Tri-State Team	July 10
12. Report Sessions	July 19, July 31, August 9
13. Solicitations completed and Final Report Session	August 16

6/14/85

CAPITAL PROJECT COSTS

I. Total Construction $19,901,000

      Site Preparation
      Financing Costs
      Contingencies

II. Remodeling   3,264,000

III. Equipment   2,200,000

                                                  $25,365,000

CAPITAL PROJECT SOURCES

Project Costs as stated in the
Certificate of Capital Expenditure
from State of Wisconsin $25,365,000

  A. Sources of funds including
      bonds and hospital reserves $22,865,000

  B. Public Sources required to
      complete the project (10%)
      Capital Campaign Goal   2,500,000

LUTHERAN HOSPITAL FOUNDATION

Public Phase

Gift Range Table

As an official "gifts negotiator", you play a vital role in the success of La Crosse Lutheran Hospital's Capital Campaign. As you know, the total campaign goal is $2.5 million of which one-half will be raised from the public phase or the Hospital's 18-county service area.

You and other gifts negotiators will be concerned with fellow prospective donors in either the A, B, C or D range (see Gift Range Table) to solicit pledges over a three-year period. The importance of your service in negotiating for these kinds of gifts is borne out in the Gift Range Table. This target of gift amounts needed to produce approximately $1,250,000 is based upon actual experience in successful fundraising campaigns.

LUTHERAN HOSPITAL FOUNDATION

Public Phase

Gift Range Table

Total Donors	In the Range of	Total About	Aggregate Total
2	$50,000.00	$100,000.00	
5	25,000.00	125,000.00	$225,000.00
4	20,000.00	80,000.00	305,000.00
4	15,000.00	60,000.00	365,000.00
6	10,000.00	60,000.00	425,000.00
20	5,000.00	100,000.00	525,000.00
40	3,000.00	120,000.00	645,000.00
60	1,500.00	90,000.00	735,000.00
100	1,000.00	100,000.00	835,000.00
100	900.00	90,000.00	925,000.00
50	720.00	36,000.00	961,000.00
75	540.00	40,500.00	1,001,500.00
400	360.00	144,000.00	1,145,500.00
500	180.00	90,000.00	1,235,500.00
XXX	under*	14,500.00	1,250,000.00

A — (spans rows: 2, 5, 4, 4, 6)

B — (spans rows: 20, 40, 60, 100)

C — (spans rows: 6, 20, 40, 60, 100)

D — (spans rows: 100, 50, 75)

(*estimated average of about $20 per token gift)

A = CAMPAIGN CABINET

B = BUSINESS AND PROFESSIONAL

C = INDIVIDUALS AND FAMILY FOUNDATIONS

D = TRI-STATE BUSINESS AND INDIVIDUALS

6/14/85

Time enough to give enough.

Systematic giving over three to five years makes possible substantial gifts. The tax laws are written to encourage giving. Depending on the donor's tax bracket, the net cost to the donor can be substantially decreased. Seemingly small amounts paid regularly over 36 months add up to a significant total:

Three-year Pledge	Monthly	Quarterly	Semi-Annually	Annually
$ 1,000	$ 27.78	$ 83.33	$ 166.67	$ 333.33
1,800	50.00	150.00	300.00	600.00
3,000	83.33	250.00	500.00	1,000.00
3,600	100.00	300.00	600.00	1,200.00
5,000	138.89	416.67	833.34	1,666.67
7,500	208.33	625.00	1,250.00	2,500.00
9,000	250.00	750.00	1,500.00	3,000.00
10,000	277.78	833.34	1,666.67	3,333.33
15,000	416.67	1,250.00	2,500.00	5,000.00
25,000	694.44	2,083.34	4,166.67	8,333.33
36,000	1,000.00	3,000.00	6,000.00	12,000.00

Simple Steps for a Successful Solicitation

The very best way to learn is by doing. That is why it is most important that each solicitor be present at the orientation meeting. It is also imperative that this handbook be used as a guide in the orientation process.

No special skills or "super-salesmanship" abilities are needed. There are a few facts pertinent to your task, however, that you should know. Become thoroughly familiar with them and you will have success. One thing is certain . . . obtaining a generous pledge for the "Excellence With Caring" Campaign will require a sacrifice of your time. The results, however, will be most gratifying.

I. Face-to-Face Interviews. A really meaningful gift cannot be obtained by mail or telephone. Be sure your prospect can give his undivided attention to your story. More than one visit may be necessary for his careful consideration of your presentation. Even though information has been disseminated to all prospects, do not assume that they will know all about it.

II. Know the story. Read and study all the information and literature available. Your prospect will look to you as the expert. Explain how this particular campaign will benefit all of us.

III. <u>Believe It Yourself</u>. This is undoubtedly the strongest "tool" available for you to use. This belief will, of course, be best evidenced by the telling of your own participation. Reveal frankly the factors you considered in arriving at a good decision in making your own pledge.

Remember - you are not "begging" in any sense of the word. You are offering each one an opportunity to invest in the future of La Crosse Lutheran Hospital as a caring person.

IV. <u>Study Each Prospect</u>. Try to see your "best" prospect first. Good results here will tend to set the pace for others. Give some thought in advance to each one. The right time and the right place is important. You need your prospect's full attention.

V. <u>Discuss Income Tax Advantages</u>. Naturally, a person will support the capital project because of a personal conviction in the quality of care at La Crosse Lutheran Hospital. Thus, income tax benefits are not the primary motive in making a contribution. However, this provision is there because all contributions to the project are tax deductible.

VI.   Seek Pledges. This capital campaign program is seeking large gifts over a long period of time. Most gifts will be pledged over a 3-year period with some being spread over 5 years. The advantage of pledging is that a much larger gift can be secured having payments spread over a longer period of time.

VII. Seek an Amount. A specific amount should be recommended for each prospect. Decide what the amount is before you visit with your prospect. It is also advantageous to know what information is in the case booklet.

VIII. Do Not Press for an Immediate Decision. Don't push a prospect just to meet a deadline or in order to get "x" number of calls make. In fact, your prospect may wish to consult with his family and/or business associates before making a decision. Your call is aimed primarily at providing information, stimulating interest, putting the proposal before him and laying the foundation for a generous pledge.

Anything Else?

YES!

Be Patient

Be Persistent

Be Courageous

Be Proud of your Role

Remember . . .

> You are not asking for yourself but for La Crosse
> Lutheran Hospital and all the people it serves.
> We are a caring community.

Project Description

In this capital improvement program, patient areas constructed in 1927, and expanded in 1954, will be replaced. This is significant in that it means following completion of this program no hospitalized patient will have to be cared for in facilities that are more than twenty years old. The Hospital will be serving all of its patients in modern, efficient facilities. In keeping with the changing patterns of health care delivery, the hospital's licensed bed capacity will be reduced from 447 to 380.

In addition to improving our inpatient facilities and programs, the project provides for enhancement of our outpatient areas. With the increasing demand for numerous outpatient and community services, the need for expanded and improved outpatient space is critical.

Not only will the care for all our patients improve, but every department in the hospital will share in the benefits from the project.

NEW CONSTRUCTION AREAS

General   - Two new elevator cars and, under study, a fourth floor connection between
          Gundersen Clinic and Lutheran Hospital, improving both patient and
          employees access.

Basement - New storage areas with 24 hour access for large items presently stored in
          elevator lobbies and scattered spaces throughout the hospital. This will
          unclutter nursing units and departments, yet provide for quick and easy
          access to equipment.
          - New, enlarged area for the Biomedical Electronics Department for improved
          maintenance of hospital electronic equipment.

rst
loor

- Expansion of the Outpatient Registration Department convenient to the main lobby and Trauma & Emergency Center where all outpatients can be registered
- Expansion of the Outpatient Physical Therapy Department
- Relocation of the Auxiliary Gift Shop and the Flower Mart
- Added space in the Trauma and Emergency Center for support functions

hird
Floor

- Additional office and support space for the Rehabilitation Unit
- Additional patient space for Speech Pathology
- Counseling rooms for vocational and social workers to provide privacy for patients and their families
- Added space for inpatient and outpatient rehabilitation and development disability treatment
- Space to expand our outreach activities with community business and industry

ourth
Floor

- New, consolidated Laboratory facilities in one central area at the core of patient care activity. The new facility will improve specimen processing, service to nursing units, and enhance communication among lab sections.
- Improved vertical transport system, reducing "stat" time deliveries to and from critical areas
- Adequate growth potential to permit response to the future needs of the Laboratory department
- New Satellite Pharmacy area, improving service to nursing units.
- Potential relocation of Respiratory Therapy, improved and expanded facilities to better service patients.

Fifth   - New Obstetrics Nursing Unit

Floor   - Five LDR rooms (labor, delivery and recovery) that will accommodate

normal birthing procedures as well as high risk deliveries and repairs

- Two delivery rooms for births by Caesarean sections associated with a

risk labor room and two-bed recovery room

- Up-to-date comfortable patient rooms, with private bathrooms for mother

following delivery

- Lounge area for patient and family education

- Dining area for the "Celebration of Life" Dinners

- A 16-bassinet newborn nursery, divided into two rooms, permitting

separation of isolation cases when needed

- A four-bed Pediatric special care unit and an eight-bed neonatal unit is

planned (this service presently located on two different units in the

hospital)

- Family lounges for special care and neonatal unit

Sixth   - Consolidation of all cardiology services, except cardiac surgery

Floor   - The new Cardiac Rehabilitation Nursing Unit will have 20 one-bed rooms

8 two-bed rooms, each with shower and tub facilities

- Consultation space to allow patients, their families and staff to be able t

discuss sensitive matters

- Medical coronary care unit

- Two Critical Care Special Procedures Rooms for cardiac and non-cardiac

procedures

- Centralized monitoring area

Consolidated intermediate care unit for cardiac and all other patients

requiring intermediate care services

- Rehabilitation gymnasium

- Wisconsin Heart Institute offices

DEPARTMENTS AND SERVICES THAT WILL BE RENOVATED, REMODELED
AND/OR RELOCATED:

These programs, services and departments will be provided with facilities to
improve and expand the services which they provide to both patients and
hospital staff.

- Expansion and relocation of the volunteer work room and Gift Shop storage
- Improved and enlarged Library Storage and work room
- Cafeteria expansion with added coffee shop-grill service and extended
    hours, improved surroundings and services for both meal and coffee
    breaks
- Kitchen, Dietary offices and Nutrition Clinic remodeling and expansion
- Open Heart Surgery Team Room and a Cardiac/Thoracic Surgery Unit
- Anesthesia Offices
- Employee Support Services: Personnel; Nurse Recruitment/Retention;
    Employee Health; Credit Union; Payroll
- Business Office Expansion and file area expansion
- Regional Center for Chemical Dependency Treatment - expanded office and
    treatment space
- Eye Exam Room
- Additional Speech Therapy support space
- Family Lodging within Hospital
- Social Services Offices relocation
- Sleep Laboratory
- Center Wing Nursing Unit Support - all center nursing units will be
    provided with support space (for patient and unit needs), nursing unit
    adjacent to each center wing
- Gastrointestinal/Endocopy Lab
- Marketing and Referral Services
- Nurse Educators and Nursing Specialists Offices; Offices for Unit Makers

YMCA
OF THE
GREATER HOUSTON
AREA
Second Century
Development Program
gratefully acknowledges
the gift of

Name of Contributor

Total Gift $

Payment $

Balance Due $

Solicitor

_____ 19 ___

Save this stub for your
Federal Income Tax records.

PLEDGE NO. _____   SECURED BY _____

DIVISION

DATE RECEIVED

I (we) pledge to the YMCA of the Greater Houston Area to help in the successful completion of
its Second Century Development Program. I (we) agree to make payments on the balance
of the pledge in the amounts shown and on the dates indicated below....

AMOUNT EACH PAYMENT
$

PAYMENTS TO BEGIN 19 ___

TO BE PAID:

ANNUALLY ☐ 1   SEMI-ANNUALLY ☐ 2

QUARTERLY ☐ 3   MONTHLY ☐ 4

FOR _____ YEARS,

MONTHS TO BILL:

JAN	FEB	MAR	APR	MAY	JUN
01 ☐	02 ☐	03 ☐	04 ☐	05 ☐	06 ☐
JUL	AUG	SEP	OCT	NOV	DEC
07 ☐	08 ☐	09 ☐	10 ☐	11 ☐	12 ☐

USE BACK FOR ADDITIONAL REMARKS

Total Pledged	Paid Herewith	Balance
$	$	$

SIGNATURE _____   DATE

MAILING ADDRESS

CHECKS & SECURITIES SHOULD BE MADE PAYABLE TO:

THE YMCA OF THE GREATER HOUSTON AREA

1600 Louisiana—Phone (713) 961-5092

Houston, Texas 77002

Gifts are Deductible from Federal Income Tax

IOWA ENDOWMENT 2000: A COVENANT WITH QUALITY
TESTAMENTARY PROVISION STATEMENT OF INTENTION
(Confidential)

s an indication of my support of the Major Gifts Campaign for The University of Iowa "Iowa
ndowment 2000: A Covenant With Quality," I/we are pleased to certify that I/we have made
n estate provision for The University of Iowa Foundation as follows:

_____ Outright Bequest
_____ Bequest in the Will of the Survivor of Husband and Wife
_____ Testamentary Trust
_____ Life Insurance Agreement

Description of Type/Value of Estate Provision:

General Description:_____

_____

_____

Life-Income Provisions, if any:_____

_____

_____

Definition of Value of Provision (percentage of estate, description of gift property,
specific amount, etc.):_____

_____

_____

With the understanding that values are subject to change, at this time I/we expect the value
of my/our future provision to be approximately:
                         $_____

Our Birth Dates Are: _____   _____
                        Husband   Wife

Description of Purpose of Future Gift:

_____ My/our gift is unrestricted to meet Iowa Endowment 2000 Campaign objectives as the
President of The University of Iowa and the Board of Directors of The University of Iowa
Foundation shall direct.

_____ I/we have specified that the future gift be used for the following Iowa Endowment 2000
Campaign purpose:_____

_____

Other Descriptive Information:_____

_____

A copy of the above-described testamentary provision relative to The University of Iowa
Foundation is enclosed.

It is understood that this statement is not binding upon the Donor or his or her estate as to
the value or the receipt of the provision herein described.

Signature of Donor(s)_____Date_____
                     _____Date_____

Data Documents 03-425520-01 1F2 1

```
                                              _____
                                                 CARD NO.
                                          A TOTAL GIFT OF:

                                          $ . . . . . . . . . . . . . . . . . . . . . . . .

                                          $ . . . . . . . . . . . . . . . . . . . . . . . .
                                             Payment Herewith:

                                          $ . . . . . . . . . . . . . . . . . . . . . . . .
                                             BALANCE
                                             Campaigner:
```

"MAKING A WORLD OF DIFFERENCE"

Capital Development Program

The Young Men's Christian Association of Greater St. Louis

FOR THE EXTENSION OF YMCA PROGRAMS AND IN CONSIDERATION OF THE GIFTS OF OTHERS, I / WE PLEDGE THE SUM OF:

$. . . . . To be paid as Follows:

```
---------------------------------------------------
| PAYABLE OVER A _____ YEAR PERIOD AS FOLLOWS: |
|  ☐ ANNUAL      ☐ SEMI-ANNUAL  ☐ QUARTERLY  ☐ MONTHLY |
| PAYMENT AMOUNTS              1ST PAYMENT DUE:        |
| OTHER PAYMENT ARRANGEMENTS:                          |
---------------------------------------------------
```

SIGNED: _____ DATE _____

Data Documents 03-425520-01 1F2 1

```
                                              _____
                                                 CARD NO.
                                          A TOTAL GIFT OF:

                                          $ . . . . . . . . . . . . . . . . . . . . . . . .

                                          $ . . . . . . . . . . . . . . . . . . . . . . . .
                                             Payment Herewith:

                                          $ . . . . . . . . . . . . . . . . . . . . . . . .
                                             BALANCE
                                             Campaigner:
```

"MAKING A WORLD OF DIFFERENCE"

Capital Development Program

The Young Men's Christian Association of Greater St. Louis

FOR THE EXTENSION OF YMCA PROGRAMS AND IN CONSIDERATION OF THE GIFTS OF OTHERS, I / WE PLEDGE THE SUM OF:

$. . . . . To be paid as Follows:

```
---------------------------------------------------
| PAYABLE OVER A _____ YEAR PERIOD AS FOLLOWS: |
|  ☐ ANNUAL      ☐ SEMI-ANNUAL  ☐ QUARTERLY  ☐ MONTHLY |
| PAYMENT AMOUNTS              1ST PAYMENT DUE:        |
| OTHER PAYMENT ARRANGEMENTS:                          |
---------------------------------------------------
```

SIGNED: _____ DATE _____

Sample Pledge Forms

273

CARD NO.

Make Checks Payable to:
St. Louis YMCA - Capital Campaign
1528 Locust St., St. Louis, Mo. 63103
(314) 436-1177
The YMCA of Greater St. Louis Acknowledges With Thanks The
Contribution of

Name
Amount Subscribed $
Amount Paid $
Received By
Date

PART 1

CARD NO.

1. Detach this stub.
2. **Do not show to Prospect.**
3. Contact only those for whom you hold a Prospect Card.
4. See Prospect Personally.

YMCA Affiliation:

$

Amount suggested
By Appraisal
Committee

PART 2

CARD NO.

Campaigner

Campaigner No.:

| DIV | TM | CPR |

Sign, detach and leave this
stub when you select this
Prospect Card.

PART 3

CARD NO.

Make Checks Payable to:
St. Louis YMCA - Capital Campaign
1528 Locust St., St. Louis, Mo. 63103
(314) 436-1177
The YMCA of Greater St. Louis Acknowledges With Thanks The
Contribution of

Name
Amount Subscribed $
Amount Paid $
Received By
Date

PART 1

CARD NO.

1. Detach this stub.
2. **Do not show to Prospect.**
3. Contact only those for whom you hold a Prospect Card.
4. See Prospect Personally.

YMCA Affiliation:

$

Amount suggested
By Appraisal
Committee

PART 2

CARD NO.

Campaigner

Campaigner No.:

| DIV | TM | CPR |

Sign, detach and leave this
stub when you select this
Prospect Card.

PART 3

A Pledge to
The University of Iowa Foundation for
Iowa Endowment 2000:
A Covenant with Quality

_____
name(s) (please print clearly)

_____

_____
address

_____
city, state, zip

As an investment in human resources at The University of Iowa and in consideration of the gifts of others, I (we) hereby subscribe and agree to pay The University of Iowa Foundation for the Iowa Endowment 2000 Campaign the sum of:
_____ Dollars ($_____)
to be paid in either cash, securities or other property of equivalent value.

_____   _____
signature   date

_____   _____
spouse's signature (when joint gift)   date

Total pledge $_____
Paid herewith $_____
Balance due $_____

Balance To Be Paid As Follows:

Month	Year	Amount
	19	$
	19	$
	19	$
	19	$
	19	$

Payment schedules other than annual may be arranged.

I (we) have made provisions for an estate/testamentary gift to support the Iowa Endowment 2000 Campaign. A description of the deferred gift arrangement is attached.

Please make checks payable to: **The University of Iowa Foundation.** Your gift is tax deductible.

July 2, 1985

CAMPAIGN MONEY MATTERS

"A Note to YOU"

The Foundation Office will do its best to inform each volunteer on the progress of our campaign through this weekly newsletter called "Campaign Money Matters." Important dates, report meetings, gift totals, successes, facts and everything that deals with the Excellence with Caring Campaign will be covered in this weekly newsletter. If any of you have news to share about a prospect or a success you like to tell about, inform the Foundation office. Success breeds Success --- we will be successful in our goal to raise $2.5 million.

- Jim Ash

* * * *

"Official VS Unofficial"

During every campaign there are two sets of figures that surface during the months of solicitation...official and unofficial figures. Unofficial figures comprise verbal as well as written or documented pledges while the official figures are only those that have been documented. Whenever figures are mentioned in this newsletter, the Foundation office will state whether they are official or unofficial figures.

* * * *

"Where Do We Stand"

The kickoff for the public phase of our campaign took place at Heileman Hall on Wednesday evening, June 26. The unofficial figure released then on the amount of money pledged was $1,471,000 toward the $2.5 million goal. Since that time additional pledges have brought the figure up to $1,514,000 as of July 1, 1985. We have less than $1 million to go so keep up the good work.

* * * *

Source: Excellence with Caring Campaign, La Crosse Lutheran Capital Improvement Program, Lutheran Hospital Foundation, La Crosse, Wisconsin.

MCA Of Greater St. Louis

CONTRIBUTORS' NEWSLETTER

Corporate Offices • 1528 Locust Street • St. Louis, MO 63103-1897 • 314-436-1177

SAM EDGAR
President

JULY, 1986

DIC
Vice
Dev

Thank You . . .

Your contributions to the YMCA enable children throughout the Metropolitan area to develop and grow in mind, body and spirit. You are indeed a "Partner With Youth" and this newsletter describes only a handful of benefits your generosity makes possible through Y programs.

"Y" pre-school provides important learning experiences for the future while teaching how to share both verbally and socially in a group situation.

Bright lively bundles of energy are entranced with learning new skills in tumbling and beginning gymnastics.

CAPITAL CAMPAIGN
"Down the Final Mile"

The "Making A World of Difference" capital campaig of the YMCA of Greater St. Louis is moving strongl through its final stage of solicitation. Gatherin $14,000,000 in pledges to date, 78% of the $17 million goal, determined campaigners continue the efforts to fund buildings and expand programs fc 60,000 - 70,000 more people. Projects made possib by this campaign include:

• West County Y - Construct a new family progra and fitness center.
• YMCA of the Ozarks - Build a new lodge and fami program center, replace and remodel cabins an develop new program areas.
• North County Y - Complete the Emerson Fitnes Center adding a gymnasium, indoor track an expanded locker rooms.
• Downtown Fitness Center - Renovate the existin facility and add a second fitness center east c 9th Street.
• Mid-County Y - Remodel and add additiona program space.
• Kirkwood/Webster Y - Construct a gymnasium a the Kirkwood Center and air-condition the Webste Groves Center.
• South Side Y - Improve facilities for expande latch-key and adult fitness programming.
• Carondelet Y - Enhance building access for senio citizens and revitalize existing facilities.
• Monsanto Y - Add fitness and day-care facilities
• Northwest County/Westport Y - Establish a cardic vascular center in the Westport business/residentia community.
• Washington University Campus Y - Increase th endowment supporting student services.
• Jefferson County Y - Acquire property and construc facilities to provide day-care and other communit based programs.
• St. Charles County/Wentzville Y - Acquire propert and construct a program building to serve wester St. Charles Co.

Source: YMCA of Greater St. Louis, St. Louis, Missouri.

A New Voice: Richard D. Remington

Interim President Richard Remington greets his visitor with a hearty handshake and a few disparaging comments about the heat. His desk and a worktable are piled with file folders from his recent trip to the East Coast to attend former UI President James O. Freedman's inaugural ceremony at Dartmouth College and to explore some possibilities with a distinguished professor who may be interested in Iowa's recently funded laser institute.

Remington's duties as head of The University of Iowa during the search for a new president are far more complex than merely taking temporary hold of the institutional reins. Iowa Endowment 2000 will create numerous faculty chairs and graduate fellowships at the UI. Remington, as the University's most visible representative, will take the UI's case for this support to alumni and friends throughout the country. This is also a critical time in the Iowa legislature, a time which requires vision and vigorous leadership.

Remington, who participated in the initial discussions about a possible campaign with Freedman and Darrell Wyrick of the UI Foundation, has played a key role in the campaign planning process from the start. He spoke with *Dispatch* recently about his belief in the campaign's significance— not only for the University, but for Iowa and the country as a whole.

Dispatch: What do you think the long-term effects of Iowa Endowment 2000 will be for the state of Iowa?

Remington: The linkage between the University and Iowa is a very strong one. As the state of Iowa shows itself to be hospitable to major institutions like the University, and as the UI grows in high-priority areas that relate to the purposes of the state, then both the state and the University prosper together. The UI is very active in bringing in outside money to this state, in the form of, for example, federal research grants. We have data showing that every dollar spent by the UI generates more than $3.50 in business-related activity in the state. That is quite a multiplier— three and a half to one. An investment in higher education these days, whether it's a private or a public investment, is really a very, very good investment.

Dispatch: You said something about high-priority areas. What are they?

Remington: Well, you hear a lot about laser science. That is the one we are moving on, and we have received some support from the Iowa lottery to endow it. The state has also approved funding for a $25 million building to house the laser center. But if you go in the other direction and look at things like the Writers' Workshop, you'll find that it does something very important for the state as well. The fact that we have sustained excellence in both space science and creative writing for so many years is a tribute to the diversity of the University and the state.

Dispatch: What do you think the relationship between the high-tech aspects of the University and the humanities should be?

Remington: I think that the humanities have always been important to the University. They are important to the state too, because they help people look beyond themselves, look beyond their own individual problems. The humanities give those who study them a vision and perspective on their situation that ultimately is the way problems get solved. Technology tends to be the art of developing solutions to problems that are very well-defined, very well outlined in the here and now. But when you talk about the problems of the human spirit, or the problems of society in general, there is no technology in that area. Poets and playwrights and novelists help us to understand ourselves in the long run.

Dispatch: How will the campaign affect undergraduate education?

Remington: I believe very firmly that undergraduate education is related to the quality of the faculty who deliver it, and faculty who do nothing but teach cannot deliver a high quality education for very long. Every

(continued on next page)

Source: Iowa Endowment 2000: A Covenant with Quality, University of Iowa Foundation, Iowa City, Iowa.

Resource H.
Sample Letterhead and Envelopes

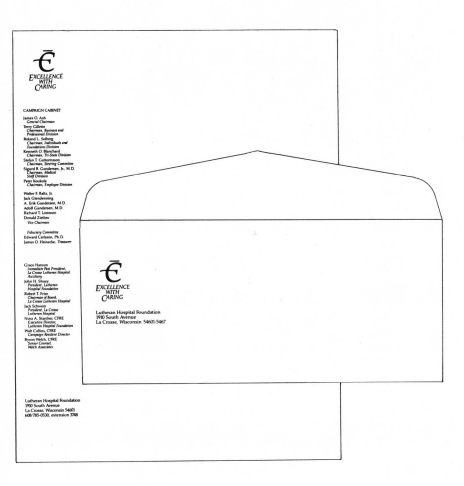

References

American Association of Fund-Raising Counsel (AAFRC). *AAFRC Directory of Members*. New York: American Association of Fund-Raising Counsel, 1986.

Anderson, G. M. "At Home on the Gift Range." *CASE Currents*, May 1986, pp. 42–44.

Baxter, F. R. "Prospect Management." Unpublished paper, University of California, Berkeley, Calif., 1987.

Billian, J. M. "Prospect Research, Evaluation, Cultivation, and Solicitation." Presentation made at annual CASE conference, Nashville, Tenn., March 1985.

Brakeley, John Price Jones, Inc. "The Challenge of Change." Corporate report. Stamford, Conn.: Brakeley Communications, 1986.

Broce, T. E. *Fund Raising*. Norman: University of Oklahoma Press, 1979.

Builta, J. *The Campaign Manuals*. Vol. 1: *The Campaign*. Cleveland, Ohio: Third Sector Press, 1984a.

Builta, J. *The Campaign Manuals*. Vol. 2: *Steps and Procedures*. Cleveland, Ohio: Third Sector Press, 1984b.

Butler, J. P., III. "Capital Giving: Transition from '80s to '90s." Presentation made at annual CASE conference, Bethesda, Md., April 1986.

Campbell, D. A., Jr. "The Capital Campaign: Soliciting the Lead Gift(s)." Presentation made at annual CASE District VI conference, St. Louis, Mo., January 1985.

Chewning, P. B. "The Attitudes of Alumni Non-Donors, Donors, and Consecutive Donors Toward Drake University." Unpublished dissertation, Drake University, Des Moines, Iowa, 1984.

Conrad, D. L. How to Solicit Big Gifts. San Francisco: Public Management Institute, 1978.

Dove, K. E. "Changing Strategies for Meeting Campaign Goals." In A. W. Rowland (ed.), Handbook of Institutional Advancement. (2nd ed.) San Francisco: Jossey-Bass, 1986.

Dunlop, D. R. "Suggestions for Working with Volunteers." Presentation made at CASE Summer Institute in Educational Fund Raising, Dartmouth College, Hanover, N.H., July 1981.

Evans, G. A. "Relationship of Capital Campaign to Annual Fund and Deferred Giving Program." Presentation made at annual CASE conference, Detroit, Mich., August 1978.

Evans, G. A. "Decisions About the Big Three." CASE Currents, March 1979, pp. 34-37.

"Fact-File: Capital Campaigns to Raise $100-Million or More." Chronicle of Higher Education, September 2, 1987, p. A76.

Gabor, A. "Fund Raising in Trying Times," U.S. News and World Report, May 4, 1987, p. 53.

The Gallup Organization. "Patterns of Charitable Giving by Individuals II." Commissioned by The 501(c)(3) Group, Independent Sector and The National Society of Fund Raising Executives, conducted by the Gallup Organization, Washington, D.C.: Independent Sector, 1982.

The Gallup Organization. "An Analysis of Charitable Contributions by Upper-Income Households for 1986 and 1987." Commissioned by the AAFRC Trust for Philanthropy, conducted by the Gallup Organization, New York: Giving USA, 1987.

Gibson, E. B. "The Role of Professional Counsel." Discussion notes from a presentation at annual CASE conference, Philadelphia, Pa., March 1983.

Grenzebach, John, and Associates, Inc. "Prerequisites for Probable Campaign Success Investigated by a J G & A Feasibility/Development Study." Corporate report, Chicago, Ill., 1986a.

Grenzebach, John, and Associates, Inc. "Preparation for a Feasibility/Planning Study." Corporate report, Chicago, Ill., 1986b.

Grenzebach, John, and Associates, Inc. "Description of the Development Program Audit Provided by John Grenzebach and Associates, Inc." Corporate report, Chicago, Ill., 1986c.

Grenzebach, John, and Associates, Inc. "Campaign Evaluation Questionnaire." Corporate report, Chicago, Ill., 1986d.

Hale, E. E. Untitled remarks made at annual CASE conference on Capital Fund Raising, Atlanta, Ga., April 1980.

Keller, G. *Academic Strategy.* Baltimore: Johns Hopkins University Press, 1983.

Kughn, J. C., Jr. "Using Volunteers Effectively." Presentation made at annual CASE conference, Nashville, Tenn., March 1982.

Livingston, H. J., Jr. "The Role of Trustees in a Capital Campaign." *Bulletin on Public Relations and Development for Colleges and Universities,* March 1984, pp. 1–4.

Lord, J. G. *The Raising of Money.* (3rd ed.) Cleveland: Third Sector Press, 1985.

Milton, J. "The Ship of the Commonwealth Is Always Under Sail." Livewell Chapman at the Crown in Popes-Head Alley: London, 1660.

National Society of Fund Raising Executives (NSFRE). "The Survey Course on Fund Raising Fundamentals." Alexandria, Va.: NSFRE Institute, 1985.

Panas, J. *Mega Gifts.* Chicago: Pluribus Press, 1984.

Pendel, M. H. *What Is a Case Statement?* Thompson and Pendel Associates, Arlington, Va., 1981.

Perkins, D. R. "Public Relations Support for the Capital Campaign." Presentation made at annual CASE conference, Nashville, Tenn., April 1985.

Pickett, W. L. "What Determines Fundraising Effectiveness?" *CASE Currents,* September 1984, pp. 45–48.

Picton, R. R. "Effective Follow Through." Presentation made at annual CASE conference, Nashville, Tenn., March 1982.

Public Management Institute. *Capital Campaign Resource Guide.* San Francisco: Public Management Institute, 1984.

Rose, S. J. *The American Profile Poster: Who Owns What, Who*

Makes How Much, Who Works Where, and Who Lives with Whom. Westminster, Md.: Pantheon Books, 1986.

Seymour, H. J. *Designs for Fund Raising.* New York: McGraw-Hill, 1966.

Smith, J. P. "Rethinking the Traditional Capital Campaign." In F. C. Pray (ed.), *Handbook for Educational Fund Raising: A Guide to Successful Principles and Practices for Colleges, Universities, and Schools.* San Francisco: Jossey-Bass, 1981.

Stuhr, R. L. *Gonser Gerber Tinker Stuhr on Development.* Chicago: Gonser Gerber Tinker Stuhr, 1977.

Thompson, D. M., and others. "Typical Outline for the Case Statement." Frantzreb, Prey, Ferner, and Thompson, Arlington, Va., 1978.

White, A. H. *The Charitable Behavior of Americans.* Washington, D.C.: Independent Sector, 1986.

Whittaker, F. M. "Prospect Research, Evaluation, Cultivation, and Solicitation." Outline of presentation at annual CASE conference, Philadelphia, Pa., March 1983.

Index

A

Accountability system, for prospect management, 112–113
Acknowledgment: of donor's major gift, 119–120; form for temporary, 141; system for, 126–128
Administration. *See* Leadership
Alabama, charitable giving less in, 9
Alger, H., 30
American Association of Fund-Raising Counsel (AAFRC), 76, 134–135, 166
American Express, 161–162
Anderson, G. M., 74
Approach system, in prospect management, 113
Area campaign, timetable for, 124–126
Arlett, A., 4
Association of Governing Boards (AGB), 135
Audiovisual materials, for marketing, 141–142
Audit, internal: areas included in, 25–27; concept of, 25; conducting, 24–28; constituency representation for, 27; purposes of, 25; report from, 27–28
Audit, postcampaign, 156–157

B

Barnes & Roche, Inc., 163
Barton, D. W., Jr., 144
Baxter, F. R., 104, 107, 109n
Bequests: including in results, 87–88; soliciting, 117
Berra, Y., 16
Billian, J. M., 95, 96, 97
Boys Town, quality and impact of, 8
Brakeley, John Price Jones, Inc., 162
Broce, T. E., 32
Budget, campaign, 129–130
Builta, J., 131
Butler, J. P., III, 163

C

California, Berkeley, University of, and prospect management system, 104
Campaign chair: acknowledgments by, 127; continuous case stating by, 143; enlistment of, 78–79; and major gifts committee, 151; recruitment of, 44–45; role of, 31–32; and training volunteers, 51
Campaign director, responsibilities of, 78, 154–155
Campaigns. *See* Capital campaigns

Campbell, D. A., Jr., 91, 115
Canada: charities registered in, 4; regional differences in, 9
Canadian Centre for Philanthropy, 4
Capital campaigns: advantages of, 167-168; announcement event for, 147; areas of development for, 163-167; as art, 138; background on, 1-5; case statement for, 56-66; categories of, by size, 4-5; components of, 1-14; comprehensive, 12, 160-161; concept of, 1; concluding and building on, 150-159; continuing major gifts programs form of, 13-14, 171; cultivation and solicitation in, 104-121; for debt retirement, 162; and development programs, 157-159; disadvantages of, 168-171; donors to, 90-103; final reports on, 154-156; forms of, 10-14; future of, 160-172; gifts table for, 67-76; goal setting for, 8, 170-171; historical form of, 11-12; importance of, 3-4; internal audit for, 24-28; internal report on, 154-155; market survey for, 18-24; marketing, 139-149; momentum from, 150-159, 170; name for, and public relations, 147; operational logistics of, 122-138; organization for, 78-80; organizational structure and solicitation process for, 77-89; organizational variables in, 6-10; preparatory steps for, 15-28; prerequisites to, 5-6, 19; public report on, 155-156; roles in, 29-42; scrapbook of, 155; single-purpose, 12-13; solution for, 171-172; strategic planning for, 15-17; trends for, 160-163; volunteer role in, 43-55. See also Fundraising
Carey, M., 3
Carnegie, A., 3
Case statement: aspects of, 56-66; background on, 56-58; concept

of, 56; future for, 163-164; governing board role in, 34; as motivational, 57-58; need for, 5; organization of, 58-59; outline of, 60-63; presenting, 64; process for, 65-66; in recruiting volunteers, 46; sample, 178-207; uses of, 63-64; in worker's kit, 52
Chairpersons. See Campaign chair; Governing board chair
Chewning, P. B., 3
Chief development officer: characteristics of, 41-42; and executive committee, 81; and major gifts committee, 151; purpose of, 41; responsibilities of, 77; role of, 40-42; and training volunteers, 51-52
Chief executive officer (CEO): acknowledgments by, 127; aspects of role of, 36-39; continuous case stating by, 143, 147; on executive committee, 81; functions of, 37-39; fundraising responsibilities of, 38-40; and major gifts committee, 151; recruitment by, 45, 79; solicitation of board by, 35; and training volunteers, 51
Chronicle of Higher Education, 5
Clemens, S. L., 144-145
Commitment: of governing board, 32; need for, 5; by solicitors, 35
Committees: of governing board, 33, 34, 80; for market survey, 24; for public relations, 148; responsibilities of, 80-82, 151
Communications advisory committee, and public relations, 148
Community: leadership from, 30, 36; and public relations plan, 148
Confidentiality: for gift rating of prospect, 141; of market survey interview, 21; and prospect evaluation committee, 81
Conrad, D. L., 119
Constituency: caliber of, 6-7; goals with appeal for, 18; internal, 24-25; and internal audit, 27; leader-

ship from, 30; size and spread of, 7; volunteers from, 44

Consultants. *See* Counsel, outside professional

Corporations: cultivating, 120-121; information needed on, 95-96; involvement of, 162; prospect research on, 95-97; rating of, 95; relationships with, 96-97; sources of information on, 96

Council for the Advancement and Support of Education (CASE), 47, 88, 135, 163, 166

Counsel, outside professional: aspects of using, 130-137; benefits and drawbacks of, 136-137, 168; for market surveys, 20; professional ethics of, 134-135; role of, 132, 134; selecting, 135-136; in single-purpose campaigns, 12

Cultivation: acknowledgment and recognition in, 119-120; aspects of, 104-121; continued, 152, 153, 154, 158-159; cycle of, for prospects, 92; and major donor solicitation guidance system, 104-114; quotient of, in prospect management system, 111-112, 114; and soliciting major gifts, 104-121; weighted system of contacts in, 113

D

Dartmouth College: conference at, 47; and gifts table, 74

Debt retirement campaigns, 162

Development program: built on capital campaign, 157-159; objectives of, 62-63. *See also* Chief development officer; Staff

Donors: acknowledgment and recognition for, 119-120; aspects of, 90-103; characteristics of, 91; continued cultivation of, 152, 153, 154, 158-159; identifying prospects for, 91-92; listings of, 156; need for, 6; rating prospective, 94-95, 99-103; recognition

of major, 119-120, 153; renewals by, 128; research on prospective, 92-99, 164-165. *See also* Prospects

Dunlop, D. R., 47

E

Economy, impact of, 10

Ethics code, 134-135

Evaluation, gifts table for, 76

Evans, G., 83, 85

Executive committee, responsibilities of, 33, 34, 81

F

Facts sheet: publication of, 140; sample, 231-233

Finance committee, role of, 33, 34

Foundations: cultivating, 120-121; information needed on, 97-98; prospect research on, 97-99; rating of, 95; sources of information on, 98

Frantzreb, Prey, Ferner, and Thompson, 60

Fundraising: essentials of, 18; evangelical aspect of, 2; history of, 2-3; previous success at, 7-8. *See also* Capital campaigns

G

Gabor, A., 4

Gallup Organization, 6, 76

General gifts and cleanup: committee for, 82; timetable for, 124

Gerber, J. J., 32

Gibson, E. B., 136

Gifts: acknowledging and reporting systems for, 126-128; asking for, 35, 54, 83-85, 115, 117; guidelines for counting toward goal, 88-89; lead, 74-75, 90, 117; nucleus, 90; planned, 84-85, 86-87, 161, 165; valuing, 88. *See also* Major gifts

Gifts table: aspects of, 67-76; constructing, 67-72; for evaluation, 76; functions of, 67; and gift needs, 72; and gift prospects, 73; as management tool, 72–75; and market survey, 67, 72–73; mathematical development of, 70–71; and rule of thirds, 68, 73; samples of, 69–72, 74–75; as score card, 73–74; trends for, 68, 73–74, 76; unworkable, 75

Girl Scouts of America, quality and impact of, 8

Giving program, range of, 7

Governing board: aspects of role of, 32–37; and continuing major gifts program, 171; cultivation of, 34–35; development committee of, 33, 34, 80; executive committee of, 33, 34; finance committee of, 33, 34; functions of, 32; investment committee of, 33; leadership from, 32, 36; recruitment by, 45; responsibilities of, 36–37; solicitation of, 35; as solicitors, 36; as volunteers, 33

Governing board chair: acknowledgments by, 127; enlistment by, 78–79; on executive committee, 81

Graves, W. B., 37

Grenzebach, J., 19, 20, 23, 25, 27, 156

Group discussion, for rating prospects, 99–100

Group/individual ratings, of prospects, 100

H

Harvard College, first fundraising by, 2–3

Hale, E. E., 46

Houston, campaign goals in, 162–163

Human factors, significance of, 9–10

I

Individual/one-on-one ratings, of prospects, 100

Individual/solitary ratings, of prospects, 100

Institutions. *See* Objectives, institutional; Organization

Internal audit. *See* Audit, internal

Investment committee, role of, 33

Involvement, investment related to, 159, 166

J

John Price Jones Corporation, 3

K

Keller, G., 17

Kughn, J. C., Jr., 45, 54

L

Lead gifts: citing, 117; concept of, 90; succeeding without, 74–75

Leadership: aspects of, 29–42; background on, 29–30; by campaign chair, 31–32; for case statement, 65; celebration for, 152–153; by chief development officer, 40–42; by chief executive officer, 37–40; in comprehensive campaigns, 12; future for, 165–166; future sources of, 159; by governing board, 32–37; need for, 5; and prospect cultivation, 112; and saving victory, 129; selection of, 30

Letter of intent: publication of, 140; sample of, 142

Livingston, H. J., Jr., 33

Lord, J. G., 16–17

M

Major gifts: acknowledgment and recognition of, 119–120; brochures on opportunities for, 139–140; continuing program for, 13–14, 170; cultivation and solicitation for, 104–121; defining, 90; donors of, 90–103; timetable for obtaining, 123-124; trends for, 162

Major gifts committee: for maintaining momentum, 151; responsibilities of, 81-82

Management, gifts table as tool for, 72-75. *See also* Operations; Prospect management system

Market survey: benefits of, 23; committee for, 24; concept of, 18; conducting, 18-24; confidential interview for, 21; consultants for, 20; and gifts table, 67, 72-73; and internal systems, 22; interview population for, 20-21; need for, 5; objectives of, 19; process of, 19-22; purposes of, 18-19, 23; report from, 22-23

Marketing: with campaign publications, 139-146; and public relations plan, 146-149

Mayo Clinic, quality and impact of, 8

Memphis, short campaign in, 122

Michigan, economy in, 10

Milton, J., 1

Mission. *See* Objectives, institutional

Mississippi College, and fundraising by chief executive officer, 39

Motivation: from case statement, 57-58; recognition as, 120; in recruiting volunteers, 45; significance of, 9-10

N

National Association of College and University Business Officers (NACUBO), 88

National Association of Hospital Development (NAHD), 135, 163, 166

National Society of Fund Raising Executives (NSFRE), 4, 56, 135, 160, 163, 166

Needs list, for market survey, 18

New York City, foundation wealth in, 9

New York University, campaign goal of, 5

Newsletters: publication of, 140; sample, 275-277

Noble, L., 39-40

North Dakota, charitable giving less in, 9

Nucleus gift, concept of, 91

O

Objectives, institutional: in capital campaign, 169; in case statement, 60-61; need for, 5

Operations: for acknowledging and reporting gifts, 126-128; aspects of, 122-138; for campaign budget, 129-130; critical difference in, 138; with professional counsel, 131-137; and reporting forms, 130-133; for stewardship, 128; timetable for, 122-126; and victory, 128-129

Oregon, economy in, 10

Organization: age of, 6; development objectives of, 62-63; future directions for, 61-62; location of, 8-9; quality and impact of, 8; record of accomplishment by, 61; sponsorship of, 63

P

Pamphlet, and case statement, 66

Panas, J., 9, 10

Pendel, M. H., 57-58, 63

Perkins, D. R., 148

Philadelphia, first community chest drive in, 3

Pickett, W. L., 7

Picton, R. R., 128, 150, 152

Pierce, L. L., 3

Planned gifts: solicitation for, 84-85, 86-87; trends for, 161, 165. *See also* Major gifts

Planning. *See* Strategic planning

Pledge card: ears for, 141; publication of, 140-141; sample, 270-274; in solicitation visit, 117

Policy committee, responsibilities of, 80-81
Postcampaign audit, 156-157
Pre-public announcement phase, timetable for, 123
Priority system, for prospect management, 110-112
Professional fundraisers. *See* Counsel, outside professional
Program brochure: and case statement, 65-66; sample, 209-210
Proposal, written, for major gift solicitation, 116
Prospect evaluation committee, responsibilities of, 81
Prospect management system: accountability system for, 112-113; approach system for, 113; concept of, 104; data elements for, 107-109; guidance system for, 104-114; objectives of, 105-106; priority system for, 110-112; rating system for, 110-111; report system in, 113-114; subsystems of, 110-114; tracking system for, 106-107
. Prospects: concept of, 91; contact records for, 93-94; corporations as, 95-97; cultivating and soliciting, 104-121; cultivation cycle for, 92; foundations as, 97-99; future for, 164-165; giving potential of, 94-95, 99-103; identifying, 91-92; information needed on, 93, 95-96, 97-98; objections of, during solicitation, 117-118; progress reporting and control system for, 77-78; publications on, 94, 96, 98; rating of, 94-95; research and evaluation on, 92-99, 164-165; sources of information on, 94, 96, 98; status summary chart for, 133. *See also* Donors
Public Management Institute, 119, 131
Public relations: and campaign name, 147; communications advisory committee for, 148; communications materials checklist for, 176-177; director of, 149; for maintaining momentum, 152, 153; and marketing, 146-149; methods for, 147; objective of, 146; resources on, 176-279; steps in, 148-149
Publications, on prospects, 94, 96, 98
Publications, campaign: aspects of, 139-146; continuity in, 143; designing, 145-146; first, 3; for market segments, 142-143; preparing, 143-146; style of, 144-145; types of, 139-143

R

Ratings: confidentiality of, 81, 141; of giving potential, 94-95, 99-103; manageable sessions for, 103; system of, 110-111; techniques for, 99-101
Recognition: of major gift, 119-120, 153; for volunteers, 156
Recruitment, checklist for, 45-46
Reporting: forms for, 130-133; system for, 77-79, 113-114, 126-128
Rockefeller, J., 3
Rockefeller Brothers Fund, 6
Rose, S. J., 76
Rule of thirds, 68, 73

S

Seneca, 16
Seymour, H. J., 29, 49, 56, 68, 151
Shrinkage, loss from, 130
Simic, C. R., 65
Smith, G. T., 91-92
Smith, J. P., 167, 171
Solicitation: for annual giving, 83-85, 86; and asking for gifts, 35, 53-54, 83-85, 115, 117; for bequests, 87-88; for capital gifts, 83-86; and cultivation, 104-121; with double ask, 83-84; errors in, 119; by governing board, 35-36; and making visit, 116-119; for

planned giving, 84-85, 86-87; and preparing for visit, 115-116; process of, 82-85; prospect objections during, 117-118; and reluctance, 53-54; and report on visits, 118-119; scope of, 85-89; with separate ask, 83; by teams, 35, 53-54, 115; timing of, 115; with triple ask, 84-85

South Dakota, charitable giving less in, 9

Special gifts committee, responsibilities of, 82. *See also* Major gifts

Staff: as account executive, 112; future for, 166-167; and prospect ratings, 94-95, 99-103; and prospect research, 92; and report system, 113-114; responsibilities of, 77; scrapbook compilation by, 155; trends for, 163; worker's kit prepared by, 52; and working with volunteers, 46-50

Standards-of-giving chart. *See* Gifts table

Stanford University: campaign goal of, 5; national campaign of, 7

Statue of Liberty, 162

Stewardship, operations for, 128

Strategic planning: concept of, 17; and continuing major gifts program, 13; need for, 5; as preparatory step, 15-17

Structure: aspects of, 77-89; background on, 77-78; of campaign organization, 78-80; and committee responsibilities, 80-82; for maintaining momentum, 150; and scope of solicitation, 85-89; and solicitation process, 82-85

Stuhr, R. L., 32, 37, 39, 40

T

Table. *See* Gifts table

Tax and estate planning brochure, publication of, 139-140

Team solicitation: by governing board, 35; for reluctant solicitors, 53-54; for major gifts, 115

Texas: economy in, 10; foundation wealth in, 9; goal setting in, 162-163

Thirds, rule of, 68, 73

Thompson, D. M., 60, 63

Timetable: for area campaign, 124-126; for operations, 122-126

Trustees. *See* Governing board

Twain, M., 144-145

U

United Way, impact of, 8

V

Victory: celebrating, 152-154; dinner and report for, 147-148; saving, 128-129

Volunteers: acknowledgments by, 127; aspects of, 43-55; background on, 43-44; celebration for, 153; characteristics of, 44; competition for, 29-30; concept of, 43; continued involvement of, 158-159; and corporate prospects, 97; educating, 50-54; expectations for, 54; future for, 165-166; governing board as, 33; guide for, 52-53, 140, 146; in historical campaigns, 11; job descriptions for, 79; maintaining momentum for, 150-152; for market survey committee, 24; organization for, 80; orientation session for, 50-51; prospects assigned to, 80, 112, 129; rating prospects by, 99-103; recognition for, 156; recruiting, 44-46; reluctance by, 53-54; remembering, 154; sample handbook for, 233-269; services for, 54-55; trends for, 162; weekly campaign report for, 127-128, 132; worker's kit for, 52; working with, 47-50; workshops for, 52

W

Ward, C. S., 3, 14
White, A. H., 6
Whittaker, F. M., 93
Winship, A. L., II, 70, 74

Y

Yankelovich, Skelley and White, 6
YMCA, early fundraising by, 3
YMCA/YWCA: and importance, 9;
    quality and impact of, 8